DAVID HUME
DIALOGUES CONCERNING
NATURAL RELIGION
in focus

Based on the original handwritten manuscript, this book provides a new, accurate edition of Hume's important work, faithful to his original text, marginal notes, and changes. Stanley Tweyman's comprehensive introduction gives an interpretation of the *Dialogues* as a whole, as well as close analysis of each of the work's twelve parts. Hume's views on evil are discussed in four previously published articles and the volume concludes with an extensive bibliography.

Stanley Tweyman is Professor of Philosophy at York University, Toronto, Canada.

ROUTLEDGE PHILOSOPHERS IN FOCUS SERIES

General Editor: Stanley Tweyman
York University, Toronto

GÖDEL'S *THEOREM* IN FOCUS
Edited by S. G. Shanker

J. S. MILL: *ON LIBERTY* IN FOCUS
*Edited by John Gray
and G. W. Smith*

CIVIL DISOBEDIENCE IN FOCUS
Edited by Hugo Adam Bedau

JOHN LOCKE: *LETTER ON TOLERATION*
IN FOCUS
Edited by John Horton and Susan Mendus

DAVID HUME

DIALOGUES CONCERNING NATURAL RELIGION
in focus

A new edition, edited and with an introduction by Stanley Tweyman

London and New York

First published 1991
by Routledge
11 New Fetter Lane, London EC4P 4EE

Simultaneously published in the USA and Canada
by Routledge
a division of Routledge, Chapman and Hall, Inc.
29 West 35th Street, New York, NY 10001

Typeset in 10/12pt Bembo by
Witwell Ltd, Southport
Printed in Great Britain by
Biddles Ltd, Guildford, Surrey

British Library Cataloguing in Publication Data
Hume, David, *1711–1776*
David Hume: Dialogues concerning natural religion in
focus. – (Routledge philosophers in focus series)
1. Scottish philosophy
I. Title   II. Hume, David; Dialogues concerning natural
religion, *1711–1776*
192

Library of Congress Cataloging in Publication Data
Hume, David, 1711–1776.
[Dialogues concerning natural religion]
David Hume: Dialogues concerning natural religion in focus/
edited by Stanley Tweyman.
p.   cm. — (Routledge philosophers in focus series)
Includes bibliographical references.
1. Natural theology—Early works to 1800.   I. Tweyman, Stanley,
1942–   .   II. Title.   III. Title: Dialogues concerning natural
religion.   IV. Series.
B1493.D52   1991
210—dc20   90–33166

ISBN 0 415 02013 1
ISBN 0 415 02014 X (pbk)

CONTENTS

PUBLISHING HISTORY
Editions of Hume's *Dialogues*
Concerning Natural Religion

The first mention of the *Dialogues* is in a letter to Gilbert Elliot of March 1751, where Hume sends Elliot a 'sample' of the work.

The first edition was printed in 1779, in Edinburgh, supervised by Hume's nephew, 152 pages.

The second edition was also printed in 1779, 264 pages. According to Price, this edition was entered in the Stationer's Register on 10 May, 1779. (See J. V. Price, 'The First Publication of David Hume's *Dialogues Concerning Natural Religion.*' *Papers of the Bibliographical Society of America*, 68, 1974, 119–27.)

A third edition was published in 1804, consisting of the second edition text and a new title page.

The *Dialogues* was reprinted as part of Hume's collected works in editions of 1782, 1788, 1821, and 1826 (the last edited by Hume's nephew). The Green and Grose collection was published in 1874–5.

PREFACE

This edition of David Hume's *Dialogues Concerning Natural Religion* attempts to provide an accurate reproduction of the handwritten manuscript housed in the National Library in Edinburgh.

With the exception of minor grammatical changes, (e.g. "tis' to 'it is', 'which' to 'that'), all Hume's revisions are included. Hume's editorial changes are indicated in the text by the use of footnotes, and, in the case of word or phrase substitutions, both the deleted and the added text are given. Major additions to the text are noted by the use of two asterisks at the beginning and end of the added passage, and by a footnote giving Hume's directions for insertion. Hume's own footnotes are printed in italics. The original punctuation has been retained throughout; in most cases, though, spelling has been modernized and his general capitalization of nouns has been omitted. Hume uses Arabic numbers in his text for numbering the twelve Parts, and this style has been retained in this edition in the text of the *Dialogues* and in the Introduction.

The Introduction contains an interpretation of the *Dialogues* which I first began developing in a number of published papers, and in my *Scepticism and Belief in Hume's Dialogues Concerning Natural Religion* (Kluwer, Dordrecht, Netherlands, 1986). The current study of the *Dialogues* differs from this earlier work in a number of significant ways. Whereas the earlier book confined itself to a detailed analysis of Parts 1 through 8 and 12 (Cleanthes' Argument from Design and Philo's criticisms of this argument), this Introduction provides an analysis of all twelve parts of the *Dialogues*. Furthermore, whereas *Scepticism and Belief* attempted to relate the *Dialogues* to Hume's treatment of 'natural belief' in the *Treatise of Human Nature* and to his discussion of 'scepticism' in the' *Enquiry Concerning Human Understanding*, the current study omits entirely the treatment of natural belief, and deals only briefly with the material in the first *Enquiry* on scepticism. I continue to believe in the importance of the 'natural belief' doctrine in the *Treatise* and of Hume's analysis of sceptism in the first *Enquiry* to a full understanding of Parts 1 through 8 and 12 of the *Dialogues*. However, since I have previously recorded my thoughts on these matters, I can only recommend that the reader consult my *Scepticism and Belief* for a more detailed account than I am able to offer here of Hume's treatment of Cleanthes' Argument from Design. Kluwer has been highly supportive of my work on Hume: I would like to thank the publishers for their encouragement in regard to this edition of the *Dialogues*.

In addition to the text of the *Dialogues Concerning Natural Religion* and an Introduction, this volume contains a number of articles which should assist the reader in understanding the debate in the *Dialogues*. These papers were originally presented as a symposium at the Edinburgh Hume Conference, 25–30 August 1986, and subsequently appeared in *Hume Studies*, 13, 1987. An extensive bibliography is also included.

I have been extremely fortunate to have had Beryl Logan assisting me at every stage of this project. Her love of the *Dialogues* and overall philosophic good sense are evident throughout this volume.

My efforts in this book, as always, are dedicated to my parents, Fay and Dave Tweyman, my wife Barbara, my daughter Justine Susan, and my brother Martin.

INTRODUCTION

PART 1

The debate in the *Dialogues* is centred around Cleanthes, Philo, and Demea. Of the three, Cleanthes maintains that there can be a religion of nature, that is, that knowledge of God can be obtained by examining what God has designed – the world. Cleanthes holds that God can be understood anthropomorphically, in human terms. Within the *Dialogues*, the two anthropomorphic claims which Cleanthes defends are that the Designer of the world is an intelligent being (discussed in Parts 2 through 8 and Part 12) and that the Designer is benevolent (Parts 10 and 11).

Philo is the main critic of Cleanthes' arguments. Cleanthes interprets Philo's criticisms to be of the extreme sceptical or pyrrhonian variety. According to Cleanthes, Philo's critical arguments generate 'undistinguished scruples with regard to the religious hypothesis, which is founded on the simplest and most obvious arguments, and, unless it meet with artificial obstacles, has such easy access and admission into the mind of man' (D. 104). As well, Philo's objections pay no heed to common sense and the plain instincts of nature (D. 118). As such, Philo's objections are intended more for amusement than for the pursuit of truth.

Philo's attitude to the arguments he puts forth reveals that the arguments are presented in a serious manner, and with a view to dealing seriously with Cleanthes' position in natural religion. At one point in Part 1, Cleanthes compares the extreme sceptics or Pyrrhonians with the Stoics. The mind, through stoical reflections, can be elevated into a sublime enthusiasm for virtue, such that no bodily pain can triumph over this high sense of duty. But he points out that such a state of mind cannot have a lasting effect upon us. Similarly, Cleanthes urges, pyrrhonian objections can have a momentary effect upon us, but, thereafter, we will return to our ordinary ways of dealing with the world. Therefore, there is, according to Cleanthes, no lingering effect to pyrrhonism. Philo responds to Cleanthes by saying that the comparison of Sceptics to Stoics is apt. However, Cleanthes fails to understand that there is a lingering effect to each of these: the effects of the Stoic's reasoning will appear in his conduct in common life, and through the whole tenor of his actions; similarly, those who are familiar with sceptical considerations on the uncertainty and narrow limits of reason will be found different in all their philosophical principles and reasoning from those who have never considered pyrrhonian objections on various topics.

The view to be adopted in this Introduction is that our reading of Philo's pyrrhonian objections should be guided by his comments to Cleanthes in various passages on the value of pyrrhonism, and by Hume's views on pyrrhonism when these arguments are constructive in nature.[1] Although pyrrhonian objections may generate undistinguished doubts – in Part 12 Philo characterizes this as a lack of caution in argumentation – nevertheless, the value of such objections is to show that we have gone beyond what human reason and the senses can properly examine. In Part 1, Philo tells Cleanthes that pyrrhonian objections are intended to counterbalance those arguments which run wide of common life and experience, and are designed to produce a suspense of judgement. In Section XII of the first *Enquiry*,[2] Hume urges that such counterbalancing arguments should be directed against philosophical dogmatists: '. . . while they see objects only on one side, and have no idea of any counterpoising argument, they throw themselves precipitately into the principles, to which they are inclined; nor have they any indulgence for those who entertain opposite sentiments' (E. 161). The intent of such counterbalancing arguments is to rid the mind of prejudice: only after this has been accomplished can inquiry be directed to determining whether there is anything on the topic under discussion which is in accordance with either common sense (also referred to at times as instinct) or reason. In the first *Enquiry*, this is referred to as mitigated scepticism – the type of scepticism to which Hume himself subscribes.

---

1 For a more detailed analysis of Hume's views on scepticism, see my *Scepticism and Belief*, pp. 3–10 and 24–30.
2 References to the first *Enquiry* are taken from Hume's *Enquiries Concerning Human Understanding and Concerning the Principles of Morals*, edited by L. A. Selby-Bigge, second edition (Oxford, Clarendon Press, 1902).

Demea, the third member of the dialogue, is characterized as a mystic, as one who holds a belief in God, but who also believes that nothing whatever can be known about God. In Part 9, Demea offers an *a priori* proof of God's necessary existence. (The place of Part 9 in the debate between Cleanthes and Philo is discussed later in this Introduction, pp. 60-8.)

The narrative of the dialogue is provided by Pamphilus, a student of Cleanthes, who had spent a summer with his teacher. It was during this period that he was present at the discussion which forms the subject matter of the book. Pamphilus relates to Hermippus (we are told nothing about the latter) the content of the discussion which took place among Cleanthes, Philo, and Demea.

PART 2

As Part 2 opens, we find all three speakers agreeing that the existence of God is certain and self-evident. Of the three, Philo and Demea agree that, beyond this claim, nothing more can be known about God. At one point, Philo asserts: 'And it is a pleasure to me . . . that just reasoning and sound piety here concur in the same conclusion, and both of them establish the adorably mysterious and incomprehensible nature of the Supreme Being' (D. 108). Only Cleanthes maintains that something can be learned of the nature of God. The argument he presents is the Argument from Design: through this argument he attempts to establish, by analogy, that the cause of the design of the world resembles human intelligence.

Cleanthes' version of the Argument from Design reads as follows:

Look round the world: Contemplate the whole and every part of it: You will find it to be nothing but one great machine, subdivided into an infinite number of lesser machines, which again admit of subdivisions, to a degree beyond what human senses and faculties can trace and explain. All these various machines, and even their most minute parts, are adjusted to each other with an accuracy, which ravishes into admiration all men, who have ever contemplated them. The curious adapting of means to ends, throughout all nature, resembles exactly, though it much exceeds, the productions of human contrivance; of human design, thought, wisdom, and intelligence. Since therefore the effects resemble each other, we are led to infer, by all the rules of analogy, that the causes also resemble; and that the

Author of Nature is somewhat similar to the mind of man; though possessed of much larger faculties, proportioned to the grandeur of the work, which he has executed. By this argument *a posteriori*, and by this argument alone, do we prove at once the existence of a Deity, and his similarity to human mind and intelligence. (D. 109)

Since the argument begins with a reference to finding the world 'to be nothing but one great machine, subdivided into an infinite number of lesser machines', it is tempting to hold that the claim that the world is a machine is a premise in this argument. However, this is not a correct reading of Cleanthes' argument. First, when Philo begins his criticism of Cleanthes' argument, he makes the point that resemblances between human artifacts and the universe are not sufficient to justify the claim that they are effects of the same kind:

If we see a house, Cleanthes, we conclude, with the greatest certainty, that it had an architect or builder; because this is precisely that species of effect, which we have experienced to proceed from that species of cause. But surely you will not affirm, that the universe bears such a resemblance to a house, that we can with the same certainty infer a similar cause, or that the analogy is here entire and perfect. The dissimilitude is so striking, that the utmost you can here pretend to is a guess, a conjecture, a presumption concerning a similar cause; (D. 110)

Cleanthes, however, does not appear bothered by this; he has recourse to the adaptation of means to ends and coherence of parts which are present in all machines and throughout the design of the world to support his claim:

It would surely be very ill received, replied Cleanthes; and I should be deservedly blamed and detested, did I allow, that the proofs of a Deity amounted to no more than a guess or conjecture. But is the whole adjustment of means to ends in a house and in the universe so slight a resemblance? The economy of final causes? The order, proportion, and arrangement of every part? (D. 110)

Second, the principle employed within the Argument from Design to establish the resemblance between the Deity and us is 'like effects prove like causes'. And when Philo puts forth his version of the Argument from Design two pages later (Cleanthes acknowledges that Philo's version provides a fair representation of the Argument), he states clearly that 'the adjustment of means to ends is alike in the universe, as in a machine of human contrivance.' By this statement, he is acknowledging that the comparison within the argument is between the means to ends relations and coherence of parts present in the design of machines and the world, and not simply between machines and the world.

Stated formally, Cleanthes' argument can be put in the following way:

Argument I:

$P_1, P_2, P_3 \ldots P_n$ (human artifacts)	have	A	(means to ends relations),
		B	(coherence of parts).
Q (the universe)	has	A	(means to ends relations),
		B	(coherence of parts).

$P_1, P_2, P_3 \ldots P_n$ (human artifacts)	have	C	(mind or intelligence as their cause of design).
Q (the universe)	also has		C (mind or intelligence as its cause of design).

Argument II:

$P_1, P_2, P_3 \ldots P_n$ (human artifacts)	have	C	(mind or intelligence as their cause of design).
Q (the universe)	has	C	(mind or intelligence as its cause of design).

$P_1, P_2, P_3 \ldots P_n$ (human artifacts)	have	D	(an external cause of design).
Q (the universe)	also has		D (an external cause of design).

That the world is a machine is a conclusion to which the Argument leads, and not a premise from which it begins. That is, it is only upon knowing that the means to ends relations and coherence of parts throughout the design of the world have resulted from intelligence that we can infer that the world is a machine. Knowing that the design of the world can be reduced to means to ends relations and a coherence of parts is not sufficient to classify the world as a machine.

A second version of the Argument from Design is put forth by Philo, ostensibly in response to Demea's uneasiness with Cleanthes' version of this argument. (As we will see, this second version is the version against which Philo's objections are directed in Part 8.) Philo's version of the Argument from Design is the following:

> Were a man to abstract from every thing which he knows or has seen, he would be altogether incapable, merely from his own ideas, to determine what kind of scene the universe must be or to give the preference to one state or situation of things above another. For as nothing, which he clearly conceives, could be esteemed impossible or implying a contradiction, every chimera of his fancy would be upon an equal footing; nor could he assign any just reason, why he adheres to one idea or system, and rejects the others, which are equally possible.
>
> Again; after he opens his eyes, and contemplates the world, as it really is, it would be impossible for him, at first, to assign the cause of any one event; much less, of the whole of things or of the universe. He might set his fancy a rambling; and she might bring him in an infinite variety of reports and representations. These would all be possible; but being all equally possible, he would never, of himself, give a satisfactory account for his preferring one of them to the rest. Experience alone can point out to him the true cause of any phenomenon.
>
> Now according to this method of reasoning, Demea, it follows (and is, indeed, tacitly allowed by Cleanthes himself) that order, arrangement, or the adjustment of final causes is not, of itself, any proof of design; but only so far as it has been experienced to proceed from that principle. For ought we can know *a priori*, matter may contain the source or spring of order originally, within itself, as well as mind does; and there is no more difficulty in conceiving, that the several elements, from an internal unknown cause, may fall into the most exquisite arrangement, than to conceive that their ideas, in the great, universal mind, from a like internal, unknown cause, fall into that arrangement. The equal possibility of both these suppositions is allowed. But by experience we find (according to Cleanthes) that there is a difference between them. Throw several pieces of steel together, without shape or form; they will never arrange themselves so as to compose a watch: Stone, and mortar, and wood, without an architect, never erect a house. But the ideas in a human mind, we see, by an unknown, inexplicable economy, arrange themselves so as to form the plan of a watch or house. Experience, therefore, proves, that there is an original principle of order in mind, not in

matter. From similar effects we infer similar causes. The adjustment of means to ends is alike in the universe, as in a machine of
human contrivance. The causes, therefore, must be resembling.
(D. 111–12)

For purposes of analysis, it is useful to set out Philo's version of the
Argument in a more rigorous form, adding steps which make explicit
some of the conclusions which Philo appears to want to draw on
Cleanthes' behalf:

(1) Experience or observing objects constantly conjoined can alone
show us the true cause of any event.

(2) (from (1)) Therefore, the presence of order, arrangement, or the
adjustment of final causes does not by itself prove that the
principle of the design is mind or intelligence.

(3) (from (1)) *A priori*, matter may contain the source or spring of
order originally within itself, as well as mind.

(4) If matter contains the source or spring of order of the universe,
then the source or spring of design is internal to the design; and, if
mind or intelligence contains the source or spring of order of the
universe, then the source or spring of design is external to the
design.

(5) By experience, or observing objects constantly conjoined, we find
(according to Cleanthes) a principle of order in mind, and no
principle of design in matter.

(6) (from (1) and (5)) Therefore, mind or intelligence contains a
principle of order; matter does not.

(7) (from (6)) Therefore, design is evidence of mind as the principle
of design.

(8) The universe everywhere shows signs of design.

(9) (from (7) and (8)) Therefore, the principle of design in the
universe is mind.

(10) (from (4) and (9)) Therefore, the principle of design of the
universe is external to the universe.

(11) Like effects prove like causes.

(12) In machines of human contrivance, we find an adjustment of
means to ends (i.e. a design of a certain kind).

(13) In the universe, we find an adjustment of means to ends (i.e. a
design of the same kind).

(14) (from (11), (12), and (13)) Therefore, the cause of the design of the
universe resembles the cause of the design of machines of human
contrivance.

(15) The cause of the design of machines of human contrivance is human intelligence.

(16) (from (14) and (15)) Therefore, the cause of the design of the universe resembles human intelligence.

In setting out the argument in this way, we are able to see the complex nature of Cleanthes' commitment. For this rendering shows us that Cleanthes actually holds to two points regarding mind or intelligence. From step (6), we learn that Cleanthes holds that all design must stem from mind or intelligence, since we cannot find an alternative cause of order in matter itself. But he is not, according to this argument, committed to holding that *all* order is the result of something resembling *human* intelligence; this is something which requires additional argumentation through the principle (step (11)) that like effects prove like causes. Hence, the two points which the argument makes regarding mind are that all order or design is the product of intelligence, and to show that the particular intelligence in question is like ours requires the use of the principle 'like effects prove like causes'. It is possible to disagree with the first claim, and yet to hold to the second, i.e., although denying mind as the cause of all order, it is possible to claim that a particular event has a cause which resembles human intelligence. It is important to realize, therefore, that Philo's version of Cleanthes' argument lends itself to the possibility of accepting a part of the total argument while rejecting the other part. As I have set the argument out, the crucial point in the argument comes between steps (10) and (11). It is possible to accept steps (11) through (16) without also accepting steps (6), (7), (9), and (10).

The longer version of the argument also makes explicit the various points which must come under scrutiny. They are:

(a) Is intelligence always responsible for order or arrangement?
(b) Is an external cause always responsible for order or arrangement?
(c) Is there a resemblance between the universe and machines of human contrivance sufficient for claiming that their respective causes resemble each other?
(d) Is the claim of resemblance between the causes of the world and machines of human contrivance (assuming that a positive answer can be given to question (c)) sufficient to justify the claim that the cause of the design of the world is external to the world itself?

I now turn to Philo's criticisms in Part 2. In his first criticism, he focuses on the principle 'like effects prove like causes'. While not taking issue with the principle itself, he does challenge Cleanthes' use of the principle:

> Unless the cases be exactly similar, they repose no perfect confidence in applying their past observation to any particular phenomenon. . . . But can you think, Cleanthes, that your usual phlegm and philosophy have been preserved in so wide a step as you have taken, when you compared to the universe houses, ships, furniture, machines; and from their similarity in some circumstances inferred a similarity in their causes? (D. 112–13)

In this initial criticism, we begin to see Philo's meaning when he earlier told Demea that he argues with Cleanthes 'in his own way' (D. 111). For Philo, while not challenging the principle 'like effects prove like causes', demands that it be used in a certain way. The principle, Philo insists, can be used with maximum confidence where the object into whose cause we are enquiring bears so close a resemblance to other objects whose cause is known that it can be classified as an object of that type.

Now, Cleanthes would not find Philo's criticism relevant to his use of the principle 'like effects prove like causes'. Cleanthes, as we have seen, discounts all differences between the world and machines, and focuses instead on the resemblances which are found: it is the adaptation of means to ends and the coherence of parts throughout the design of machines and the world which countenances the use of this principle and the inference to similar causes of design. In this initial criticism, we also begin to see Philo's 'lack of caution' in presenting his position against Cleanthes: while asserting his own position, Philo pays no attention to the similarities between the world and machines which Cleanthes' argument utilizes, and the relevance of these similarities to Cleanthes' use of the principle 'like effects prove like causes'. What Philo's initial criticism does accomplish is to reveal the source of the disagreement between Philo and Cleanthes: Philo insists that a classification of the world as a machine of a given sort whose cause is known must precede the employment of the principle 'like effects prove like causes'; Cleanthes insists that the presence of means to ends relations and a coherence of parts is all the resemblance required between a given item and machines to countenance employment of the principle 'like effects prove like causes'. Further argumentation is required to determine the force of each position.

In Philo's second criticism, he urges that thought or intelligence, as we understand it, is but one principle within the universe. How then do we justify transferring a conclusion from parts to the whole? Does not the great disproportion between machines and the world bar all comparison and inference?

This criticism goes further than the first in that it makes explicit the reality of additional springs and principles within the world itself. The question to raise is why Cleanthes is not moved by this to the point of questioning his own argument. The answer is that Philo's criticism, as it is formulated in Part 2, does not prove that other springs and principles, by themselves, are capable of producing effects which manifest means to ends relations and a coherence of parts. All that Philo has established is that the principles which he mentions – heat and cold, attraction and repulsion – and those to which he alludes are similar to thought in that they are active causes 'by which some particular parts of nature, we find, produce alterations in other parts' (D. 113). Philo has not established that any principle other than thought is capable of yielding a design such as we find in the world. Hence, Cleanthes is not troubled by Philo's point regarding additional springs and principles in the world.

The third, fourth, fifth, and sixth criticisms are all amenable to a similar analysis. The third criticism asks how we select reason or intelligence as the principle of design in the world, even if we could use the origin of one part of nature as the basis for the inference concerning the origin of the whole. In the fourth, Philo points out that not only cannot one part of nature form the basis for a conclusion concerning the whole, the operations of one part of nature often do not provide the basis for an inference concerning another part. Philo's fifth criticism questions whether we can justly attribute thought as the principle of design of the whole world in its embryo state, even if it were the only principle of design discovered in the world once it has achieved its given constitution and arrangement. As a sixth criticism, Philo points out the multiplicity of springs and principles we discover in the world, and he raises the possibility of nature using 'new and unknown principles' in 'so new and unknown a situation, as that of the first formation of a universe' (D. 114).

In each of these criticisms, Philo pays no heed to the likenesses apparent in the design of the world and machines of human contrivance which Cleanthes' argument utilizes; he does not show that any other principle could plausibly be suggested as capable of designing a world such as the present one; therefore, he has not disproved Cleanthes' claim that, on the basis of the exact resemblance between the world and machines in terms of means to ends relations and a coherence of parts, thought or intelligence is the only principle capable of producing a design such as we find in the world. Accordingly, Cleanthes continues to hold that his analogical argument is convincing. Philo's criticisms here are not compelling: to constitute a challenge to Cleanthes' position, Philo's criticisms must establish, with at least as much plausibility as the Argument from Design possesses, that a design such as we find in the world could have been caused by springs and principles other than thought.

In his last criticism, Philo recalls the importance of seeing two species of objects constantly conjoined when we engage in causal reasoning.

> But how this argument can have place, where the objects, as in the present case, are single, individual, without parallel or specific resemblance, may be difficult to explain. And will any man tell me with a serious countenance, that an orderly universe must arise from some thought and art, like the human; because we have experience of it? To ascertain this reasoning, it were requisite, that we had experience of the origin of worlds; and it is not sufficient surely, that we have seen ships and cities arise from human art and contrivance . . . (D. 115)

This criticism, as it is presented by Philo, is inappropriate. In it he asserts, but does not prove, that God and the world are not members of classes, and, therefore, the point is no stronger than Cleanthes' claim that God and the world can be so classified. Philo's criticism is making, but not arguing, the point that the principle 'like effects prove like causes' is inapplicable to God and the design of the world.

Also, as with the other criticisms which Philo advances in Part 2, no weight is given to the resemblances between the effects. The criticism is phrased as though the principle 'like effects prove like causes' is entirely inapplicable in the present discussion. Philo does not show that this is so, nor does he examine how the principle might be applied, given the resemblances which do exist between the world and a machine.

PART 3

In Part 2, Cleanthes maintained that the similarities between the works of nature and those of human contrivance, namely, the presence of means to ends relations and a coherence of parts, are sufficient to enable us to reason analogically to the conclusion that the cause of the

11

design of the world resembles human intelligence. Philo objects to this on a number of grounds, and it falls to Cleanthes in Part 3 to try to strengthen his own case. He seeks to do so through two illustrative analogies: the articulate voice heard in the clouds and the vegetable library. At this stage I will not assess the illustrations, but rather examine why Cleanthes believes they are able to support his case, and to show that they actually add a new factor to his position which Philo must address, if he is to deal with Cleanthes' total position.

The articulate voice analogy

In the first illustration, Cleanthes asks us to suppose that a voice was heard in the clouds, and that 'this voice were extended in the same instant over all nations, and spoke to each nation in its own language and dialect'; the words spoken 'not only contain a just sense and meaning, but convey some instruction altogether worthy of a benevolent Being, superior to mankind'; in the next paragraph we are told that what is heard is 'a rational, wise, coherent speech'. Now Cleanthes asks:

> Could you possibly hesitate a moment concerning the cause of this voice? And must you not instantly ascribe it to some design or purpose? Yet I cannot see but all the same objections (if they merit that appellation) which lie against the system of theism, may also be produced against this inference.
>
> Might you not say, that all conclusions concerning fact were founded on experience: That when we hear an articulate voice in the dark, and thence infer a man, it is only the resemblance of the effects, which leads us to conclude that there is a like resemblance in the cause: But that this extraordinary voice, by its loudness, extent, and flexibility to all languages, bears so little analogy to any human voice, that we have no reason to suppose any analogy in their causes: And consequently, that a rational, wise, coherent speech proceeded, you knew not whence, from some accidental whistling of the winds, not from any divine reason or intelligence? You see clearly your own objections in these cavils; and I hope too, you see clearly, that they cannot possibly have more force in the one case than in the other. (D. 117–18)

Cleanthes appears to be maintaining that the articulate voice heard from the clouds can be held to have an intelligent designer or cause, because of the resemblances which we find between it and ordinary human voices. If so, then his argument here takes exactly the same form as his attempt in Part 2 to show that the cause of the design of the world is an intelligent being. In both cases, the arguments are based on noted resemblances. To the extent that this is the position which he is defending, his position can be schematized as follows:

(1) $\dfrac{\text{Ordinary voices (effects)}}{\text{Intelligent beings (causes)}}$ (3) $\dfrac{\text{Works of human contrivance}}{\text{Intelligent beings (causes)}}$

$=$

(2) $\dfrac{\text{Articulate voice (effect)}}{\text{Superior intelligent being}}$ (cause)   (4) $\dfrac{\text{Works of nature}}{\text{Superior intelligent being}}$ (cause)

Since (4) is alleged to stand to (3) as (2) is held to stand to (1), if we deny (4) even granting (3) then we must deny (2) even granting (1). But, since we do not want to deny (2), we cannot deny (4).

The obvious attack on this position is to establish some fundamental difference between (1) and (2) on the one hand and (3) and (4) on the other, which would enable us to accept (2) on the basis of (1), while rejecting (4) on the basis of (3). It can be argued that the characteristics appealed to in the case of what is heard from the clouds are sufficient to classify what is heard as a voice, and, since voices are found constantly conjoined with intelligent beings as their cause, we can reason by analogy regarding the intelligence of the cause of what is heard from the clouds. However, Philo's criticisms in Part 2 make reference to alternative principles of order; hence he questions whether, in fact, the world is machine-like. To know that the world is a machine requires knowing of an intelligent cause of design, whereas knowing of an articulate *voice* does not require knowing that the cause is intelligent. Therefore, we can reason analogically from the voice to an intelligent designer, whereas to call the world a machine requires knowing of an intelligent designer. However, as I pointed out earlier, his argument focuses on means to ends relations and a coherence of parts in order to make the inference to an intelligent designer, and not on whether we can begin with the classification of the world as a machine. A reappraisal of Cleanthes' illustrative analogy is therefore in order.

In the two paragraphs in which Cleanthes expounds his views on the articulate voice, he appears to be making two different points. The first deals with the possibility of *reasoning* analogically from the observed resemblances in the effects to resembling causes. Within these two paragraphs and scattered throughout his entire discussion in Part 3, and later in Part 12, mention is also made by Cleanthes of an immediate or instantaneous inference to an intelligent cause of design:

> Could you possibly hesitate a moment concerning the cause of this voice? And must you not instantly ascribe it to some design or purpose? (D. 117)

> Consider, anatomize the eye: survey its structure and contrivance; and tell me, from your own feeling, if the idea of a contriver does not immediately flow in upon you with a force like that of sensation. The most obvious conclusion surely is in favour of design; and it requires time, reflection and study to summon up those frivolous, though abstruse, objections, which can support infidelity. (D. 119)

On p. 118, he refers to such arguments as 'natural' arguments. He acknowledges that such natural arguments have an irregularity to them, since they appear to contravene the principles of logic:

> And if the argument for theism be, as you pretend, contradictory to the principles of logic; its universal, its irresistible influence proves clearly, that there may be arguments of a like irregular nature. Whatever cavils may be urged; an orderly world, as well as a coherent, articulate speech, will still be received as an incontestable proof of design and intention. (D. 119)

In seeking to understand 'natural arguments', we can begin by asking for their form. And this is easily answered. According to Cleanthes, such arguments proceed directly from the data to the conclusion without the need for constant conjunction to link the data and conclusion. The conclusion strikes us as obvious, given the data. In Part 2, Philo made the point that, to know the nature of the cause of the design of the world, worlds would have to be formed under our eyes. Cleanthes' position in Part 3 suggests that there are other causal inferences to an intelligent cause of design (e.g. the articulate voice, the eye) where this requirement of constant conjunction is waived, and he is further suggesting that the case of God and the world is another instance of this.

What proof does he offer for this latter suggestion? To grasp this, it must be kept in mind that his original argument employed means to ends relations and a coherence of parts as evidence for an intelligent cause of the design of the world, and Philo's criticisms in Part 2 sought to deny, or at least to question, a knowledge of God based only on the aforementioned characteristics in the effect. Hence, the challenge to Cleanthes is one of showing how these characteristics support a belief in an intelligent designer. The voice is regarded as 'rational, wise, and coherent'. Now, at least part of rationality and wisdom consists in the proper adaptation of means to ends, and the feature coherence indicates that all such adaptations of means to ends work together as well as individually, precisely the point made of the means to ends relations in the world. To convey 'a just sense and meaning' again indicates an adaptation of means to ends: the words spoken are the means whereby the just sense and meaning are conveyed. But the coherence of parts must also be included if the words are to function in concert in conveying this sense and meaning. We were also told that the words delivered 'convey some instruction altogether worthy of a benevolent being', and it might be thought that here the comparison with the world breaks down, since in Parts 10 and 11 Hume maintains that the world does not appear to be the product of a benevolent designer. However, this can be answered if we take into account the type of benevolent instruction which Hume allows that the world manifests and which is articulated in the Principle of the Uniformity of Nature, a principle which we believe obtains of the world. By experience we learn what causes what, and we are led to believe that causal relations which obtained in the past will continue to obtain: therefore, the world instructs us in regard to those matters which we should pursue and those to be avoided. The instruction of the voice discloses means to ends relations; our experiences in the world disclose such relations as well. And both sources are conducive to our well-being.

Accordingly, all the characteristics which Cleanthes assigns to the articulate voice are reducible to the characteristics which form the basis of the inference regarding an intelligent designer of the world, and Cleanthes' point is that, just as there is an immediate inference from the means to ends relations and coherence of parts in the voice to an intelligent cause of design, so there should be a similar inference to an intelligent designer of the world. Cleanthes emphasizes that Philo fails to grasp this because of 'too luxuriant a fertility, which suppresses your natural good sense, by a profusion of unnecessary scruples and objections' (D. 120).

Cleanthes does not consider natural arguments to be rational arguments. At one point he compares such arguments to 'some beauties in writing we may meet with, which seem contrary to rules, and which

15

gain the affections, and animate the imagination, in opposition to all the precepts of criticism and to the authority of the established masters of art' (D. 119), indicating that natural arguments, like these maverick beauties, also appeal to the affections and imagination. His concern in discussing natural arguments is to discuss their 'universal' and 'irresistible influence', even allowing for Philo's claim that they are 'contradictory to the principles of logic' (D. 119). In short, his concern is with how such arguments are received, and not with their rationality.

It should not be thought that, in accepting the natural argument leading to a belief in an intelligent designer, Cleanthes has abandoned his analogical argument presented in Part 2. In a passage in Part 12, he makes it clear that both routes (as well as a third, education) are available:

> A false, absurd system, human nature, from the force of prejudice, is capable of adhering to, with obstinacy and persever-ance: But no system at all, in opposition to a theory, supported strong and obvious reason, by natural propensity, and by early education, I think it absolutely impossible to maintain and defend. (D. 174)

Why does Cleanthes continue to defend the version of the Argument from Design presented in Part 2, granting Philo's criticisms of it in that section? Part of the answer can be gathered from his belief in the success of his illustrative analogy. We saw that, in presenting the articulate voice analogy, Cleanthes suggests a possible line of criticism based on the dissimilitudes between this voice and ordinary human voices. His position, however, is that the standard which this suggested criticism applies is greater than that normally employed; therefore, this line of criticism, in the voice example, does not move us to reject the argument about an intelligent cause. Cleanthes maintains that the suggested line of criticism against the voice example is on a par with Philo's objections to the Argument from Design. Therefore, he believes that Philo's criticisms in Part 2 are also setting a standard which is too high. It is not that the Design Argument cannot be criticized; it is rather the case that it should not be criticized. Both arguments, according to Cleanthes, meet the usual standards applied to analogical arguments.

The other reason why Cleanthes continues to defend the Design Argument can be gathered by recalling what Philo has accomplished in Part 2. A close look at that section shows that, although Philo introduces alternative principles of order, nothing which he says there proves that any principle of order can produce an effect like the effects known to stem from intelligence, namely, those displaying means to ends relations and a coherence of parts. In fact, this is only accomplished by the end of Part 8.

If this account of the voice analogy is correct, then it is evident that the task confronting Philo is more complicated than is usually supposed. For he must deal with Cleanthes' claim that a knowledge of God is possible both through an analogical argument and through a natural argument, and not just through the analogical argument. But the task of the commentator is now also seen to be more complicated, inasmuch as an understanding of the *Dialogues* requires not only seeing the connection between the analogical argument presented in Part 2 and the final pronouncement in Part 12 'that the cause or causes of order in the universe probably bear some remote analogy to human intelligence' (D. 184), but also determining the connection (if any) between the natural argument advocated in Part 3 and this final pronouncement.

The vegetable library analogy

Cleanthes' second illustration begins with two assumptions: 'Suppose, that there is a natural, universal, invariable language, common to every individual of human race, and that books are natural productions, which perpetuate themselves in the same manner with animals and vegetables, by descent and propagation' (D. 118). With these assumptions in mind, he asks whether upon viewing these volumes containing 'the most refined reason and most exquisite beauty' you could

> doubt, that its original cause bore the strongest analogy to mind and intelligence. . . . When it reasons and discourses; when it expostulates, argues, and enforces its views and topics; when it applies sometimes to the pure intellect, sometimes to the affections; when it collects, disposes, and adorns every consideration suited to the subject: Could you persist in asserting, that all this, at the bottom, had really no meaning, and that the first formation of this volume in the loins of its original parent proceeded not from thought and design? (D. 118)

Cleanthes continues by affirming that any difference between the case of the imagined vegetable library and the universe is to the advantage of the latter: 'The anatomy of an animal affords many stronger instances of design than the perusal of Livy or Tacitus' (D. 118). Cleanthes also urges that the illustration of the vegetable library, which he assumes Philo (and everyone else) will accept, is equally vulnerable to Philo's earlier objection regarding the cause of the design of the world: 'And any objection which you start . . . by carrying me back to so unusual and extraordinary a scene as the first formation of worlds, the same objection has place on the supposition of our vegetating library' (D. 118). He concludes this second illustration by offering the following alternatives: 'Choose, then, your party, Philo, without ambiguity or evasion: Assert either that a rational volume is no proof of a rational cause, or admit of a similar cause to all the works of nature' (D. 118).

The vegetable library analogy is usually criticized by commentators on two grounds. First, the library example employs organisms to illustrate the force of the Design Argument, and, as it has been repeatedly urged, this appeal cannot succeed. For example, Kemp Smith writes:

> What is peculiarly characteristic of the argument from design – at once its strength and its greatest weakness – is that it has always professed to find its chief and most convincing evidence precisely in the field where the analogy to which it appeals is least applicable, namely, in the field of animal and vegetable life. The organic is not only organized; it is self-organizing. Organisms are self-developing, self-maintaining, self-regulating, self-propagating. Their 'form', that is to say, is as native and natural to them as is the 'matter' of which they are composed. In an artificial product, on the other hand, the form, so far from being native to it, depends for its existence on an external artificer.[3]

It would appear, then, that since organisms have internal unintelligent principles of order, the appeal to organisms is doomed to failure in seeking support for the Design Argument.

Secondly, the organic library example raises a question about whether the object appealed to can be called a book. As Kemp Smith puts it:

> It is precisely the differences between 'project and forethought' as revealed in articulate speech, in a book, or in a machine, and 'order and final causes' as exhibited in plants and animals, that

3 Norman Kemp Smith, *Hume's Dialogues Concerning Natural Religion* (Indianapolis; Bobbs-Merrill, 1947), p. 102.

have to be reckoned with. In Cleanthes' illustration they are confounded together, not distinguished. If a book is really a book it is due to 'project and forethought', *not* to propagation; if, on the other hand, it is due to propagation it must be vegetable or animal, and to term it a book is to insist on a resemblance while refusing the conditions which can alone make it relevant.[4]

To the extent that Cleanthes' illustration is intended to establish, through analogical reasoning, the similarity of the cause of the vegetable library to human intelligence, what form would the argument take, or more specifically, to what is the vegetable library being compared? On Kemp Smith's reading, Cleanthes' vegetable library would be compared to other vegetables, and this is what leads Kemp Smith to hold that this analogy is inapplicable, inasmuch as vegetables have internal unintelligent principles of order, and the Design Argument is intended to show that the cause of the design of the world is external to the world and intelligent.

However, it is an error to read Cleanthes' illustration in this way. What has repeatedly been overlooked is that Cleanthes recognizes that the library has as its *immediate* cause 'descent and propagation'. In other words, the way the illustration is set up, the role of unintelligent internal principles of order is acknowledged. Now at this point, it might be said that this simply shows Cleanthes' inability to recognize how the library example hurts his case, by calling attention to alternative principles of order. However, Cleanthes is attempting to make certain points which he believes will support his case about the world. In the first place, in maintaining the inference to an intelligent cause for the vegetable library, Cleanthes does not focus on what the books are, namely, natural productions or organisms, but rather on what they do. It is when one of the books is opened and we discover that it reasons and discourses, that it expostulates, argues, and enforces its views and topics, that it applies sometimes to the pure intellect, sometimes to the affections, and that it collects, disposes, and adorns every consideration suited to the subject – it is then, according to Cleanthes, that the inference to an intelligent cause is justified. Second, Cleanthes' concern is not with the immediate cause of design of the volumes. His concern is with the *original cause*, with 'the first formation of this volume in the loins of its original parent'. The basis for comparison, therefore, appears to be the rational activities of this

4 ibid., p. 103.

vegetable library and identical rational activities in ordinary volumes. His argument would then be that, since rational activities have always been observed to stem from intelligent beings, we can, by analogy, infer that the rational vegetable volumes also have an intelligent cause. The immediate cause of the volumes does not satisfy what experience has shown to be the cause of rational activity. Hence, the immediate cause cannot of itself account for what the volumes do. The only way to account for what the volumes do is to distinguish between the immediate cause of a particular volume and the original parent, that is, that which so structured the process of 'descent and propagation' that each volume would have the capacity for rational activity.

But a further point must be made. In arguing analogically to an intelligent cause for the volumes, we do not require that we experience a constant conjunction between the original parent of the volumes and particular volumes. The reasoning appears satisfactory, even though we do not have access to the original cause. This accounts for Cleanthes' challenge to Philo:

> And any objection which you start in the former case, by carrying me back to so unusual and extraordinary a scene as the first formation of worlds, the same objection has place on the supposition of our vegetating library. . . . Assert either that a rational volume is no proof of a rational cause, or admit of a similar cause to all the works of nature.' (D. 118)

Two questions must be raised here: first, how does the inference from the activities of the volumes to an intelligent original cause, even if allowed, illustrate that the world had an intelligent cause of design, and, second, what reason does Cleanthes have for tying the activity to organic volumes?

In addressing the first question, it is clear that the illustration will be successful provided that there are sufficient similarities between the activities of the volumes and the world to enable us to infer the cause of one through arriving at the cause of the other. How, then, do the activities of the volumes resemble the world? The only answer is in terms of means to ends relations and a coherence of parts. All the activities cited for the volumes can be reduced to the very characteristics used by Cleanthes in connection with seeking to establish that there is an intelligent cause for the design of the world, namely, means to ends relations and a coherence of parts. This is particularly evident in the reference to the opened volume in so far as it 'collects, disposes, and adorns every consideration suited to the subject', although it fits the other activities as well. 'To reason and discourse, to expostulate, argue, and enforce views and topics' – all these activities involve the proper adaptation of means to ends relations and a coherence of parts. In applying 'sometimes to the pure intellect, sometimes to the affections', the volume puts itself forth as a means of dealing with these capacities. Hence, the force of the illustration can be schematized as follows:

$$
\frac{\text{Rational activity in ordinary volumes (means to ends relations and a coherence of parts)}}{\text{Intelligent principle of order}} \div \frac{\text{Rational activity in the vegetable library (means to ends relations and a coherence of parts)}}{\text{Intelligent principle of order}} = \frac{\text{Rational activity in machines (means to ends relations and a coherence of parts)}}{\text{Intelligent principle of order}} \div \frac{\text{Rational activity in the world (means to ends relations and a coherence of parts)}}{\text{Intelligent principle of order}}
$$

The second question raised was why the activities cited in the example are tied to organic volumes. One part of the answer lies in the fact that, if successful, we are made aware that the immediate cause may not suffice in accounting for design, and that we can reason by analogy to an original cause of design even where we have not had any experience of such an original cause conjoined with the item in question. We have never seen a vegetable library designed by its original cause; yet, Cleanthes claims, having seen rational volumes designed by intelligence, we can reason to the original cause of the organic volumes. But there is another part to the answer, and it is emphasized by Cleanthes himself:

> But if there be any difference, Philo, between this supposed case and the real one of the universe, it is all to the advantage of the latter. The anatomy of an animal affords many stronger instances of design than the perusal of Livy or Tacitus. (D. 118)

In other words, the organic volumes themselves display the features of design which the activities of the volumes display, and, therefore, the volumes *qua* organic existences require an intelligent original cause of design just as they require an intelligent original cause of design in virtue of their activities. Hence, animals and vegetables for Cleanthes

21

can now be seen to require an intelligent original cause of design. The organisms in the world, therefore, can be used as evidence that the original cause of design is an intelligent being, and organisms do not appear to conflict with the thesis of the Design Argument.

It is now clear why Cleanthes would not be bothered by the first objection cited earlier by Kemp Smith regarding the self-organizing character of organisms, namely, he holds that their design is evidence of an intelligent original designer. It is also clear why Cleanthes would not be bothered by Kemp Smith's second criticism. For Cleanthes believes that the vegetable library example shows that no distinction can be made between the results of 'project and forethought' (the activities of the volumes) and 'order and final causes' (the structure of the organisms) which is adequate to establish that the causes of each are different. Means to ends relations and a coherence of parts, wherever they are found, Cleanthes is saying, require an intelligent principle of order. Kemp Smith's point, therefore, that if a book is really a book it stems from project and forethought and not propagation, and if it is due to propagation it is not a book, would be regarded by Cleanthes as an assertion by someone who fails to distinguish between immediate and original causes. The immediate cause of the volumes, 'descent and propagation', enables us to regard what comes about as organic. But the original cause which is inferred is what enables us to regard the result as a book. Hence, for Cleanthes there is nothing odd in speaking of organic books.

We can now understand why Philo's objections in Part 2 are not seen as effective criticisms by Cleanthes. For Cleanthes' position acknowledges alternative principles of design, and it requires that, even where experience discloses a non-intelligent principle as the immediate cause of intelligent contrivance (means to ends relations and a coherence of parts), we should not regard this principle as adequate for the production of the design; rather, we should, by analogy, insist on an intelligent original principle of order. This shows us that a refutation of Cleanthes' position cannot be accomplished by simply pointing to non-intelligent immediate causes for rationally designed effects. By ignoring this illustrative analogy, or by interpreting it as Kemp Smith has done, the full challenge to Philo, the critic of the argument, is missed.

Cleanthes' 'natural' or 'irregular' argument must also be examined. As in the case of the articulate voice example, there is a direct inference from the data to the conclusion, and again here, as in the former case, there is no appeal to constant conjunction. His position is that, once the volumes are observed, we could not doubt that their

22

original cause greatly resembles intelligence. If we are to be persuaded by his natural argument, there must be sufficient similarities not only in the argument forms employed in the case of the vegetable library example and the design of the world, but also in what is compared, namely, the organic volumes and the world. As shown earlier when discussing the vegetable library as an instance of analogical reasoning, the similarities which Cleanthes emphasizes are understood in terms of means to ends relations and a coherence of parts. The same features are emphasized with respect to the natural argument. The rational activities of the volume lead immediately to a belief in an intelligent original cause. Furthermore, the rational design of the volumes does exactly the same thing.

PART 4

At the beginning of Part 4, Cleanthes insists that the ideas which we have of mind are 'just, and adequate, and correspondent' to God's nature. Philo, who throughout the discussion has insisted on 'the adorable mysteriousness' of the divine nature, responds to Cleanthes by saying he will prove 'that there is no ground to suppose a plan of the world to be formed in the divine mind, consisting of distinct ideas, differently arranged; in the same manner as an architect forms in his head the plan of a house which he intends to execute' (D. 124). Philo characterizes this as an 'inconvenience' of anthropomorphism.

He begins by claiming that nothing is gained by Cleanthes' position whether it is assessed by 'reason' or by 'experience'. The judgement of reason is

> that a mental world or universe of ideas requires a cause as much as does a material world or universe of objects; and if similar in its arrangement must require a similar cause. For what is there in this subject, which should occasion a different conclusion or inference? In an abstract view, they are entirely alike; and no difficulty attends the one supposition, which is not common to both of them. (D. 124)

Similarly, experience cannot 'perceive any material difference in this particular, between these two kinds of worlds, but finds them to be governed by similar principles, and to depend upon an equal variety of causes in their operations' (D. 124–5). Philo concludes that the type of argument employed by Cleanthes leads to an infinite regress:

How therefore shall we satisfy ourselves concerning the cause of that Being, whom you suppose the Author of Nature, or, according to your system of anthropomorphism, the ideal world, into which you trace the material? Have we not the same reason to trace that ideal world into another ideal world, or new intelligent principle? (D. 125)

He then suggests that we should not go beyond the material world itself:

But if we stop, and go no farther; why go so far? Why not stop at the material world? How can we satisfy ourselves without going on *in infinitum*? And after all, what satisfaction is there in that infinite progression? Let us remember the story of the *Indian* philosopher and his elephant. It was never more applicable than to the present subject. If the material world rests upon a similar ideal world, this ideal world must rest upon some other; and so on, without end. It were better, therefore, never to look beyond the present material world. (D. 125)

In suggesting that it is better never to look beyond the material world, what precisely is it that Philo is advocating? George Nathan maintains that 'Cleanthes is unaware that Philo is trying to eliminate only the externality of the cause. He is not trying to deny its intelligence.'[5]

Certain questions suggest themselves regarding Nathan's position. First, what does Nathan mean by the intelligence of the cause? Second, what evidence is there that Hume does not want to deny the intelligence of the cause? And, third, is Nathan correct in maintaining that Philo only wants to deny the externality of the cause, and not its intelligence?

To understand Nathan's sense of the terms 'rationality' and 'intelligence' (he treats these as synonyms in this context, see his article p. 421), we must examine what he says in other parts of his paper. The first clue to Nathan's interpretation occurs when he discusses the vegetable library illustration. He points out that there is an essential ambiguity in the word design throughout the *Dialogues*: 'At some stages the meaning of "design" is taken to be that of the rational or intelligent order which is produced by an external agent or the intentions and plans of that agent. However, "design" can also mean only the rational

5 George Nathan, 'Hume's Immanent God.' In *Hume: A Collection of Critical Essays*, ed. V. C. Chappell (New York: Doubleday & Co. Inc., 1966), pp. 396–423. Further references will be cited in the text.

order itself without any further assumptions about external causes' (p. 404). To determine whether an object has a rational order, Nathan suggests the following:

> Just as we call a mind rational because of its particular order, and not because of its cause, likewise we determine whether any other thing has an intelligent order by examining its structure and not by looking for the cause. For Hume, the way of determining such order is by comparing something to objects which are acknowledged to be rationally ordered and then ascertaining what points of analogy are present in both. If the aspects which are found in the ordered product are also found in the item in question, then we can pronounce that item rational. Of course, human artifacts suggest themselves as the obvious paradigm for such comparisons. (pp. 407–8)

Nathan maintains that the rational order in human artifacts derives from the fact that there are 'parts which are related to each other by the reciprocal relation of cause and effect and which also contribute to some general purpose of the object as a whole' (p. 421). Hence, on Nathan's reading of Hume, non-human products can be regarded as rationally ordered provided they also possess these features. To be rationally ordered, therefore, there is no requirement of conscious design on the part of the cause. Nathan goes further and holds that, where an effect displays the features which entitle us to regard it as rational or intelligently ordered, we can conclude that its cause is rational or intelligent, regardless of whether the cause is internal or external. Commenting on the effects of causal reasoning in man and similar results achieved through instinct in other animals (cases of external causes), Nathan writes:

> Judging from the marvellous adaptation of means to ends which men evidence, we must equally acknowledge a similar process on the part of animals. If man exhibits rationality, then so do other creatures. The fact of rationality is not diminished by the revelation that instinct is the cause of this amazing adaptive process. Rather, we are led to the conclusion that instinct possesses a rationality of its own. (p. 407)

Speaking in connection with the vegetable library illustration, which Nathan maintains must be regarded as having internal ordering principles, he writes: 'even though the propagation of the natural volumes does not depend on conscious design, nevertheless the volumes

25

are rational and are due to a rational cause. The character of the volumes remains unchanged, even if they did not have an external cause' (p. 407).

Regarding the second question I raised in connection with Nathan's thesis, namely, is there evidence that Hume does not want to deny the intelligence or rationality of the cause of the design of the world, he argues as follows: 'The . . . principle which is responsible for the order in the universe has already been characterized as rational. It is rational or intelligent because its effects resemble the intelligently ordered objects of human artifice' (p. 421). We are now able to see why he holds that in Part 4 only the externality of the cause of the design of the world is being attacked: since Nathan holds that Hume ascribes rationality to causes the effects of which have a relation of parts to each other and to a general purpose, and since these features are not questioned in regard to the design of the world in Part 4, he concludes that nothing said by Philo in this part is critical of the rationality of the ordering cause. Now, although it is true that nothing said by Philo in Part 4 challenges the claim that the world is rationally or intelligently ordered, this is not sufficient to confirm Nathan's position. For his argument is that Hume *nowhere* challenges the rationality of the cause of the design of the world, and, therefore, Nathan's major effort is to show that Hume is arguing for a rational (in Nathan's sense) internal principle of order for the world. Therefore, I propose to turn to the third question raised in connection with Nathan's paper to determine whether Philo wants only to deny the externality of the cause. This is best approached by determining whether Philo ever criticizes the rationality or intelligence of the design of the world.

In proceeding with this problem, it is best to advance in two stages. First, I will examine passages which are held by Nathan (and others) to establish that Philo accepts the rationality of the world, and therefore of its designing cause, and I will show that these passages do not support Nathan's view. In the second stage, I will turn to the text to show that there are passages in which Philo shows why the rationality of the design of the world and of its cause cannot be established. One more point before we begin. Nathan maintains, as we saw (and I believe that this is correct), that for an effect to be considered rational, and, therefore, for the cause of that effect to be considered rational, the effect must be so ordered that it satisfies two conditions, namely, there must be a relation of parts to each other and to a general purpose. It is reasonable to hold that, if the second condition is satisfied, then the first condition is also satisfied. That is, if the parts are so ordered that they lend themselves to some overall purpose, then the parts must be related to each other. Hence, claims of purposiveness allow us to conclude the existence of means to ends relations. Philo never denies that the design of the world exhibits means to ends relations. However, it is far from obvious that the existence of means to ends relations allows us to claim that there is a general purpose to whatever possesses these relations. As we shall see, it is this very point with which Hume is struggling in seeking to determine whether the order we find in the world is a rational order. Philo will deny that reason can ever establish that the design of the world is purposive.

The first passage quoted by Nathan appears in Part 10. Philo asserts: 'You ascribe, Cleanthes (and I believe justly), a purpose and intention to nature' (D. 157). At first glance, this passage appears to support the view that the design of the world is a rational one. However, I believe that the situation is somewhat more complex, and to show this I want to return to a passage spoken by Philo in Part 2 in which he speaks – as he does in the passage from p. 157 – of 'ascribing justly'. Philo there tells Demea and Cleanthes:

> as all perfection is entirely relative, we ought never to imagine, that we comprehend the attributes of this Divine Being, or to suppose, that his perfections have any analogy or likeness to the perfections of a human creature. Wisdom, thought, design, knowledge; these we justly ascribe to him; because these words are honourable among men, and we have no other language or other conceptions, by which we can express our adoration of him. But let us beware, lest we think, that our ideas any wise correspond to his perfections, or that his attributes have any resemblance to these qualities among men. (D. 108)

At least in connection with divine attributes, 'justly ascribing' certain attributes to God does not involve any accuracy on our part in regard to such ascriptions: just ascription, in this case, is linked with a complete lack of comprehension of divine attributes, and a denial of any likeness between human perfections and those of God.

The passage spoken by Philo at p. 157, in which he acknowledges a purpose and intention to nature, is expressed in a manner similar to the way in which he expressed his views about divine attributes in Part 2. And, therefore, in reading the passage in Part 10, we should be open to the possibility that, when Philo consents to a 'just ascription of a purpose and intention to nature', he does not believe either that we understand the purpose and intention in nature, or that purposiveness as far as we understand it has any likeness to what is true of the world. In any case, the passage at p. 157 cannot be taken *simpliciter* as evidence that Philo holds that there is a purpose and intention to nature.

The second passage quoted by Nathan occurs at the end of Part 10:

> In many views of the universe, of its parts, particularly the latter, the beauty and fitness of final causes strike us with such irresistible force, that all objections appear (what I believe they really are) mere cavils and sophisms; nor can we then imagine how it was ever possible for us to repose any weight on them. (D. 160)

In assessing this passage, the sentence preceding what I have quoted is relevant. Philo tells Cleanthes that 'Formerly, when we argued concerning the natural attributes of intelligence and design, I needed all my sceptical and metaphysical subtlety to elude your grasp.' The full point that Philo is making, therefore, is that in attacking the claim of intelligence and design, he employed sceptical (pyrrhonistic) arguments. However, often our perception of the world, particularly the adaptation of means to ends, strikes us so irresistibly that we can no longer deny the rationality of the world, even though we have been exposed to the sceptical arguments against the rationality of the world. In fact, the sceptical arguments now appear to us as mere cavils and sophisms (and are such).

The structure of Philo's point does not lend itself to interpreting him as holding that there are reasonable (or analogical) grounds for believing in a purpose and intention to nature. Rather, what he says supports the view that a belief in purposiveness is instinctive or a natural tendency. Notice that the concession to purposiveness follows the presentation of sceptical arguments. And notice further that it is a particular view of the world 'striking' us with 'irresistible force' which gives rise to the belief in purposiveness.

A third passage relevant to our discussion occurs in Part 12, where Philo again appears to assent to the purposive nature of the world:

> A purpose, an intention, a design strikes every where the most careless, the most stupid thinker. (D. 172)

In understanding this passage it should be recalled that 'carelessness' for Hume is a technical term which is used to characterize that state of mind which enables us to ignore the arguments of the sceptic and to be moved by our natural tendencies. At the conclusion of the section 'Of Scepticism with regard to the senses' in the *Treatise*,[6] Hume writes:

> This sceptical doubt, both with respect to reason and the senses, is a malady, which can never be radically cured, but must return upon us every moment, however we may chace it away, and sometimes may seem entirely free from it. 'Tis impossible upon any system to defend either our understanding or senses; and we but expose them further when we endeavour to justify them in that manner. As the sceptical doubt arises naturally from a profound and intense reflection on those subjects, it always increases, the farther we carry our reflections, whether in opposition or conformity to it. Carelessness and in-attention alone can afford us any remedy. For this reason I rely entirely upon them; and take it for granted, whatever may be the reader's opinion at this present moment, that an hour hence he will be persuaded there is both an external and internal world. (T. 218)

The passages we have examined lend themselves to the interpretation that a belief in the rationality of the design of the world is not something which reason can establish. It is usual with Hume in his effort to establish a belief as natural to show why reason is unable to establish the belief in question. I will now show that this standard practice of Hume's is also present in the case of the claim regarding the rationality of the design of the world.

The challenge to Philo to determine whether the world possesses a rational design is made by Cleanthes at the end of Part 5: 'by the utmost indulgence of your imagination, you never get rid of the hypothesis of design in the universe; but are obliged, at every turn, to have recourse to it' (D. 132). Cleanthes' challenge is met by Philo in Part 8. In this section, Philo proposes the following:

> Suppose . . . that matter were thrown into any position, by a blind, unguided force; it is evident that the first position must in all probability be the most confused and most disorderly imaginable, without any resemblance to those works of human contrivance, which, along with a symmetry of parts, discover an adjustment of means to ends and a tendency to self-preservation. If the actuating force cease after this operation, matter must

---

6 References to the *Treatise* are taken from Hume's *Treatise of Human Nature*, edited by L. A. Selby-Bigge, second edition (Oxford, Clarendon Press, 1978), and are cited by 'T.' followed by relevant page numbers.

remain for ever in disorder, and continue an immense chaos, without any proportion or activity. But suppose, that this actuating force, whatever it be, still continues in matter, this first position will immediately give place to a second, which will likewise in all probability be as disorderly as the first, and so on, through many successions of change and revolutions. . . . Thus the universe goes on for many ages in a continued succession of chaos and disorder. But is it not possible that it may settle at last, so as not to lose its motion and active force . . . yet so as to preserve an uniformity of appearance, amidst the continual motion and fluctuation of its parts? This we find to be the case with the universe at present. Every individual is perpetually changing, and every part of every individual and yet the whole remains, in appearance, the same. May we not hope for such a position, or rather be assured of it from the eternal revolutions of unguided matter, and may not this account for all the appearing wisdom and contrivance, which is in the universe? Let us contemplate the subject a little, and we shall find, that this adjustment, if attained by matter, of a seeming stability in the forms, with a real and perpetual revolution or motion of parts, affords a plausible, if not a true solution of the difficulty. (D. 145-6)

A blind unguided force of the sort which this hypothesis postulates could not be considered a rational designing principle in Nathan's sense. Now, if reason will always be confronted with the possibility that the cause of the design of the world is not a rational principle of order, and if only a rational principle of order can produce a rationally ordered effect, it follows that reason cannot establish that the world is a rationally ordered effect. The question we must now answer is why can reason not be convinced that the design of the world is a rational one.

Hume's answer to this must be that means to ends relations and a coherence of parts – features of the world which we can verify – do not ensure that there is a general purpose to whatever it is that possesses these features; for, if they did, then their presence would rule out the possibility that the cause of design is a 'blind, unguided force'. The point Hume is anxious to make is that purposiveness is not reducible to means to ends relations and a coherence of parts, nor do these features ensure purposiveness. If means to ends relations and a coherence of parts were either the same as a general purpose or features ensuring a general purpose, then these features would ensure that the object is rationally designed, and hence has a rational cause. But, since we can deny the rationality of the cause even when these characteristics are present, it follows that a general purpose cannot be known or inferred merely from the presence of these features. If we take a machine or an organism as items which satisfy the requirements of a rational design, much can be learned about Hume's views on purposiveness and rational design. Machines and organisms all possess means to ends relations and a coherence of parts as well as a rational design, and, therefore, Hume's point is that it is a common error to confuse these characteristics with the notion of a general purpose, or to believe that these characteristics ensure a general purpose. Nathan himself has fallen into this confusion when he tells us that

> For Hume the way of determining such order is by comparing something to objects which are acknowledged to be rationally ordered and then ascertaining what points of analogy are present in both. If the aspects which are found in the ordered product are also found in the item in question, then we can pronounce that item rational. Of course, human artifacts suggest themselves as the obvious paradigm for such comparisons. For this reason Cleanthes' illustrations are especially apt. His comparison of the universe to machines, houses and books is useful because they all exhibit an intelligent structure. (pp. 407–8)

What Hume is trying to show is that the presence of means to ends relations and a coherence of parts is not sufficient to claim that an object possesses a rational structure and a rational cause, and that, therefore, more is required before such a rational structure can be confidently affirmed. What more is needed?

A clue to answering this is provided by Hume in a passage in Part 8 which immediately follows the one we have been discussing. Philo asserts:

> It is in vain, therefore, to insist upon the uses of the parts in animals or vegetables and their curious adjustment to each other. I would fain know how an animal could subsist, unless its parts were so adjusted? Do we not find, that it immediately perishes whenever this adjustment ceases, and that its matter corrupting tries some new form? It happens, indeed, that the parts of the world are so well adjusted, that some regular form immediately lays claim to this corrupted matter: And if it were not so, could the world subsist? Must it not dissolve as well as the animal, and

31

pass through new positions and situations; till in a great, but finite succession, it fall at last into the present or some such order? (D. 146)

According to this passage, means to ends relations and a coherence of parts are necessary for an object's existence: without these features nothing can exist. Where an object comes into existence through a 'blind, unguided force', the object and its particular set of causal relations are not brought into existence purposively. On the other hand, where an object and its particular set of causal relations come into existence through some guiding force (or principle), the resulting design is purposive. For the designing principle to bring about such an object, it is not necessary, according to Hume, that it be aware of the object it is designing.

A tree bestows order and organization on that tree, which springs from it, without knowing the order: An animal, in the same manner, on its offspring: A bird on its nest. And instances of this kind are even more frequent in the world, than those of order, which arise from reason and contrivance. (D. 141)

What is required in order to say that the design is purposive is this: we must find the cause of design and the item constantly conjoined. It is precisely the absence of this constant conjunction in the case of God and the design of the world which allows Philo to suggest a 'blind, unguided force' as the origin of the design of the world. Therefore, we find ourselves returning to Philo's earlier objection in Part 2: without seeing worlds formed under our eyes, it is impossible to comment on the cause of the design of the world – and this includes its rationality. Without the required constant conjunction it will never be possible to answer the question, 'Why does the world exhibit this particular set of means to ends relations?' Without an answer to this, the problem of the general purpose served by its design cannot be answered, with the result that we cannot establish the rationality of the design of the effect or of its cause. In Part 8, Philo is suggesting that, so long as we are unable to establish that the design of the world and its cause of design are both rational (in the sense discussed earlier), it will be impossible to determine if the question, 'What is the purpose of the design we find in the world?' is well formed, since there may not be a purpose to the design.

It can now be seen, therefore, that Nathan is mistaken in holding that only the externality of the cause is being attacked by Hume, and not its rationality (in Nathan's sense of this term). The particular insight which Philo has revealed is that the presence of means to ends relations and a coherence of parts does not establish or guarantee a general purpose, and, therefore, these features alone cannot be used to establish the rationality of the effect and of the cause.

Some commentators[7] maintain that, when Philo urges that it were better never to look beyond the present material world in accounting for the design of the world, what Philo means is that we should eliminate altogether the requirement for a causal account of the order in the world. By considering the present order as an ultimate fact, no explanation of it is required, and no regress is generated. The text, however, does not support this interpretation. In one passage, Philo argues that to say that the parts of the material world fall into order of themselves, and by their own nature, is 'really to talk without any precise meaning' (D. 125) – a strange admission on his part if this is the position he is defending. In a related passage, Philo insists that to say 'that *such* is the nature of material objects, and that they are all originally possessed of a *faculty* of order and proportion . . . are only more learned and elaborate ways of confessing our ignorance' (D. 126), thereby revealing his opposition to the theory under discussion.

Perhaps, then, in the passage under discussion, Philo is advocating that the world should be supposed to have an internal (as opposed to an external) principle of order. The one passage which is relevant to our present discussion appears toward the end of Part 6. Philo says:

> And were I obliged to defend any particular system of this nature (which I never willingly should do) I esteem none more plausible, than that which ascribes an eternal, inherent principle of order to the world; though attended with great and continual revolutions and alterations. This at once solves all difficulties; and if the solution, by being so general, is not entirely complete and satisfactory, it is, at least, a theory, that we must, sooner or later, have recourse to, whatever system we embrace. How could things have been as they are, were there not an original, inherent principle of order somewhere, in thought or in matter? And it is very indifferent to which of these we give the preference. Chance has no place, on any hypothesis, sceptical or religious. Every thing is surely governed by steady, inviolable laws. And were the inmost essence of things laid open to us, we should then discover a scene, of which, at present, we can have no idea.

---

7 See, for example, Nelson Pike, *David Hume: Dialogues Concerning Natural Religion*, edited and with commentary (Indianapolis: Bobbs-Merrill Co. Inc., 1970).

Instead of admiring the order of natural beings, we should clearly see, that it was absolutely impossible for them, in the smallest article, ever to admit of any other disposition. (D. 136–7)

Philo is making the following points:

(1) If he were to defend any theory, it would be that advocating an eternal inherent principle of order, but he would never willingly do it. This solution, by being so general, is not in a finished form or wholly acceptable as it stands.

(2) An original inherent principle of order seems both necessary and sufficient for explaining the world, but we cannot determine whether this inherent principle is in thought (i.e. in an external principle of order) or in matter (i.e. an internal principle of order).

(3) He suggests that, if we could penetrate the essences of things, we would find that they cannot have any order other than the order they do have.

Each of these three points deserves some comment. In the case of (1), the inclusion of the term 'eternal' is important, for it shows that Philo realizes that the infinite regress cannot be stopped merely by positing an internal principle of order. On the other hand, if the cause is eternal, then the infinite regress criticism ceases to be effective: now it makes no sense to ask for the cause of this cause.

The hypothesis of an 'eternal inherent principle of order' avoids the problem of how the world is to be characterized (a criticism which Philo brought against Cleanthes' Argument from Design), and it makes no reference whatever to what the ordering principle is. This explains Philo's assertion that the solution possesses too great a generality; this also explains why Philo denies completeness and full acceptability to this hypothesis. What Philo believes is that, rather than offering a solution to the problem of the divine nature, he has, by asserting that the design of the world requires as its cause an eternal inherent principle of order, provided the 'form' which he regards the most plausible solution to possess.

If the world could be characterized as having a 'specific resemblance' to certain things found in the world, for example, if it could be characterized as machine-like, it would be possible to argue by analogy to the type of ordering principle it has, and this includes whether the ordering principle is internal or external. The claim of generality to the hypothesis in (1) when coupled with Philo's claim in

(2) that it is indifferent whether we opt for an internal or an external ordering principle establishes that he believes that such a characterization of the world is not possible.

Even though we cannot, according to Philo, determine whether the ordering cause of the world is in thought or matter, it appears as though some success has been obtained in the realization that no more plausible solution can be proposed to the problem of how the world achieved its design than that of an eternal inherent principle of order. Why, then, does Philo say that he would never willingly defend this position? In the passage under discussion, he says that the theory of an eternal inherent principle of order is one we must sooner or later have recourse to 'whatever system we embrace'. In other words, all systems of cosmogony are open to the criticism of an infinite regress, and, therefore, all must, in the end, posit an eternal inherent principle of order, for only in this way can the regress be stopped. But to argue in this way is to argue as Demea does in Part 9: to explain the contingent, Demea argues, a modal jump is required to a necessarily existent being; otherwise, we become involved in an infinite regress, in which case no existent can be satisfactorily accounted for. I submit that Philo recognizes that, to stop the regress to which all systems of cosmogony lead, we must have recourse to Demea's *a priori* argument in Part 9. However, since Philo holds that this argument is ill-grounded, he is obviously unwilling to defend the claim of an eternal inherent principle of order to the world.

The third point raised by Philo in the passage under discussion, namely, that, if we could penetrate the essences of things, we would find that they cannot have any order other than the order they have, can also be explained by turning to a passage in Part 9. Toward the end of this part, Philo asserts:

> It is observed by arithmeticians, that the products of 9 compose always either 9 or some lesser product of 9; if you add together all the characters, of which any of the former products is composed. Thus, of 18, 27, 36, which are products of 9, you make 9 by adding 1 to 8, 2 to 7, 3 to 6. Thus 369 is a product also of nine; and if you add 3, 6 and 9 you make 18, a lesser product of 9. To a superficial observer, so wonderful a regularity may be admired as the effect either of chance or design; but a skillful algebraist immediately concludes it to be the work of necessity, and demonstrates, that it must for ever result from the nature of these numbers. Is it not probable, I ask, that the whole economy of the universe is

conducted by a like necessity, though no human algebra can furnish a key, which solves the difficulty? And instead of admiring the order of natural beings, may it not happen, that, could we penetrate into the intimate nature of bodies, we should clearly see why it was absolutely impossible, they could ever admit of any other disposition? (D. 150–1)

This passage makes it clear that Philo is not claiming that the order in the world is necessary. What he is saying is that, although we cannot establish the claim that the order of things in the world is necessary, it is also not possible to disprove it. And since this claim cannot be disproved (given that we cannot penetrate into the intimate nature of bodies) we will always be ignorant of whether a principle of order is required to account for the order in the world: the inclusion of principles of order presupposes that the order in the world is contingent, and that, therefore, the order arises from something other than the very nature of what is ordered.

I argued earlier that Philo refuses to defend the hypothesis of an eternal inherent principle of order to the world because this would involve him with the type of argument Demea employs in Part 9, and he holds this argument to be defective. We can now see an additional reason for his unwillingness to defend an eternal inherent principle of order to the world, namely, he would have to establish that the order in the world is contingent, and this he believes he cannot do.

To sum up, if the order in the world is contingent, then the ordering cause must be regarded as necessary to stop the infinite regress charge. And if not contingent, then the order must be necessary. In either case, our ignorance will continue, since we can neither understand nor demonstrate necessity as it relates to existence.

An ironic element in the debate between Philo and Cleanthes is apparent. Philo has shown that Cleanthes' Argument from Design ultimately rests on the *a priori* proof presented by Demea in Part 9. Yet it is Cleanthes who offers the bulk of the critique against this *a priori* proof. By so doing, he shows that the 'inconvenience' of his Argument from Design, as developed by Philo, is something he cannot remedy.

PART 5

As part of Philo's attack on Cleanthes' Argument from Design, we find two sections, Part 4 and Part 5, devoted to elaborating certain 'inconveniences' in the anthropomorphism of Cleanthes' argument. I will now be concerned with Philo's critique in Part 5, and, in particular, with his *reductio ad absurdum* of Cleanthes' anthropomorphism in this part.

Philo's *reductio* begins with Cleanthes' commitment to an anthropomorphic conception of God:

> And what say you to the discoveries in anatomy, chemistry, botany? – These surely are no objections, replied Cleanthes: They only discover new instances of art and contrivance. It is still the image of mind reflected on us from innumerable objects. Add, a mind *like the human*, said Philo. I know of no other, replied Cleanthes. And the liker the better, insisted Philo. To be sure, said Cleanthes. (D. 129)

He now offers the first stage of his argument:

> Now, Cleanthes, said Philo, with an air of alacrity and triumph. Mark the consequences. *First.* By this method of reasoning, you renounce all claim to infinity in any of the attributes of the Deity. For as the cause ought only to be proportioned to the effect, and the effect, so far as it falls under our cognizance, is not infinite; What pretensions, have we, upon your suppositions, to ascribe that attribute to the divine Being? (D. 129)

It might be thought that Philo's argument is not permissible both because of his pyrrhonism, and because of his (Hume's) account of causality which does not allow for *a priori* knowledge of causes. In fact, however, the argument put forth by Philo does not represent his own view (hence it is not in conflict with his pyrrhonism), and, to the extent that it involves a causal claim, Philo recognizes that it does so incorrectly. That this first step does not represent Philo's views can be seen from the fact that he prefaces his remarks with the words 'by this method of reasoning' and begins his conclusion with 'upon your suppositions', indicating that this first step follows from *Cleanthes'* position. But why does Philo present this argument; that is, what has Cleanthes said that leads Philo to put this argument forth as representing Cleanthes' position? The answer is to be found in Cleanthes' version of the Argument from Design in Part 2. He argues: 'Since therefore the effects resemble each other, we are led to infer, by all the rules of analogy, that the causes also resemble; and that the author of nature is somewhat similar to the mind of man; though possessed of much larger faculties, *proportioned to the grandeur of the work, which he has executed*' (D. 109, italics added). It is, therefore, Cleanthes who, early in the debate, proposed 'proportioning the cause to the effect' in those cases where only the effect can be observed.

But it might be argued that I have not yet established conclusively that Philo is not committed to the view of a finite Deity on the basis of a finite effect (the design of the world). It could be argued that when Philo asserts that 'the cause ought only to be proportioned to the effect' he is to be interpreted as accepting this principle, and employing it to establish a finite Deity for the design of the world. Philo, on this account, is not himself bothered by this consequence but, as his *reductio* will reveal, this consequence will adversely affect Cleanthes' position. In other words, Philo regards the proportioning of causes to effects as legitimate, and then turns this against Cleanthes, who, in Philo's opinion, must be able to establish that God is infinite to prevent having the *reductio* applied against the position he holds.

That this is an incorrect reading can be learned by noting that, toward the end of Part 5, Philo expresses what he regards as following from Cleanthes' hypothesis, and in so doing he omits any reference to God as finite or infinite:

> In a word, Cleanthes, a man, who follows your hypothesis, is able, perhaps, to assert, or conjecture, that the universe, some time, arose from some thing like design: But beyond that position he cannot ascertain one single circumstance, and is left afterwards to fix every point of his theology, by the utmost licence of fancy and hypothesis. (D. 131)

What this passage also reveals is that Philo urges that Cleanthes also should not hold to the hypothesis of a finite Deity: even if we were to grant Cleanthes' mode of seeking a knowledge of God by comparing the design of the world to the design of machines, the inference to a finite Deity cannot be countenanced – and this obtains even though 'the effect, so far as it falls under our cognizance, is not infinite'.

Why does Philo refuse to allow the inference to the finitude of the Deity? No direct answer is provided by Philo in Part 5. However, there are other passages – in Section XI of the first *Enquiry* – in which Hume indicates why he will not accept arguments like the one Philo has presented in Part 5 regarding a finite Deity. It will be seen that Philo has all along echoed Hume's reasons when arguing against Cleanthes.

In Section XI of the first *Enquiry*, Hume examines the principle concerning the proportioning of causes to effects where the cause is to be known only through the effect:

When we infer any particular cause from an effect, we must proportion the one to the other, and can never be allowed to ascribe to the cause any qualities, but what are exactly sufficient to produce the effect. . . . If the cause, assigned for any effect, be not sufficient to produce it, we must either reject that cause, or add to it such qualities as will give it a just proportion to the effect. (E. 136)

He then goes on to entertain a use for this principle in learning about the Deity:

Allowing, therefore, the gods to be the authors of the existence or order of the universe; it follows, that they possess that precise degree of power, intelligence, and benevolence, which appears in their workmanship; but nothing farther can ever be proved, except we call in the assistance of exaggeration and flattery to supply the defects of argument and reasoning. So far as the traces of any attributes, at present, appear, so far may we conclude these attributes to exist. (E. 137)

Throughout this discussion, the principle regarding the proportioning of causes to effects is treated quantitatively: it is proposed that by examining the effect, we can calculate how much of a particular attribute must be present in its cause – there may, of course, be a greater degree of the attribute in the cause, but this cannot be known by examining the effect.

However, this interpretation of the principle is rejected by Hume, and he denies that a cause can be known only through its effect, where the effect cannot be classified as being a member of a species whose cause is known:

I much doubt whether it be possible for a cause to be known only by its effect (as you have all along supposed). . . . It is only when two *species* of objects are found to be constantly conjoined, that we infer the one from the other; and were an effect presented, which was entirely singular, and could not be comprehended under any known species, I do not see, that we could form any conjecture or inference at all concerning its cause. If experience and observation and analogy be, indeed, the only guides which we can reasonably follow in inference of the nature; both the effect and cause, must bear a similarity and resemblance to other effects and causes, which we know, and which we have found, in many instances, to be conjoined with each other. (E. 148)

For Hume, therefore, the proper application of the principle regarding the proportioning of causes to effects is based on observing effects and their causes constantly conjoined: to proportion a cause to an effect means assigning as the cause of an effect what we have found to be the cause of an effect of that sort. To offer a quantitative analysis of this principle without the requisite constant conjunction is to corrupt the principle.

Now, Philo refuses to infer a finite Deity even though the effect presents itself as finite. He has, throughout the discussion, given full support to the Humean claims that causal knowledge requires observing cause and effect constantly conjoined, and that the design of the world does not enable us to classify the world under any known species. Philo could accept a finite Deity on the basis of an effect which appears finite where the advantage of observing cause and effect constantly conjoined is not present if and only if he accepts a purely quantitative analysis of the principle enjoining the proportioning of causes to effects. Since he refuses the former, he must be denying the latter as well. Therefore, Philo's refusal to infer a finite Deity establishes his refusal to treat the proportioning principle in a purely quantitative manner. According to Philo, Cleanthes' position lacks the required constant conjunction for causal knowledge of God, and misuses the principle that causes ought to be proportioned to their effects.

Pike writes that, even if Philo has shown that Cleanthes is committed to a finite Deity, this should not disturb Cleanthes, for at no time did he seek to deny this:

> The question of interest is whether Cleanthes should be disturbed by Philo's contention. . . . I think we can agree that Cleanthes would not be distressed in the least. . . . Cleanthes holds that God's attributes far exceed their counterparts in men, but he explicitly denies that they are infinite. At this point we should expect Cleanthes to be quite content with the claim that the argument from design will establish the existence of an extremely intelligent (and extremely powerful) creator although it does nothing to show that the intelligence (and power) involved in this cause is infinite. (Pike, pp. 166–7)

Pike makes two errors in his interpretation. First, Philo denies that the inference to a *finite* Deity is countenanced inasmuch as the requisite constant conjunction is absent in the case of God and the world. And, second, Pike fails to realize – what Philo correctly points out to

Cleanthes – that the *reductio* in Part 5 is possible only if the finitude of the Deity is granted:

> From the moment the attributes of the Deity are supposed finite, all these [absurdities] have place. And I cannot, for my part, think, that so wild and unsettled a system of theology is, in any respect, preferable to none at all. (D. 132)

Philo's *reductio* can now be seen in a clear light. Allowing 'A' to stand for 'The Deity is a mind like the human mind,' 'F' to stand for 'The Deity is finite,' and '$R_1 \cdot R_2 \cdot R_3 \cdot R_4 \cdot R_5$' to stand for the absurdities which Philo will draw from Cleanthes' position, Philo's argument against Cleanthes can be represented as follows:

$$(A \rightarrow F) \cdot [(A \cdot F) \rightarrow (R_1 \cdot R_2 \cdot R_3 \cdot R_4 \cdot R_5)] \tag{C}$$

In the first conjunct above, 'A' must be represented as implying 'F' since the finitude of the Deity is, for Cleanthes (D. 128), 'a consequence of' his anthropomorphism. That is to say, when Cleanthes argues for the intelligence of the designer of the world through the principle 'like effects prove like causes', he is maintaining that this principle can be employed only if the principle of proportioning causes to effects is also employed. Cleanthes' anthropomorphic conception of God is the result of a former principle; the claim that the Deity is finite results from the latter principle. Accordingly, we can regard his anthropomorphism to imply the finitude claim.

In the second conjunct, the antecedent must be represented as '$A \cdot F$' and not simply as 'F', inasmuch as otherwise Philo would be represented as holding that the absurdities follow simply from the claim of the finitude of the Deity, and this is not the position for which he is arguing. Philo is not claiming that all representations of the Deity which include the finitude claim lead to absurdities. He urges that Cleanthes' anthropomorphism implies the finitude claim, and that these two doctrines lead to absurd conclusions regarding the Deity. Hence, the representation of the argument which I have offered above.

Philo's primary aim in Part 5 is to discredit anthropomorphism. Part 5 opens with Philo indicating that he will show Cleanthes 'more inconveniences' in his anthropomorphism. How Philo accomplishes this is easily seen by determining what follows from (C).

(1) $(A \rightarrow F) \cdot [(A \cdot F) \rightarrow R_1 \cdot R_2 \cdot R_3 \cdot R_4 \cdot R_5)]$ P (C)
(2) $(A \cdot F) \rightarrow (R_1 \cdot R_2 \cdot R_3 \cdot R_4 \cdot R_5)$ 1, Simplification

(3) $A \rightarrow F$ 1, Simplification
(4) $A \rightarrow (A \cdot F)$ 3, Absorption
(5) $A \rightarrow (R_1 \cdot R_2 \cdot R_3 \cdot R_4 \cdot R_5)$ 4,2 Hypothetical
                                                            Syllogism

Given premise (1) (C) above, it follows that the absurdities which Philo draws are implied by the claim that 'the Deity is a mind like the human mind', and Cleanthes' anthropomorphism is seen to be unacceptable.

None of the following propositions, however, can be inferred from (C):

(1) 'The Deity is not finite': $(\sim F)$
(2) 'The Deity is finite': (F)
(3) 'The Deity is a mind like the human mind and
      the Deity is not finite': $(A \cdot \sim F)$
(4) 'The Deity is a mind like the human mind and
      the Deity is finite': $(A \cdot F)$

In other words, within this argument nothing has been settled regarding whether the Deity is or is not finite, and nothing has been established about the acceptability or unacceptability of anthropomorphism *simpliciter*. Philo has only established that Cleanthes' anthropomorphism leads to certain absurd results, once the Deity is held to be finite. Cleanthes cannot, of course, conjoin his anthropomorphism with the claim of an infinite Deity even though this would avoid the *reductio*, since he has no evidence for the hypothesis of an infinite Deity. Furthermore, in one passage (at the beginning of Part 11) he indicates his resistance to the ascription of the term 'infinite' to the Deity:

> I scruple not to allow, said Cleanthes, that I have been apt to suspect the frequent repetition of the word, infinite, which we meet with in all theological writers, to savour more of panegyric than of philosophy, and that any purposes of reasoning, and even of religion, would be better served, were we to rest contented with more accurate and more moderate expressions. (D. 161)

What are the absurdities which follow from Cleanthes' position? Philo lists five. First, once the Deity is supposed finite we cannot ascribe perfection to Him, since the product, from which our knowledge of the Deity is to be inferred, contains 'many inexplicable difficulties' (D. 129). Second, even if the world is a perfect production,

42

we cannot determine whether the perfections of the work can be ascribed to the workman. Very often, the one who brings a designed product about is 'a stupid mechanic, who imitated others, and copied an art, which, through long succession of ages, after multiplied trials, mistakes, corrections, deliberations, and controversies, had been gradually improving' (D. 130). Third, on Cleanthes' hypothesis, we cannot establish that there is only one Deity: several deities may have co-operated in framing this world. Fourth, men are mortal and renew their species by generation: why should this feature, which 'is common to all living creatures', be excluded from the deities? Finally, why not become a perfect anthropomorphite, and assert that the deities are corporeal, a position which accords with the fact that we have never seen reason except in a human figure?

Pike interprets these five points as constituting a 'fanciful hypothesis', and he holds that Philo's intention in putting it forth is to suggest that this fanciful hypothesis is as good as, or better than, the hypothesis of design in accounting for the design of the world (Pike, p. 165). We have already seen that this is a misreading of Philo, since his concern is to demonstrate, through these five claims, what Cleanthes' hypothesis of design yields, once the Deity is supposed to be finite. Therefore, these five points do not constitute an alternative to Cleanthes' position: they follow from it. To maintain the hypothesis of design such that it will be compatible with his theism, Cleanthes must give up the claim of the finitude of the Deity.

Philo's *reductio*, therefore, does not constitute a criticism of Cleanthes' Argument from Design, and, in particular, it does not attack the position that the design of the world stems from intelligence. The essential argument in the Argument from Design, namely, Cleanthes' attempt to establish that the cause of the design of the world resembles human intelligence because both the world and machines of human contrivance exhibit means to ends relations and a coherence of parts, has yet to be attacked decisively by Philo.

PARTS 6 TO 8

Within Part 5, Philo has demonstrated the absurdities which follow from Cleanthes' anthropomorphism, once the Deity is regarded as finite. In the final paragraph of Part 5, Cleanthes responds to Philo's *reductio*:

These suppositions I absolutely disown; cried Cleanthes. They strike me, however, with no horror; especially when proposed in that rambling way, in which they drop from you. On the contrary, they give me pleasure, when I see, that, by the utmost indulgence of your imagination, you never get rid of the hypothesis of design in the universe; but are obliged, at every turn, to have recourse to it. To this conception I adhere steadily; and this I regard as a sufficient foundation for religion. (D. 132)

This passage is important, primarily because it discloses that Philo's *reductio* has moved Cleanthes to yield on certain points to which he formerly held, and it shows that Cleanthes realizes those elements within his position which Philo has not yet attacked successfully. It is clear that Cleanthes realizes that Philo has not yet succeeded in attacking his characterization of design in the world and the manner in which he regards this characterization to support his claim of an intelligent designer, namely, that the mere presence of means to ends relations and a coherence of parts in machines and the world countenances reasoning analogically to an intelligent designer for the world. Along with this, of course, goes Cleanthes' belief that Philo has not shown that natural theology cannot be founded on the principle 'like effects prove like causes'. What Cleanthes must be willing to give up in the light of Philo's *reductio* is that the Design Argument establishes that the Designer of the world is finite. For, without the finitude claim, Philo's *reductio* is eliminated. The final paragraph in Part 5 reveals no adamancy on Cleanthes' part to retain the finitude claim.

The crucial challenge has now been presented to Philo: to establish the principal error in Cleanthes' position, in so far as the argument he advanced maintains that means to ends relations and a coherence of parts are always evidence of intelligent contrivance.

Philo begins his attack on this claim by introducing the Principle of Co-existence, 'that where several known circumstances are *observed* to be similar, the unknown will also be *found* similar' (D. 133). Philo urges that this principle is similar to Cleanthes' principle 'like effects prove like causes' in that it is 'no less certain, and derived from the same source of experience'. Cleanthes' principle is concerned with making causal inferences, given specific resemblances in the effects observed. Philo's principle, on the other hand, is not a principle enabling us to make causal inferences. Just what Philo intends by his principle can be learned from the particular examples he offers of the employment of the principle:

Thus, if we see the limbs of a human body, we conclude that it is also attended with a human head, though hid from us. Thus, if we see, through a chink in the wall, a small part of the sun, we conclude, that, were the wall removed, we should see the whole body. (D. 133)

In both examples, there is a concern with inferring something to be co-present with what is being observed, based on our past experience of such items being co-present. Philo maintains that the Principle of Co-existence is at least as certain as Cleanthes' principle 'like effects prove like causes', since both principles derived their level of certainty from the same source – the observation of constant conjunction. The Principle of Co-existence requires that the observations obtained bear a specific resemblance to portions of objects (Philo's examples are confined to natural objects) previously observed. What the principle countenances is an inference to those portions of that type of object which cannot be observed. If the principle countenances such inferences, then it must also countenance inferring that the observations obtained are those of an object of a certain sort. The usefulness of the Principle of Co-existence can, therefore, be stated in two ways: given the appropriate constant conjunction, the principle enables us to infer the presence of an object of a certain sort, or the presence of the unobserved portion of that sort of object.

I now proceed to Philo's employment of this principle against Cleanthes' position. Philo argues:

Now if we survey the universe, so far as it falls under our knowledge, it bears a great resemblance to an animal or organized body, and seems actuated with a like principle of life and motion. A continual circulation of matter in it produces no disorder: A continual waste in every part is incessantly repaired: The closest sympathy is perceived throughout the entire system: And each part or member, in performing its proper offices, operates both to its own preservation and to that of the whole. The world, therefore, I infer, is an animal, and the Deity is the SOUL of the world, actuating it, and actuated by it. (D. 133)

Allowing A, B, C, and D to stand for the four characteristics which the world has in common with an animal or organized body, Philo's argument can be stated as follows:

(1) A, B, C, and D have been found by experience to be characteristics of animals. The world possesses A, B, C, and D. Therefore, from

45

the Principle of Co-existence, it follows that the world is an animal.

(2) A, B, C, and D have been found by experience to be joined to mind. The world possesses A, B, C, and D. Therefore, from the Principle of Co-existence, it follows that the world is joined to a mind.

Cleanthes uses the Principle of Co-existence to take issue with Philo's argument:

> [I]t seems to me, that, though the world does, in many circumstances, resemble an animal body, yet is the analogy also defective in many circumstances, the most material: No organs of sense; no seat of thought or reason; no one precise origin of motion and action. In short, it seems to bear a stronger resemblance to a vegetable than to an animal; and your inference would be so far inconclusive in favour of the soul of the world. (D. 135)

Commentators are in general agreement that the concession by Cleanthes, that the world bears a greater resemblance to an organism than to a machine, effectively destroys his case regarding an intelligent cause of design for the world. However, in the light of our previous discussion on the vegetable library analogy, it is clear that his position cannot yet be taken as refuted, inasmuch as he concedes that organisms have, as their immediate cause, internal unintelligent designing principles, but insists that the original cause of organisms is intelligence. Hence, he believes his anthropomorphism to be secure, regardless of whether the design of the world resembles the design of machines or the design of organisms.

At the beginning of Part 7, Philo enquires into the cause of the design of the world, in light of his examination in Part 6, which sought to examine that the world is an organism. He argues:

> If the universe bears a greater likeness to animal bodies and to vegetables than to the works of human art, it is more probable, that its cause resembles the cause of the former than of the latter, and its origin ought rather to be ascribed to generation or vegetation than to reason or design. Your conclusion, even according to your own principles, is therefore lame and defective.' (D. 138)

That the universe bears a greater resemblance to animals and vegetables than to machines is asserted by Philo in three different passages – p. 138, line 5; p. 139, lines 27–8; p. 133, lines 25–6. Hence, it is a claim which must be taken seriously. The evidence for this claim is difficult to determine. That the world resembles an organism is based on the Principle of Co-existence. But this, by itself, does not establish that the resemblance is greater with respect to organisms than it is with respect to machines. To substantiate his position, either Philo must show that the very evidence employed by Cleanthes in his argument to establish that the world resembles a machine is, in fact, more supportive of Philo's claim that the world resembles an organism, or he must show that the data he has offered in support of his position are (in some sense) superior to the data employed by Cleanthes to support the intelligence claim.

Cleanthes' sole basis for arguing an intelligent cause of design for the world is the presence of means to ends relations and a coherence of parts. Now, each of the characteristics cited by Philo as evidence that the world resembles an organism is reducible to these very features: the first ('a continual circulation of matter in it produces no disorder' (D.133)), third ('the closest sympathy is perceived throughout the entire system' (D.133)), and fourth ('each part or member, in performing its proper offices, operates both to its own preservation and to that of the whole' (D. 133)) are clear cases of means to ends relations and a coherence of parts, while the second – 'a continual waste in every part is incessantly repaired' (D. 133) – is nothing but a display of means to ends relations. Philo makes the point that the four features cited in support of the world-as-an-organism hypothesis are gained by surveying the universe 'so far as it falls under our knowledge' (D.133), thereby indicating that these are characteristics which are confirmed by scientific investigation.

Cleanthes had insisted that they proceed scientifically. Philo urges that investigating the world scientifically reveals some resemblances between the world and organisms – resemblances which have their basis in the means to ends relations and a coherence of parts which are discovered. This gives us the insight we require to determine why Philo believes that the resemblance between the design of the world and organisms is greater than that between the world and machines: whereas scientific investigation reveals *specific* similarities between the world and organisms in terms of the means to ends relations and a coherence of parts which are found, no comparable specific similarities based on these features are found by science between the world and machines. That science cannot establish that the world resembles a machine is the very point Philo had maintained in the first four paragraphs of Part 5. In Parts 6 and 7, he elaborates on this through the Principle of Co-existence, that is, the particular means to ends relations and coherence of parts in the design of the world appear to allow for the classification of the world as an organism, whereas no comparable classification of the world as a machine is countenanced through this principle (or for that matter through any other principle of inference). It should also be recalled that at the end of Part 5, Cleanthes challenged Philo by insisting that nothing which Philo has argued refutes 'the hypothesis of design' in the universe, and that this – which amounts to the presence of means to ends relations and a coherence of parts – he regards 'as a sufficient foundation for religion'. It is entirely reasonable for Philo to address this challenge by showing that the very features of design cited by Cleanthes are, in fact, more supportive of the view of the world as an organism than they are of Cleanthes' view of the world as a machine.

Should Philo be regarded as believing that the claim that the design of the world arose from generation or vegetation is more acceptable (in terms of the evidence provided) than Cleanthes' hypothesis of design? Philo does appear to be maintaining that his argument is stronger than Cleanthes' Design Argument:

> [T]here are other parts of the universe (besides the machines of human invention) which bear still a greater resemblance to the fabric of the world, and which therefore afford a better conjecture concerning the universal origin of this system. These parts are animals and vegetables. The world plainly resembles more an animal or vegetable than it does a watch or a knitting loom. Its cause, therefore, it is more probable, resembles the cause of the former. The cause of the former is generation or vegetation. The cause, therefore, of the world, we may infer to be something similar or analogous to generation or vegetation. (D 138)

In another passage, however, he explains precisely how the superiority of his position over Cleanthes' is to be understood. His account is offered while replying to a question raised by Demea: the latter asks 'is the slight, imaginary resemblance of the world to a vegetable or animal sufficient to establish the same inference with regard to both? Objects, which are in general so widely different; ought they to be a standard for each other?' (D. 139). And Philo replies:

> Right! . . . This is the topic on which I have all along insisted. I

48

have still asserted that we have no *data* to establish any system of cosmogony. Our experience, so imperfect in itself, and so limited both in extent and duration, can afford us no probable conjecture concerning the whole of things. But if we must needs fix on some hypothesis; by what rule, pray, ought we to determine our choice? Is there any other rule than the greater similarity of the objects compared? And does not a plant or an animal, which springs from vegetation or generation, bear a stronger resemblance to the world, than does any artificial machine, which arises from reason and design? (D. 139)

Philo is asserting (a) that, strictly speaking, evidence for classifying the world in order to enable us to infer its cause of design is not available; and (b) but, if, in the face of this absence of adequate evidence to classify the world, we persist in forming hypotheses about it, then we should opt for that hypothesis which is based on the strongest resemblance between the world and certain items found in the world. Hence, since the world bears a stronger resemblance to an organism than it does to a machine, the machine hypothesis must be rejected. Philo holds that neither position is actually tenable; but, if we are forced to choose, our selection should be guided by what it is that the world most closely resembles.

By examining the world we find that it bears some resemblances to an animal or vegetable, but not enough to justify classifying it as one or the other. Philo does not enumerate what other characteristics the world would have to possess to justify classifying it as an organism. However, from other things which he says, we can understand why such a list is not included. In Part 2, Philo expresses misgivings about Cleanthes' position, partly because he saw no justification for concluding that thought is the productive principle of the whole world: there are other productive principles as well, and Philo was at a loss to know how they are to be ruled out. In Parts 6 and 7, the discussion centres around means to ends relations and a coherence of parts which are found in organisms, and which originate from generation and vegetation. Hence, the mere presence of these characteristics does not guarantee that the productive principle involved is thought. Other principles may also be responsible for design which manifests these characteristics:

In this little corner of the world alone, there are four principles, *reason, instinct, generation, vegetation,* which are similar to each other, and are the causes of similar effects. What a number of other principles may we naturally suppose in the immense extent and variety of the universe, could we travel from planet to planet and from system to system, in order to examine each part of this mighty fabric? Any one of these four principles abovementioned (and a hundred others, which lie open to our conjecture) may afford us a theory, by which to judge of the origin of the world; and it is a palpable and egregious partiality to confine our view entirely to that principle, by which our own minds operate. (D. 140)

We also know how Philo (and Hume) hold that the productive principle can be inferred and others ruled out: we must find a close correspondence (or specific resemblance) between the features exhibited by the object in question, and other objects whose cause is known; it is this which provides for the proper employment of the principle 'like effects prove like causes'. In short, for Philo, the concern in causal reasoning is with classification at the level of species ('when two species of objects have always been observed to be conjoined together, I can infer, by custom, the existence of one whenever I see the existence of the other' (D. 115)). And no classification of the world with respect to species is possible, because of the absence of the relevant (specific) resemblance between the design of the world and known species of objects. If this classification according to species is not forthcoming, then a classification according to genus is not permissible. This, then, explains why Philo does not provide a list of features which, if exhibited by the world, would enable us to classify it as an organism: the only lists of features which are relevant are those pertaining to species of objects, and there is no species within the world to which the world bears so close a resemblance that it can be regarded as another member of that species.

It is clear that, in Parts 6 and 7, Philo has effectively destroyed Cleanthes' efforts within the Argument from Design itself to establish the legitimacy of a causal inference to an intelligent Designer merely through the presence of means to ends relations and a coherence of parts. The issue of classification shows Cleanthes' procedure in the argument to be defective. From our treatment of the articulate voice, it can now be established that this illustrative analogy is without force in strengthening Cleanthes' position. The means to ends relations and coherence of parts apprehended in what is heard from the clouds are precisely what justify an inference to the belief that what is heard is a voice. With this classification and our knowledge of the cause of voices, we are justified in concluding that the cause of what is heard from the clouds is intelligence. However, since a similar classification of the world as a machine on the basis of the means to ends relations and coherence of parts which we find is not possible, it follows that the voice analogy is not helpful in illustrating Cleanthes' position. The voice analogy does, in fact, illustrate Philo's claim that, unless the features of design exhibited allow a proper classification of what is being observed under a known species, an inference to the cause of design is not justified.

Philo has succeeded in showing that a classification of the world which would allow the use of the principle 'like effects prove like causes' cannot be accomplished. And in this respect Cleanthes' efforts have failed. But what Philo has conceded is that, if we still persist in our efforts at classification, then 'Is there any other rule than the greater similarity of the objects compared?', and, on this method of proceeding, we find that the world bears a stronger resemblance to a plant or animal than it does to a machine (D. 133). What Philo must now show is that, even if this is the most convincing claim we can make about the nature of the world, it will not assist Cleanthes in seeking to establish that the cause of the design of the world is an intelligent being. We know that Cleanthes is not bothered by a classification of the world as an organism: in the vegetable library analogy, he argued that when reasoning by analogy about the cause of the design of the vegetable library, we must acknowledge that only intelligence, posited as the *original* cause of the vegetable library, can adequately explain the activities and design of the vegetable volumes. But the activities of the volumes and their particular design exhibit means to ends relations and a coherence of parts, and, to the extent that any organism displays these features, the same original cause must be posited. It is at this point, therefore, that Philo must address the second of Cleanthes' illustrative analogies. This, then, is (at least part of) what Philo's argument has thus far not challenged.

That Philo is about to address the vegetable library analogy can be learned from the fact that the central claim of that analogy is re-introduced in Part 7 as a challenge to Philo:

> But methinks, said Demea, if the world had a vegetative quality, and could sow the seeds of new worlds into the infinite chaos, this power would be still an additional argument for design in its author. For whence could arise so wonderful a faculty but from design? Or how can order spring from any thing, which perceives not that order which it bestows? (D. 140)

Philo's answer is given in two parts, and his answer addresses two inconsistent positions adopted earlier by Cleanthes.

At times, Cleanthes insists that the immediate cause which experience discloses for a particular phenomenon should be regarded as a satisfactory causal account for that phenomenon, even though we are unable to trace that cause further back to its cause, and so on. This is particularly evident in Part 4, when Cleanthes is confronted with the cause of the ideas in God's mind.

> Even in common life, if I assign a cause for any event; is it any objection, Philo, that I cannot assign the cause of that cause, and answer every new question, which may incessantly be started? And what philosophers could possibly submit to so rigid a rule? philosophers, who confess ultimate causes to be totally unknown, and are sensible, that the most refined principles, into which they trace the phenomena, are still to them as inexplicable as these phenomena themselves are to the vulgar. The order and arrangement of nature, the curious adjustment of final causes, the plain use and intention of every part and organ; all these bespeak in the clearest language an intelligent cause or author. The heavens and the earth join in the same testimony: The whole chorus of nature raises one hymn to the praises of its Creator: You alone, or almost alone, disturb this general harmony. You start abstruse doubts, cavils, and objections: You ask me, what is the cause of this cause? I know not; I care not; That concerns not me. I have found a Deity, and here I stop my enquiry. Let those go farther, who are wiser or more enterprising. (D. 126–7)

Now, to the extent that this is Cleanthes' position, Philo urges that vegetation and generation must be accepted as the causes of organisms, and, therefore, as the causes of the organic library, since these are the designing principles which are found constantly conjoined with the resultant organisms. Experience discloses that design (means to ends relations and a coherence of parts) can originate from non-intelligent sources:

> A tree bestows order and organization on that tree, which springs from it, without knowing the order: An animal, in the same manner, on its offspring: A bird on its nest: And instances of this kind are even more frequent in the world, than those of order, which arise from reason and contrivance. (D. 141)

Philo correctly points out that, if, in the case of organisms, the

52

immediate cause is not regarded as providing an adequate causal account – a position Cleanthes maintained when putting forth the vegetable library analogy – and an intelligent original cause is posited, then we have begged the question. Philo explains this in the following way:

> To say that all this order in animals and vegetables proceeds ultimately from design is begging the question; nor can that great point be ascertained otherwise than by proving *a priori*, both that order is, from its nature, inseparably attached to thought, and that it can never, of itself, or from original unknown principles, belong to matter. (D. 141)

Cleanthes has insisted throughout that support for hypotheses be sought within experience. In his discussion of the organic library, he also insisted that the ultimate cause of the organic volumes be sought. It is Philo's answer to this line of enquiry which constitutes the second part of his answer to the vegetable library analogy.

Philo argues that, once the question of ultimate causes is raised, Cleanthes will find that his reasoning has no empirical support:

> Judging by our limited and imperfect experience, generation has some privileges above reason: For we see every day the latter arise from the former, never the former from the latter. (D. 141)

Again, in the next paragraph Philo points out that 'Reason, in innumerable instances, is observed to arise from the principle of generation, and never to arise from any other principle.' (D. 142)

If Cleanthes insists on seeking an ultimate cause, the problems which arise are clear: if we begin with the view of the world as an organism, there is no support in experience for an intelligent original cause, and, if we begin with the world as a machine, there is some support for the claim that it ultimately arose from generation. Therefore, on this mode of proceeding, Cleanthes can have either no support for his intelligence claim, or an ultimate cause (generation/vegetation) which cannot serve his purpose.

Ultimately, therefore, Philo confronts Cleanthes with a dilemma from which he believes Cleanthes cannot escape – a dilemma which is based on Cleanthes' two assertions, namely, that a satisfactory causal account can be obtained from the immediate cause, and that a satisfactory causal account can be obtained only by tracing the phenomenon back to an ultimate or original cause.

At this stage, therefore – the end of Part 7 – Philo has effectively destroyed any plausibility in Cleanthes' position, in so far as the latter holds that we can reason analogically to an intelligent cause for the design of the world. Philo's success covers the Argument from Design as well as Cleanthes' two illustrative analogies. Cleanthes finds that he has no answer to any of the objections raised by Philo. At the end of Part 7, Cleanthes says:

> I must confess, Philo, replied Cleanthes, that, of all men living, the task which you have undertaken, of raising doubts and objections, suits you best, and seems, in a manner, natural and unavoidable to you. So great is your fertility of invention, that I am not ashamed to acknowledge myself unable, on a sudden, to solve regularly such out-of-the-way difficulties as you incessantly start upon me: Though I clearly see, in general, their fallacy and error. And I question not, but you are yourself, at present, in the same case, and have not the solution so ready as the objection; while you must be sensible, that common sense and reason is entirely against you, and that such whimsies, as you have delivered, may puzzle, but never can convince us. (D. 142)

It seems appropriate, therefore, that Philo's critique should cease with Part 7. In Part 8, however, we find him continuing his attack on Cleanthes' position: Philo prefaces his remarks in this section by addressing Cleanthes' claim that the doubts and objections which Philo has raised are 'natural and unavoidable' given his 'fertility of invention':

> What you ascribe to the fertility of my invention, replied Philo, is entirely owing to the nature of the subject. In subjects, adapted to the narrow compass of human reason, there is commonly but one determination, which carries probability or conviction with it; and to a man of sound judgement, all other suppositions, but that one, appear entirely absurd and chimerical. But in such questions, as the present, a hundred contradictory views may preserve a kind of imperfect analogy; and invention has here full scope to exert itself. (D. 143)

What Philo has yet to show is the extent to which we can be sceptical in trying to understand the nature of God.

Part 8 reveals that Philo is intent on proving that our scepticism can be extended well beyond what was argued up to Part 7, where attention was confined to a determinate number of designing principles. That Philo believes he is proceeding empirically in Part 8 is learned from the opening paragraph where he claims that, in such questions as the present, a hundred contradictory views may preserve a kind of imperfect analogy, and that he could propose other systems of cosmogony which would have some faint appearance of truth.

He begins by pointing out that matter always appears to us to be in motion: 'And whatever the causes are, the fact is certain, that matter is, and always has been in continual agitation, as far as human experience or tradition reaches. There is not probably, at present, in the whole universe, one particle of matter at absolute rest' (D. 144). The number of sources of motion in matter – actual or possible – Philo refuses to specify, given our limited experience of the world. And this – the absence of a definitive list of the sources of motion in matter – works to the advantage of the sceptic. For, as we will see, Philo will argue that any source of motion in matter could have contributed to bringing about the present order. Further, since we lack a knowledge of all such sources of motion, he will argue his position through the presence of motion itself, without any reference to, or knowledge of, the actual causes of motion. In short, Philo will account for the order of the world through the mere presence of motion in matter – a feature of matter which appears to have no exceptions – without taking into account how matter acquired motion, and he will argue that his account possesses at least as much empirical support as the Argument from Design possesses.

Since he has already shown, in Parts 6 and 7, that the means to ends relations and coherence of parts which we find do not allow us to classify the world (in any strict sense) according to a known species or genus, his concern in Part 8 need not, and, in fact, will not be to show additional known species to which the world bears some (imperfect) analogy. Part 8 is silent on the matter of such classifications, and, therefore, we can conclude that Philo believes that he has offered enough on this. As such, it becomes evident that Part 8 will not concern itself with *Cleanthes'* version of the Argument from Design – the first version presented in the *Dialogues*, p. 109 – wherein certain features that the world exhibits in its design are compared to the same features in machines of human contrivance. It will be recalled that Part 2 contained two versions of the Argument from Design: the second version (D. 111–12) is the one which avoids the concern with classification, and emphasizes that matter appears to be unable to arrange itself so as to form an object displaying means to ends relations and a coherence of parts, whereas we find that the human mind can arrange its own ideas so as to form the plan of objects possessing design. Part 8, therefore, is largely concerned with the second version of the Argument from Design, and will show that experience supports the claim that design can arise in matter without an intelligent source of order.

The passage in the original argument where the issue of intelligence and matter as sources of design is raised reads:

> For ought we can know *a priori*, matter may contain the source or spring of order originally, within itself, as well as mind does; and there is no more difficulty in conceiving, that the several elements, from an *internal unknown cause*, may fall into the most exquisite arrangement, than to conceive that their ideas, in the great, universal mind, from a like *internal, unknown cause*, fall into that arrangement. The equal possibility of both these suppositions is allowed. (D. 111–12, italics added)

From the italicized portion of this passage we learn that no allowance is made for inquiring into the cause of the order exhibited in mind or matter: the extent of the inquiry is simply whether order can be observed to originate in each. The original argument claims that order can be observed to originate only in mind, not in matter (premise 5, see p. 7 of this Introduction):

> But by experience we find (according to Cleanthes) that there is a difference between them. Throw several pieces of steel together, without shape or form; they will never arrange themselves so as to compose a watch: Stone, and mortar, and wood, without an architect, never erect a house. But the ideas in a human mind, we see, by an unknown, inexplicable economy, arrange themselves so as to form the plan of a watch or house. Experience, therefore, proves, that there is an original principle of order in mind, not in matter. (D. 112)

Therefore, if Philo can establish that order can be observed to originate in matter, he will have provided an alternative account to that in the original argument which possesses at least as much empirical support as that argument possesses.

The relevant experience (or analogy) is found in the matter of organisms which both exhibits design, and which, upon the destruction of a particular form, 'tries some new form'.

> It is in vain, therefore, to insist upon the uses of the parts in animals or vegetables, and their curious adjustment to each other.

56

I would fain know how an animal could subsist, unless its parts were so adjusted? Do we not find, that it immediately perishes whenever this adjustment ceases, and that its matter corrupting tries some new form? It happens, indeed, that the parts of the world are so well adjusted, that some regular form immediately lays claim to this corrupted matter: And if it were not so, how could the world subsist? Must it not dissolve as well as the animal, and pass through new positions and situations; till in a great, but finite succession, it falls at last into the present or some such order? (p. 146)

According to Philo, the behaviour of matter from which organisms are formed is typical of what is observed to be the case with matter generally. Wherever matter achieves an arrangement so that an adjustment of means to ends results, the arrangement has a tendency to self-preservation (an expression used one page earlier); wherever the adjustment of means to ends is disturbed, the arrangement has a tendency to self-destruction; and, wherever the destruction of such an arrangement occurs, the 'corrupted matter' continues on until it becomes part of another adjustment of means to ends relations. In short, experience discloses that design can originate in matter in motion in addition to (what was never disputed by Philo) intelligence.

Besides offering a counter claim to the fifth premise in the second version of the Argument from Design, the passage quoted establishes that there are no general characteristics by which we can determine whether order originated in mind or in matter: the very features which Cleanthes regards as evidence of design originating from mind – means to ends relations and a coherence of parts – are seen to be a feature of all design, regardless of origin, inasmuch as without these features no design can exist. Without the presence of means to ends relations and a coherence of parts, no design can come into existence or continue to exist, whereas with these features the design has a tendency to self-preservation. Accordingly, both mind and matter are bound by the same conditions in yielding design.

From Philo's argument in Part 8, we learn that any source of motion in matter could have originated the present order, and, therefore, it is in vain to attempt to provide a determinate list of principles through which the world could have achieved its design. But Philo is saying much more than that a determinate list of designing *principles* is not obtainable. Given that matter is always in motion, and that stability in arrangement depends only on matter achieving an adaptation of means to ends and coherence of parts, what appears to be the result of some designing principle may, in fact, originate in a 'blind unguided force'. A designing principle for Hume is a force – albeit one whose essence is unknown by us – which, when exerted, is disposed to produce effects of a certain type. A blind unguided force, on the other hand, would be one which also causes motion in matter, but it would not, each time it is exerted, be disposed to produce effects of a certain type. Philo's point is that, even if matter were set in motion by a blind unguided force, a stability in arrangement would be reached once the parts of matter achieved means to ends relations and a coherence of parts. Hence, the design of the world could appear to be the result of a designing principle, either in mind or matter, and actually stem from a force which has no disposition or tendency to design at all. Therefore, what Philo is challenging in Part 8 is not only the view that means to ends relations and a coherence of parts are evidence of mind as the principle of design; he is also challenging a datum accepted by Cleanthes, namely, that design is evidence of a *principle* of design. Philo urges that, given the manner in which matter is found to behave in terms of design coming into existence, passing out of existence, and abiding, the design of the world can be accounted for (at least as well as the Design Argument is able to do so) without reference to a principle of design; hence, the plausibility of the Epicurean account as Philo restates it (D. 143). Accordingly, we cannot even decide whether the present order originates from a designing principle or a blind unguided force in matter: the present order is compatible with both alternatives and appears to support both equally. (The mysteriousness of the causes of order in mind and in matter has already been discussed by Philo in Part 4 of the *Dialogues*.)

In the account of matter in which there is no employment of designing principles in explaining the present order, it must also be the case that the regularities which are observed within the world, from which the account of the design of the whole world is fashioned, are to be explained without reference to principles of design. All generation, stability, and decay of forms may be the result of an arrangement which all matter has assumed, which permits the present order to continue, but which has not been achieved through any designing principles. This explains why, in delivering his version of the Epicurean hypothesis, no reference whatever is made to designing principles – either with regard to the whole world or within the world. The distinction between principles of order and forces generating motion in matter is, therefore, understood not to be one which can be made simply through an examination of the effects – even when generation and decay are observed to occur in a regular manner. This, of course, stems from our complete ignorance of principles and forces, and is not a position adopted by common sense. Common sense will always treat regularities in nature as resulting from certain principles of order. The sceptic, however, can exploit our ignorance of principles of design in nature, and provide an account of design which omits all reference to these principles.

Given that the sceptic is able to attack one of the data of the Design Argument, namely, that design is evidence of a principle of design, Philo is able to complete his sceptical attack on this argument, inasmuch as he is able to challenge the principle 'like effects prove like causes' (premise 11) and the principle enjoining the observation of constant conjunction as the guide to causal knowledge (premise 1). The principle regarding constant conjunction assumes that observed regularities are evidence of a power in one object to bring about the observed effect in the second; and the principle 'like effects prove like causes' assumes that, where effects are similar, we are entitled to infer similar principles of order or guides for matter as their cause. However, on the Epicurean account which Philo offers in Part 8, both are challenged: observed regularities in nature are not regarded as evidence of a power in one object to bring about the effects observed in the one regularly conjoined with it, and similar effects are not taken as evidence of similar principles of order in objects which bring them about. The regularities and similarities observed are all accounted for through the adaptation of means to ends relations and a coherence of parts which matter has achieved in accordance with the tendency we observe in matter to hold forms achieving such adaptations, and the tendency of matter to arrange itself so as to accommodate all matter when a particular form is upset. Hence, on the Epicurean hypothesis, no object is accurately called a 'cause' of another, and similar effects are not actually the products of similar *principles* of order. Once the use which Cleanthes makes of these principles is challenged by the Epicurean hypothesis, we are made to see that Philo's objections to the Design Argument go beyond the particular principle of order for which Cleanthes has argued, and include any principle of order which we might select. The order of the world may have resulted from a designing principle or it may not have so resulted, and Philo's point is that we cannot, on the basis of data available, decide between these.

Toward the end of Part 8, Cleanthes raises a number of criticisms against Philo's hypothesis – criticisms which Philo acknowledges to be relevant. After pointing out additional difficulties in Cleanthes' Design Argument, Philo cautions that, because of the subject matter, those with opposing views should not condemn each other. Since no system of cosmogony can be defended satisfactorily, in the end victory belongs to the sceptic, and a suspense of judgement is the only reasonable position:

> all of them, on the whole, prepare a complete triumph for the sceptic who tells them, that no system ought ever to be embraced with regard to such subjects: For this plain reason, that no absurdity ought ever to be assented to with regard to any subject. A total suspense of judgement is here our only reasonable resource. And if every attack, as is commonly observed, and no defence, among theologians, is successful; how complete must be *his* victory, who remains always, with all mankind, on the offensive, and has himself no fixed station or abiding city, which he is ever, on any occasion, obliged to defend? (D. 147)

Part 8 closes with this passage. Cleanthes has now been shown that the argument he advances and attempts to support is no stronger than a variety of others which account for the design of the world in many different ways. By the end of Part 8, he is made to see that reasoning by analogy will not yield knowledge of the nature of God. Although Cleanthes' suspense of judgement has been brought about by Philo's sceptical or pyrrhonian objections to the Design Argument, there is a clear indication in the last passage quoted above that with the argument in Part 8 now complete, Philo will no longer participate in the discussion *as a pyrrhonian*[8]. When commenting on the sceptic's victory in this passage, Philo signals a shift from excessive scepticism by referring to the victory of the sceptic as 'his' victory (the word 'his' in the text is italicized by Hume for emphasis). Thus, we find that, prior to Part 12 where the concern with the claim of the intelligence of the Deity is once again brought up for discussion, Philo alerts us to an impending alteration in his position. On our reading, the shift will be to mitigated scepticism – the position which Hume explained in the first *Enquiry* as resulting from pyrrhonism, or excessive scepticism, 'when its undistinguished doubts are, in some measure, corrected by common sense and reflection' (E. 161).

8 For a discussion of the shift in Philo's procedure in Parts 10 and 11, see my 'Hume's Dialogues on Evil', and replies by Davis ('Going Out the Window: A Comment on Tweyman'), Nathan ('Comments on Tweyman and Davis'), and Wadia ('Commentary on Professor Tweyman's "Hume on Evil" ') included in this volume.

PART 9

One way to read Part 9 is to see it as included for completeness. Until this point in the debate, the only argument which has been examined is the *a posteriori* Argument from Design. In light of Philo's criticisms (in Parts 2 and 4–8), this argument appears to lose all plausibility. In Part 9, Demea, in proposing his *a priori* argument, is suggesting that of the two available approaches to God through argumentation – the *a posteriori* and the *a priori* – the latter approach is superior to the former in two ways. First, whereas the Argument from Design proceeds by analogy and can, at most, offer a conclusion which is probable, Demea's *a priori* argument, if valid and devoid of any false premises, offers a conclusion which must be true. Second, in Part 5, Philo had shown that the Design Argument cannot establish the infinity or the unity of the Designer. Demea maintains at the beginning of Part 9 that the *a priori* approach will not be subject to the difficulties encountered by the Argument from Design, and that, in fact, it will be found to be acceptable to all. After Demea presents his *a priori* argument, Cleanthes proceeds to offer a number of criticisms of this argument – criticisms which Demea does not attempt to answer. Hence, one way to read Part 9 is to treat it as included in order to show why Hume believed that neither the *a posteriori* approach nor the *a priori* approach can establish claims about God.

Now, while agreeing that Hume had little regard for Demea's argument in light of the criticisms put forth by Cleanthes, I submit that Part 9 has an additional role to play – a role which is supported by the text of this part, and which reveals that the inclusion of Part 9 is relevant to our understanding of Cleanthes' position in the context of his dialogue with Philo on the topic of the Argument from Design.

Demea offers the following version of the *a priori* argument:

> Whatever exists must have a cause or reason of its existence; it being absolutely impossible for any thing to produce itself, or be the cause of its own existence. In mounting up, therefore, from effects to causes, we must either go on in tracing an infinite succession, without any ultimate cause at all, or must at last have recourse to some ultimate cause, that is *necessarily* existent: Now that the first supposition is absurd may be thus proved. In the infinite chain or succession of causes and effects, each single effect is determined to exist by the power and efficacy of that cause, which immediately preceded; but the whole eternal chain or succession, taken together, is not determined or caused by any

thing: And yet it is evident that it requires a cause or reason, as much as any particular object, which begins to exist in time. The question is still reasonable, why this particular succession of causes existed from eternity, and not any other succession, or no succession at all. If there be no necessarily existent Being, any supposition, which can be formed, is equally possible; nor is there any more absurdity in nothing's having existed from eternity, than there is in that succession of causes, which constitutes the universe. What was it, then, which determined something to exist rather than nothing, and bestowed being on a particular possibility, exclusive of the rest? *External causes*, there are supposed to be none. *Chance* is a word without a meaning. Was it nothing? But that can never produce any thing. We must, therefore, have recourse to a necessarily existent Being, who carries the REASON of his existence in himself; and who cannot be supposed not to exist without an express contradiction. There is consequently such a Being, that is, there is a Deity. (D. 148-9)

The chief critic of this argument is Cleanthes, and he begins with the following (Humean) criticism:

I shall begin with observing, that there is an evident absurdity in pretending to demonstrate a matter of fact, or to prove it by any arguments *a priori*. Nothing is demonstrable, unless the contrary implies a contradiction. Nothing, that is distinctly conceivable, implies a contradiction. Whatever we conceive as existent, we can also conceive as non-existent. There is no Being, therefore, whose non-existence implies a contradiction. Consequently there is no Being, whose existence is demonstrable. I propose this argument as entirely decisive, and am willing to rest the whole controversy upon it. (D. 149)

This is the well-known criticism which Hume presented in Section XII of the first *Enquiry* and in the first book of the *Treatise*. However, if looked at in the context of Demea's *a priori* argument, it becomes somewhat less than compelling. Recall that Demea had said, in the course of presenting his *a priori* argument, that the Deity 'cannot be supposed not to exist without an express contradiction'. In other words, if we accept Demea's claim that (at least for him) the non-existence of the Deity is inconceivable, then he would have satisfied the condition in Cleanthes' argument that a proposition is demonstrable, provided that its denial is inconceivable. One is also reminded of Descartes who writes in the fifth meditation:

> But, nevertheless, when I think of it with more attention, I clearly see that existence can no more be separated from the essence of God than can its having its three angles equal to two right angles be separated from the essence of a [rectilinear] triangle, or the idea of a mountain from the idea of a valley; and so there is not any less repugnance to our conceiving a God (that is, a Being supremely perfect) to whom existence is lacking (that is to say, to whom a certain perfection is lacking), than to conceive of a mountain which has no valley.[9]

The upshot of this is the realization that the most Cleanthes has accomplished with his argument is to show that, in the case of those who find the non-existence of the Deity conceivable, the argument offered by Demea should be rejected as a demonstration of God's necessary existence. On the other hand, those who find the non-existence of the Deity inconceivable can reject Cleanthes' initial criticism as being without force against Demea's argument. In fact, for these people, his first criticism actually countenances a proof like Demea's *a priori* proof!

Cleanthes' second criticism achieves no greater success than the first. He argues:

> It is pretended, that the Deity is a necessarily existent Being; and this necessity of his existence is attempted to be explained by asserting, that, if we knew his whole essence or nature, we should perceive it to be as impossible for him not to exist as for twice two not to be four. But it is evident, that this can never happen, while our faculties remain the same as at present: It will still be possible for us, at any time, to conceive the non-existence of what we formerly conceived to exist . . . .. The words, therefore, *necessary existence* have no meaning; or, which is the same thing, none that is consistent. (D. 149)

However, as in the case of his first criticism, this criticism presupposes that the non-existence of the Deity is conceivable. However, for those, like Demea, who find the non-existence of God inconceivable, this criticism supports the view that necessary existence is as meaningful

9 *The Philosophical Works of Descartes*, trans. E. Haldane and G. R. Ross (Cambridge: Cambridge University Press, 1911), vol. I, 181.

when applied to the Deity as it is when applied to a mathematical equation.

Cleanthes' third criticism appears to be no stronger than the previous ones we have examined:

> But farther; why may not the material universe be the necessarily existent Being, according to this pretended explication of necessity? We dare not affirm that we know all the qualities of matter; and for aught we can determine, it may contain some qualities, which, were they known, would make its non-existence appear as great a contradiction as that twice two is five. I find only one argument employed to prove, that the material world is not the necessarily existent Being; and this argument is derived from the contingency both of the matter and the form of the world. 'Any particle of matter', it is said, 'may be *conceived* to be annihilated; and any form may be *conceived* to be altered. Such an annihilation or alteration, therefore, is not impossible.' But it seems a great partiality not to perceive, that the same argument extends equally to the Deity, so far as we have any conception of him; and that the mind can at least imagine him to be non-existent, or his attributes to be altered. It must be some unknown, inconceivable qualities, which can make his non-existence appear impossible, or his attributes unalterable: And no reason can be assigned, why these qualities may not belong to matter. As they are altogether unknown and inconceivable, they can never be proved incompatible with it. (D. 149–50)

Cleanthes is arguing that, even if we accept Demea's conclusion that the contingent can exist only if a necessary being exists, this cannot establish that the necessary being must be external to the totality of contingent beings, and, therefore, the material world may be the necessarily existent being. But, for those, like Demea, who find the non-existence of the Deity inconceivable, Cleanthes' criticism loses all force, since it is not the case, to use Cleanthes' words, 'that the same argument extends equally to the Deity, so far as we have any conception of him'. The hypothesis of an external necessary being as the ultimate cause of the universe, on this view, has a decided advantage over the hypothesis of an internal necessary being as the ultimate cause of the universe. On the other hand, for those who find Demea's argument compelling in so far as it shows the need for an ultimate necessary cause of the world, but who, nevertheless, find the non-existence of an external ultimate necessary cause of the world conceivable and the non-existence of an internal ultimate necessary cause of the world equally conceivable, Cleanthes' third criticism shows that there is no decision procedure by which to select one of these over the other.

Cleanthes' fourth criticism makes the point that, if the chain of causes and effects is eternal (as Demea maintains), then 'it seems absurd' to require a First Cause for the chain: 'How can any thing, that exists from eternity, have a cause; since that relation implies a priority in time and a beginning of existence?' (D. 150). In this criticism, Cleanthes is utilizing elements of Hume's account of causation, namely, that causes must exist prior to their effects, and that an effect is a new existent. However, to bring this analysis to bear on the *a priori* proof, as Cleanthes has done, is question-begging. For, if Demea is correct, that the chain of causes and effects and the matter out of which this chain is formed are contingent, then the fact that the chain is eternal may not remove the need to provide a causal account as to why it (and no other possible chain, or no chain at all) exists. If matter is contingent, then the chain may require a causal explanation, regardless of how far back in time it reaches. It is logically possible for there to exist two eternal beings with one being necessary and the cause or ground of the other. It can be argued that it is the modality of the entity, and not how long it has existed, which reveals whether it requires a cause. Cleanthes' (Humean-type) criticism would be acceptable only if we were assured that the eternity of matter precludes its having a cause, and Cleanthes offers no argument to support this. Cleanthes' hesitation in putting forth this criticism can be discerned by the words 'it seems absurd' which preface his remarks.

In Cleanthes' last criticism, he argues:

> In such a chain too, or succession of objects, each part is caused by that which preceded it, and causes that which succeeds it. Where then is the difficulty? But the WHOLE, you say, wants a cause. I answer, that the uniting of these parts into a whole, like the uniting of several distinct counties into one kingdom, or several distinct members into one body, is performed merely by an arbitrary act of the mind, and has no influence on the nature of things. Did I show you the particular causes of each individual in a collection of twenty particles of matter, I should think it very unreasonable, should you afterwards ask me, what was the cause of the whole twenty. That is sufficiently explained in explaining the cause of the parts. (D. 150)

Cleanthes is arguing that the 'world' or 'whole' which is formed by the succession of causes and effects is not a thing in the way that the individual members of the chain are things. The 'world' is a concept or 'arbitrary act of the mind', and as such need only be explained through concept formation. Rather than providing a decisive criticism of Demea's argument, Cleanthes has shown Demea a competing interpretation of the succession of causes and effects, but he has not provided a means of deciding between his position and Demea's. That is, Demea has argued that the modality of the chain is identical to the modality of the members of the chain, and, therefore, a causal account of each member of the chain through contingent predecessors in the chain can never account for why the chain exists. Causal accounts within the chain assume the existence of the chain, and provide causal explanations for individual members. Cleanthes argues that the question of a cause for the chain is not well-formed, given that all that exists are individual members of the chain, and these are adequately explained through the contingent causes which precede them. However, beyond asserting his position and providing an illustration ('Did I show you the particular causes of each individual in a collection of twenty particles of matter, I would think it very unreasonable should you afterwards ask me, what was the cause of the whole twenty') which may or may not be accurate, Cleanthes offers no means of deciding whether Demea's position or his position is the correct one.

Having now gone through Cleanthes' five criticisms of Demea's argument, we are able to see a pattern in his approach. In no instance has he been able to demonstrate or prove that an error is present in Demea's proof. Rather, in each instance, he has revealed to Demea – and to Philo, who is also in attendance – that Demea has failed to examine alternative views to the ones he is presenting and attempting to defend in his *a priori* argument.

This approach of Cleanthes' regarding Demea's *a priori* argument is analogous to Philo's approach to Cleanthes' *a posteriori* Design Argument. When Cleanthes argued by analogy that the Designer of the world is an intelligent being, he emphasized the resemblance between the world and machines in terms of means to ends relations and a coherence of parts. Philo argued that these features are present, not only in those cases where intelligence is the cause of design, but also when non-intelligent causes (e.g. generation, vegetation) are the source of design. Hence, to show that the design of the world has an intelligent cause, Cleanthes must establish that the design of the world bears a sufficient resemblance to a particular type of machine, so that the world can be classified as a machine of a certain sort. Only in this way, Philo insists, can the principle 'like effects prove like causes' be employed to prove that God resembles human intelligence. Within the discussion, Philo shows that the features of design present in the world are insufficient to classify the world as a (particular kind of) machine, and, for that matter, as any kind of object whose cause of design is known. Accordingly, Philo argues that all arguments by analogy fail to establish the nature of the cause of the design of the world. And, therefore, when he puts forth any arguments of this sort (Parts 6, 7, and 8), it is not done to support a particular hypothesis about the design of the world, but to argue against Cleanthes' Design Argument.

Cleanthes' efforts in Part 9 are similar to Philo's in the earlier sections of the book, namely, his aim is to show Demea that the causal chain, portions of which we are able to observe, can be accounted for in ways other than the way in which Demea has proceeded – by having recourse to matter if we adhere to the view that a necessary being is required as the cause of the chain, and by eliminating a First Cause altogether if the chain is held to be eternal and every member of the chain can be accounted for causally by some precedent member(s) in the chain. Cleanthes also argues that the demonstrability and intelligibility of a First Cause who is necessarily existent is not in any way convincing to those, like himself, who are able to conceive the non-existence of whatever can be conceived to be existent.

Philo's aim in providing counter arguments against Cleanthes' Design Argument was to loosen Cleanthes from his philosophical dogmatism. Hume's suggested cure is that the dogmatist be exposed to the arguments of the Pyrrhonian; this takes place in Parts 2 through 8. Philo urged that he was arguing with Cleanthes 'in his own way' (D. 111), and showed the latter that the Argument from Design, in so far as it seeks to establish analogically the intelligence of the Deity and his externality to what He has designed, is indefensible. Cleanthes has no answer to Philo's pyrrhonian objections; at the end of this sceptical attack, Philo proclaims a complete victory for the Pyrrhonian: the only reasonable response, he urges at the end of Part 8, is a total suspense of judgement. (Once this suspense of judgement is reached, and therefore Cleanthes' dogmatic approach has been removed, Hume will be able, in Part 12, to assess his pyrrhonian objections and reach the position of mitigated scepticism – the position which he himself endorses in the first *Enquiry*.)

If Cleanthes has been turned from his dogmatic stance, and is now able to appreciate counterbalancing arguments, how would Hume proceed to show this to us? Since all the arguments leading to a suspense of judgement in regard to the Design Argument have already been presented by Philo in Parts 2 through 8, Cleanthes cannot be expected to provide additional objections against *this* argument. An alternate means of revealing this change in Cleanthes is to have him respond to a *different* argument in a manner similar to Philo's response to the Design Argument. I submit that this is at least part of Hume's motivation in including the *a priori* argument in Part 9, and in having *Cleanthes* serve as its main critic. None of Cleanthes' criticisms in Part 9 can refute Demea's argument. At most, they reveal the one-sidedness of Demea's argument, and the fact that he has not taken into account any counterbalancing arguments. The starting point of Cleanthes' *a posteriori* Argument from Design calls attention to the design present throughout the world (means to ends relations and a coherence of parts), and Philo's efforts are directed to showing that this in itself will never be adequate to establish how the design came about; the starting-point of Demea's *a priori* argument calls attention to the succession of causes and effects throughout the world, and Cleanthes' efforts are directed to showing that this in itself will never be adequate to establish how this succession came about. In other words, Cleanthes' criticisms in Part 9 serve to illustrate to Philo, and to the reader, the success which Philo has achieved with Cleanthes through his sceptical objections in Parts 2 through 8.

In Part 2 of the *Dialogues*, Cleanthes argued that the cause of the design of the world is an intelligent being. After hearing Philo's criticisms in Part 2, Cleanthes proceeds in Part 3 to address Philo's criticisms through two imaginary illustrative analogies – the articulate voice speaking from the clouds and the vegetable library. That Cleanthes utilizes imaginary examples is understandable in light of the fact that in his Design Argument he is concerned with the cause of the design of *all* there is in nature. Since the scope of the argument and of Philo's criticisms is all there is, Cleanthes cannot, in attempting to illustrate his position, have recourse to (any part of) what there is. Hence, the propriety of imaginary examples. Similarly, since Philo's objections to Cleanthes' Design Argument continue to the point where a suspense of judgement has been achieved (and therefore no further counterbalancing arguments are available), if Hume wanted to illustrate the impact which Philo's arguments have had on Cleanthes, he could not do so through the Design Argument. A new argument is needed, with which Cleanthes can proceed to deal in a manner similar to the way in which Philo has dealt with Cleanthes' Design Argument.

PARTS 10 AND 11

Parts 10 and 11 are concerned with the benevolence and power of God. In Part 10, Cleanthes urges that God is both perfectly benevolent and infinitely powerful; hence, whatever He wills must occur.

If God is infinite and benevolent, then this world should contain no evil; in fact, it should be the best of all possible worlds. However, all three speakers agree in the early pages of Part 10 that evil does exist in the world. Philo then asks: 'And is it possible, Cleanthes, said Philo, that after all these reflections, and infinitely more, which might be suggested, you can still persevere in your anthropomorphism, and assert the moral attributes of the Deity, his justice, benevolence, mercy, and rectitude, to be of the same nature with these virtues in human creatures?' (D. 156)

Cleanthes treats Philo's question seriously, and several paragraphs later replies:

> And I must confess, that you have now fallen upon a subject worthy of your noble spirit of opposition and controversy. If you can make out the present point, and prove mankind to be unhappy or corrupted, there is an end at once of all religion. For to what purpose establish the natural attributes of the Deity, while the moral are still doubtful and uncertain? (D. 157)

In his article on Part 10 of the *Dialogues*, William Capitan interprets Cleanthes in this passage as posing a challenge to Philo, that is, as though (at this stage in the discussion) Philo has to prove that mankind is unhappy or corrupted. Capitan writes: 'Now Philo is in a position not entirely satisfactory to a sceptic; he is asked to prove something and, scepticism aside, something difficult, if not impossible to prove. His next move is important, in fact, the crux of the dialogue.'[10]

I will now examine what Capitan regards as Philo's proof that mankind is unhappy or corrupted. I will show that (a) what Capitan regards as Philo's proof is not so regarded by Philo, and that (b) Philo's arguments which damage Cleanthes' position in Part 10 have already been offered *prior to* Cleanthes' claim that, if Philo can prove mankind to be unhappy or corrupted, there is an end at once to all religion.

I begin with point (a), namely, that Philo is not offering a proof of the unhappiness or corruption of mankind in the passage cited by Capitan. The passage in question is the following:

10 William Capitan, 'Part X of Hume's Dialogues,' in *Hume: A Collection of Critical Essays*, ed. Chappell, p. 390.

I must . . . admonish you, Cleanthes; that you have put this controversy upon a most dangerous issue, and are unawares introducing a total scepticism into the most essential articles of natural and revealed theology. What! no method of fixing a just foundation for religion, unless we allow the happiness of human life, and maintain a continued existence even in this world, with all our present pains, infirmities, vexations, and follies, to be eligible and desirable! But this is contrary to every one's feeling and experience: It is contrary to an authority so established as nothing can subvert: No decisive proofs can ever be produced against this authority; nor is it possible for you to compute, estimate, and compare all the pains and all the pleasures in the lives of all men and of all animals: And thus by your resting the whole system of religion on a point, which, from its very nature, must for ever be uncertain, you tacitly confess, that that system is equally uncertain. (D. 159)

A close reading of this passage reveals that Philo is not offering a proof of the unhappiness or corruption of mankind; he is alerting Cleanthes to the dangers of proposing that the sole foundation of religion is human happiness. Philo does so for two reasons. First, in a strict sense, no one can be said to be in a perpetual state of happiness; to maintain otherwise is contrary to everyone's feelings and experience. And, second, to adopt a modified position, namely, that conscious creatures tend to be happy, and to maintain that this provides a foundation for religion is to render religion vulnerable to attack by the sceptic: no accurate calculation of all pleasures and pains already experienced by conscious creatures, and those yet to be experienced, is possible by us.

But Philo did not set out in Part 10 to argue that it is a strategic error to argue for the possibility of religion on the basis of human happiness. His intention was to show that the existence of evil makes it impossible for us to provide reasonable grounds for the hypothesis of a Designer who is infinite and benevolent. This is how Philo begins the philosophically significant portion of Part 10 (D. 156, quoted earlier), and how he ends Part 10:

Here, Cleanthes, I find myself at ease in my argument. Here I triumph. Formerly, when we argued concerning the natural attributes of intelligence and design, I needed all my sceptical and metaphysical subtlety to elude your grasp . . . .. But there is no view of human life or of the condition of mankind, from which, without the greatest violence, we can infer the moral attributes, or learn that infinite benevolence, conjoined with infinite power and infinite wisdom, which we must discover by the eyes of faith alone. It is your turn now to tug the labouring oar, and to support your philosophical subtleties against the dictates of plain reason and experience. (D. 160)

Philo offers two arguments against Cleanthes' hypothesis that the design of the world provides evidence for an infinite benevolent Designer:

His power we allow infinite: Whatever he wills is executed: But neither man nor any other animal are happy: Therefore he does not will their happiness. His wisdom is infinite: He is never mistaken in choosing the means to any end: But the course of nature tends not to human or animal felicity. Therefore it is not established for that purpose. (D. 156)

To emphasize that these are not sceptical arguments of the sort employed in Parts 2 through 8, Philo concludes: 'Through the whole compass of human knowledge, there are no inferences more certain and infallible than these. In what respect, then, do his benevolence and mercy resemble the benevolence and mercy of men?' (D. 156-7)

If we set out Philo's arguments in a more formal manner, they take the following form:

ARGUMENT 1

Hypothesis:	The Deity's power is infinite, i.e. whatever He wills comes about.
Fact:	Neither humans nor other animals are happy.
Conclusion:	The Deity does not will their happiness.

ARGUMENT 2

Hypothesis:	The Deity's wisdom is infinite, i.e., He is never mistaken in choosing means to ends.
Fact:	The course of nature does not tend to human or animal felicity.
Conclusion:	The Deity does not intend the course of nature to promote human or animal felicity.

In each argument, the hypothesis of the Deity's infinitude is conjoined with a fact to draw a conclusion which is in conflict with the claim that the Designer is benevolent. Cleanthes recognizes that the conclusion of each argument must be accepted, provided that the premises of these arguments are true; therefore, in order to reject their conclusions, he takes it upon himself to show that the factual premise in each argument is false. That is, if it is true that 'neither human nor other animals are happy' and that 'the course of nature does not tend to human or animal felicity', then given that he began by accepting that the Deity is infinite, he must accept the conclusions which these argument reach respectively. On the other hand, if the factual premise in each argument can be shown to be false, then he would have no reason to accept the conclusions of the arguments. Further, as I will now show, not only does Cleanthes attempt to establish that each factual premise employed by Philo is false, he also attempts to provide a (true) factual premise for each argument that will support the hypothesis of divine benevolence. Therefore, when Cleanthes proposes to Philo, that, if he can make out the present point, and prove mankind to be unhappy or corrupted, there is an end at once of all religion, he is not challenging Philo to present such a proof. Philo's arguments against an infinite benevolent Designer have already been presented. What Cleanthes means in this passage is, if there is no way to show that Philo's factual premises are false (i.e. that mankind is unhappy or corrupted), then there is an end at once of all religion. Cleanthes will now endeavour to prove that it is false that mankind is unhappy or corrupted.

That Cleanthes is attacking the factual premises in the two arguments put forth by Philo can be seen by Cleanthes' introductory remark: 'The only method of supporting divine benevolence . . . is to deny absolutely the misery and wickedness of man' (D. 158). His denial of this misery and wickedness is argued in the following passage:

> Your representations are exaggerated: Your melancholy views mostly fictitious; Your inferences contrary to fact and experience. Health is more common than sickness: Pleasure than pain: Happiness than misery. And for one vexation, which we meet with, we attain, upon computation, a hundred enjoyments. (D. 158)

Now, if Cleanthes is correct in his description of the conditions of humans and other animals, then, obviously, the factual premise in each of Philo's two arguments is false. And, if the premises 'humans and other animals tend to be happy' and 'the course of nature tends to human or animal felicity' replace the factual premises in each of Philo's arguments, then he believes a conclusion will be reached which is supportive of divine benevolence.

ARGUMENT 1

Hypothesis:	The Deity's power is infinite, i.e. whatever He wills comes about.
Fact:	Humans and other animals tend to be happy.
Conclusion:	The Deity has willed the tendency to happiness of humans and other animals.

ARGUMENT 2

Hypothesis:	The Deity's wisdom is infinite, i.e. He is never mistaken in choosing means to ends.
Fact:	The course of nature tends to support human or animal felicity.
Conclusion:	The Deity has willed the tendency of the course of nature to promote human or animal felicity.

Philo's ensuing remarks, incorrectly interpreted by Capitan as an effort by Philo to support his own position, are directed principally against Cleanthes' claim that the course of nature tends toward the happiness of human and other animals. He offers three arguments against Cleanthes' position:

(1) Even if it is true that pain is less frequent than pleasure, it is infinitely more violent and durable. Therefore, pleasures and pains should be measured not so much by frequency, but by intensity. Cleanthes will then see that he has no basis for claiming that Philo's representations of pain and misery are exaggerated.

(2) Since the totality of pleasure and pains in the lives of all people and all animals is impossible to compute, Cleanthes' position will for ever remain uncertain, and subject to criticism by the sceptic.

(3) Even if we could calculate the totality of pleasures and pains in the lives of all people and animals, and it could be shown (as Cleanthes holds) that Philo's representations of misery and wickedness are exaggerated, nothing would yet be established in regard to divine benevolence: 'But allowing you . . . that animal, or at least, human happiness in this life exceeds its misery; you have yet done nothing: For this is not, by any means, what we expect from infinite power, infinite wisdom, and infinite goodness. Why is there any misery at all in the world?' (D. 159)

Now this was precisely the consideration with which Philo opened the philosophic portion of Part 10 (D. 156–7), namely, he had argued at that time that the descriptions of evil in the world provided by all three speakers irrefutably show that natural theology cannot establish that the Designer of the world is infinite and benevolent. In other words, Philo's case had already been made when Cleanthes said that if it can be proved that mankind is unhappy or corrupted there is an end at once of all religion.

Taking 'B' to stand for 'the Designer of the world is benevolent'; 'I' to stand for 'the Designer of the world is infinite', and 'A' to stand for 'our world is the best of all possible worlds', and using *modus tollens*, we can schematize Philo's argument as follows:

$$(I \cdot B) \rightarrow A$$
$$\frac{\sim A}{\therefore \sim (I \cdot B)}$$

In light of this conclusion, Cleanthes must decide whether to hold 'I' to be true and 'B' false, or 'I' to be false and 'B' true, or both 'I' and 'B' to be false.

Since Cleanthes continues to insist that God is benevolent, his next move is to drop the claim of infinitude. At the beginning of Part 11, he proposes that God is benevolent and finitely perfect: 'But supposing the author of nature to be finitely perfect, though far exceeding mankind; a satisfactory account may then be given of natural and moral evil, and every untoward phenomenon be explained and adjusted . . . in a word, benevolence, regulated by wisdom, and limited by necessity, may produce just such a world as the present (D. 161). The notion of finitely perfect power means that God always acts to the maximum of his finite capacity. That is, whatever is within God's power to bring about He will bring about, although His power to do so is not infinite. In order to illustrate this, and to contrast it with the world God would bring about if He were infinitely powerful and benevolent, we can use a scale of possible worlds, at the bottom end of which is a world containing nothing but evil, and at the top a world containing nothing but good.

Best of all Possible Worlds (product of an infinitely perfect benevolent Designer)

Our World (best world possible, product of a finitely perfect benevolent Designer)

Worst of all Possible Worlds (product of an infinitely perfect malevolent Designer)

If God has infinite power and is benevolent, then this should be a world devoid of all evil and possessing only good; in other words, our world should, on this hypothesis, be the best of all possible worlds. However, as God is only finitely perfect under this new hypothesis, He can only bring about the best world possible, a world in which good is maximized and evil is minimized, consistent with the Designer's power.

Why did God not try to bring about a better world than the one we have, i.e. one with an even higher proportion of good to evil? Cleanthes' answer is that, if this is the best world possible, then the design of the world contains as much good as the Designer can produce and as little evil, consistent with His nature and His power. Therefore, if God were to attempt to improve the world further, the opposite result would occur: instead of an even greater amount of good coming into existence and even less evil, more evil and less good would come about. If, however, this is not the best world possible, then any effort by the Designer to improve it (increase the quantity of good, and decrease the quantity of evil) should succeed.

How does Cleanthes account for evil in the world, given that this is the best world possible and that God is only responsible for the good? His answer is that evil is permitted by the Designer, rather than intended by Him. We can use the illustration of an automobile and its designer. Granting that the designer has nothing but benevolent intentions with respect to the automobile which is being designed, it follows that the good features of the vehicle can be ascribed to the designer. It was never the intention of the designer for that automobile to be involved in accidents. When the automobile is involved in an accident, therefore, we do not blame the designer; rather we may ascribe it to the driver, the driver in another vehicle, road conditions, and so on. We recognize that, although the designer may not be able to bring about an automobile which will not be involved in accidents, nevertheless, when accidents do occur, these are not ascribable to the designer. Similarly, if God is finitely perfect and benevolent, then the good of the world can be ascribed to God; whatever evil exists would have to be explained through the interplay of objects and forces within the world, but it cannot be ascribed to the Designer.

On Cleanthes' account, in the best world possible, God allows evil to occur, because the only way to eliminate evil would be to eliminate the world itself. The evil which is in the world remains in the world, not because God does not have the ability to remove the causes of evil, but rather because God recognizes that if He were to remove the causes of evil in the world, even more evil would occur than currently exists.

Philo proposes a means to determine whether this world is the best world possible. Good is identified in terms of that which contributes to the survival of human and other conscious creatures, and evil in terms of that which threatens our survival. Now, in an effort to decide whether this is the best world possible, Philo begins by identifying the four causes of natural evil in the world. He argues that, if Cleanthes' hypothesis is true, that is, if the Designer is finitely perfect and benevolent, and if, therefore, this is the best world possible, then, if God were to remove any of the causes of evil in the world, the quantity of evil would increase or, in other words, our survival would be threatened to an even greater extent than it is at present. On the other hand, if this is not the best world possible, then the removal of the causes of evil would be followed by an increase in the quantity of goodness and a decrease in the quantity of evil.

In discussing the four causes of evil in the world, I will proceed as follows: after identifying the individual causes of evil, I will give Cleanthes' argument as to why the Designer does not remove the causes of evil from the world, thereby providing his arguments to the effect that this is the best world possible. I will then turn to Philo's argument in which he shows that each of the causes of evil in the world can be eliminated, the result being that the quantity of good can be increased, and the quantity of evil decreased. The text leaves no doubt that Hume's sympathies on this point lie entirely with Philo's arguments.

The first cause of evil 'is that contrivance or economy of the animal creation, by which pains, as well as pleasures, are employed to excite all creatures to action, and make them vigilant in the great work of self-preservation' (D. 163). The pursuit of pleasure and the avoidance of pain are essential elements for the survival of humans and other animals.

Cleanthes: Pain and pleasure inform us regarding those things which we should pursue, and those which we should avoid. If God were to eliminate all pain, then sensible creatures would not know what to avoid. As pain operates as an avoidance mechanism, it would be a great threat to our survival if pain were eliminated: in all likelihood, we would perish. Therefore, it is not that God cannot eliminate pain (it is within His power to eliminate it), it is that God does not want to eliminate it, because of the greater evil which would result from its elimination.

Philo: Pleasure alone could be sufficient to inform us as to what to pursue and what to avoid. God could have so constructed us that those objects and situations which are beneficial would lead to an anticipation of an increase in pleasure, if pursued; those which are harmful to us would lead to an anticipation of a decrease in pleasure, if they are not avoided. Humans and animals would be in a constant state of contentment, and a diminution of pleasure would be sufficient to prompt us to act in order to avoid what is harmful to us, much as the anticipation of an increase in pain operates upon us now. We would attach as much significance to a decrease in pleasure as we currently attach to an increase in pain. Thus, if God eliminated pain (evil), more pleasure (good) would result.

The second circumstance concerns 'the conducting of the world by general laws' (D. 164). There is regularity and uniformity in nature, because of the operations of the laws of nature. The regularity in nature which results from the laws of nature enables us to make predictions that assist our survival. If events were conducted according to the Designer's 'particular volitions', we would be in a constant state of confusion and would not know how to act at a given time. However, the laws of nature also contribute to the production of evil in the world; for example, hurricanes and illness are as natural as are the good things which happen to us.

Cleanthes: Cleanthes' position is that the only way to eliminate the evil that results from the operation of these general laws of nature is to eliminate the laws themselves. However, if God did eliminate these laws, then more evil would come into the world, as conscious creatures require regularity and predictability in their lives in order to survive. Hence, although some evil results from the operation of the laws of nature, much more evil would result if God were to eliminate entirely the laws of nature.

Philo: Philo argues that it is possible for God to increase the quantity of good in the world and decrease the quantity of evil, without altering or eliminating the laws of nature. To show this, he begins by pointing out that much of the evil which results from the general laws by which the world is governed stems from uncertainties and disappointed expectations which we experience. For example, when we anticipate good health, we sometimes find sickness and death; when we expect calm seas, we sometimes find tempests. Nature is governed by general laws, and yet evil is often a result of the seeming 'accidents' in nature, which we can neither anticipate nor correct. These 'accidents' occur because we lack an understanding of the 'secret springs of the universe' (D. 164). To prevent the evil brought into the world through these accidents, there is no need to remove the general laws by which the world is governed. Since God does know the secret springs of the universe, he could, through particular volitions, alter the secret springs in particular cases whenever it is known to God that the forces already in place will lead to evil consequences.

The third circumstance concerns the great frugality with which all powers and faculties are distributed to every particular being. There is general agreement of an order of being in nature, and, therefore, it would be impious to demand that God should have given conscious creatures additional faculties and powers beyond those which He has provided.

Cleanthes: Cleanthes' argument is based on this belief in an order of being in nature for conscious creatures, and he maintains, given that each conscious creature is appropriately placed in the order of being, if the Designer had provided any member of a particular species with additional powers or faculties, these would probably prove to be pernicious to us:

> If we required the endowments of superior penetration and judgement, of a more delicate taste of beauty, of a nicer sensibility to benevolence and friendship; we might be told, that we impiously pretend to break the order of nature, that we want to exalt ourselves into a higher rank of being, that the presents which we require, not being suitable to our state and condition, would only be pernicious to us. (D. 166–7)

Hence, according to Cleanthes, the Designer has provided each species with those powers and faculties most suited to its position in the order of nature.

Philo: While Philo agrees that the order of being in nature and boundaries of species must be respected, and that more evil would befall conscious creatures if the Designer had provided us with additional powers and faculties, e.g. 'the wings of the eagle, the swiftness of the stag, the force of the ox', he argues that the quantity of good in the world could be increased and the quantity of evil decreased if the Designer had distributed throughout our species one single power which we observe many individuals are, in fact, able to attain by habit and reflection: a greater propensity to industry and labour. An increase of this power would bring about the most beneficial consequences.

Almost all the moral, as well as natural evils of human life arise from idleness, and were our species, by the original constitution of their frame, exempt from this vice or infirmity, the perfect cultivation of land, the improvement of arts and manufactures, the exact execution of every office and duty, immediately follow; and men at once may fully reach that state of society, which is so imperfectly attained by the best regulated government. (D. 166)

The fourth circumstance 'is the inaccurate workmanship of all the springs and principles of the great machine of nature' (D. 167). Philo takes up Cleanthes' analogy of the world as a machine, in which everything is purposive. For example, wind, water, and heat are necessary for our survival, but when they are not distributed in the correct proportion, evil results.

Cleanthes: His position is that in order for the Designer to eliminate the evil that results when these elements operate to excess, e.g. causing hurricanes and floods or droughts and excessive heat, He would have to eliminate the elements themselves. However, if God did do this, then more evil would result, as we require wind, water, and heat, etc. for our survival. Therefore, this world, with its periodic excesses, cannot be improved by the Designer.

Philo: Proceeding with Cleanthes' position that the world is machine-like, Philo argues that when excesses are present in a machine, for example, a clock which runs too fast or too slow, it is not necessary to dispose of the machine, but only to adjust it so that it operates accurately. Now, granting the machine-like character of the world, the excesses and deficiencies which occur can be corrected through adjustments by the Designer; accordingly, the harmful excesses and deficiencies can be prevented. Thus it is possible for God to eliminate the evil caused by these natural phenomena if further adjustments to the design of the world are undertaken and completed. Therefore, Philo maintains that the quantity of good in the world could be increased and the quantity of evil decreased if the Designer made efforts in this regard.

Having shown that the quantity of good in the world can be increased and the quantity of evil decreased if the Designer eliminated or altered the causes of evil, Philo concludes that Cleanthes has no basis for arguing that this is the best world possible. However, since this claim is entailed by the hypothesis of a finitely perfect and benevolent Deity, it follows that this hypothesis has been refuted.

Introducing 'P' to stand for 'this world is the best world possible', Philo's argument in Part 11 can be schematized as follows:

$$\frac{\begin{array}{l}(\sim I \cdot B) \rightarrow P \\ \sim P\end{array}}{\therefore \ \sim (\sim I \cdot B)}$$

Since Cleanthes continues to insist on the benevolence of the Designer, he must give up the claim that the Designer is finitely perfect.

The overall oddity in Cleanthes' position in Parts 10 and 11 can now be grasped. In Part 10, Cleanthes is forced to give up the claim of the Designer's infinite power, if he is to retain the claim of the Designer's benevolence; in Part 11, Cleanthes is forced to give up the claim of the Designer's finitely perfect power, if he is to retain the claim of the Designer's benevolence. Accordingly, Philo has shown Cleanthes that no consideration of the power of the Designer of the world – whether infinitely perfect or finitely perfect – when conjoined with a consideration of the Designer's benevolence can account for the design of the world as we experience it. We can symbolize Cleanthes' position as follows:

$$\frac{\begin{array}{l}B \rightarrow \sim(I \ v \sim I) \\ B\end{array}}{\therefore \sim (I \ v \sim I)}$$

In short, Philo has succeeded in reducing Cleanthes' benevolence claim to absurdity. Now, returning to the first premise in this argument (B → ~(I v ~ I)), since the consequent will always be false, the premise can be true if and only if the antecedent 'B' is false. However, since 'B' is precisely what Cleanthes is attempting to defend, he cannot accept this premise. The logic of his position in Parts 10 and 11 requires either that he accepts that 'B' is false, or that he eliminates all consideration of the power of the Designer of the world.

Since Cleanthes still refuses to give up the benevolence claim, he must drop all references to the Designer's power. This explains why, when Philo introduces the next hypothesis, Manichaeanism, he suggests that it 'occurs as a proper hypothesis to solve the difficulty' (D. 169), namely, the difficulty of attempting to retain the truth of the claim that the Designer of the world is benevolent, while eliminating all consideration of the Designer's power. Although Manichaeanism posits the dual hypothesis of a benevolent and malevolent original cause, no reference to the power of either original cause is included in the theory.

Thus Manichaeanism is introduced in order to make a claim with regard to God's benevolence with no consideration of God's power. This hypothesis claims that there are opposing original forces in the world, of good and of evil, that battle for supremacy of the world. The advantage of Manichaeanism over the previous hypotheses lies in the fact that it attempts to account for evil, rather than simply maintaining that it is something which the Designer allows (the position associated with the view of the Designer as finitely perfect and benevolent) or something mysterious and inexplicable (the position associated with the view of the Designer as infinitely perfect and benevolent).

Philo insists that Manichaeanism is not defensible. First, to accept Manichaeanism, we would have to find 'marks of the combat of a malevolent with a benevolent Being' (D. 169) – some evidence of a struggle between the forces of good and evil. But no such evidence is to be found: what we find instead is 'the perfect uniformity and agreement of the parts of the universe' (D. 169). That is, the same coherence in design which we find between different elements of good in nature is also to be found between elements of good and evil; the same general laws apply to the production of both.

It is true that there is – to use Philo's term at p. 169 – 'opposition' between good and evil in nature. But this, according to Philo, does not support Manichaeanism. We can see this by considering other opposites in nature, e.g. hot and cold, moist and dry, light and heavy. First, each pair results from 'an opposition of principles' (D. 169), that is, each opposite results from an opposing cause. Nevertheless, from the fact that such opposites result from an opposition of principles, we do not believe that we are justified in inferring that, for each pair of opposites, there must be opposing *original* causes. Opposites are adequately explained through their immediate causes.

In the second place, Philo argues that, where we ascribe opposing immediate causes for the presence of opposites in nature, we find no reason to hold that the original cause of design has a preference for one of the opposites. Since both appear in accordance with the general laws by which the universe is governed, the original cause seems to be entirely indifferent to the appearance of a particular opposite.

A similar treatment should be accorded the causes of good and evil, according to Philo. There is no reason to go beyond the immediate causes for each, and there is no reason to believe that the original cause of design has a preference for one over the other. The material developed above is what Philo intends in the following highly condensed passage:

> There is indeed an opposition of pains and pleasures in the feelings of sensible creatures: But are not all the operations of nature carried on by an opposition of principles, of hot and cold, moist and dry, light and heavy? The true conclusion is, that the original source of all things is entirely indifferent to all these principles, and has no more regard to good above ill than to heat above cold, or to drought above moisture, or to light above heavy. (D. 169)

Philo concludes his discussion by putting forth four hypotheses regarding the original cause or causes of the universe: that they are perfectly good, perfectly evil, both good and evil, neither good nor evil. The first leaves evil unexplained; the second leaves good unexplained; the operation of general laws in the production of good and evil rules out the third. The fourth, therefore, seems the most plausible – that the cause of the design of the world is indifferent to the presence of good and evil.

Philo has thus shown Cleanthes that his various attempts to establish the benevolence of the Designer of the world do not succeed.

PART 12

In Part 12, Philo and Cleanthes return to Cleanthes' Design Argument (first presented in Part 2). Philo had offered a series of sceptical or pyrrhonian objections against this argument in Part 2, and Parts 4 through 8. Philo urged that he was arguing with Cleanthes 'in his own way', and showed the latter that the Argument from Design, in so far as it seeks to establish analogically the intelligence of God, is indefensible. The Argument from Design was shown to involve an infinite regress (Part 4), to be susceptible of reduction to absurdity (Part 5), and to utilize data which are equally supportive (and therefore not supportive at all) of an open-ended list of alternative hypotheses to a Designer of the world who is intelligent and external (Parts 6 to 8). Cleanthes has no answer to Philo's sceptical or pyrrhonian objections; at the end of this sceptical attack, Philo proclaims a complete victory for the sceptic; the only reasonable response, he argues at the end of Part 8, is a total suspense of judgement.

The problem with Philo's pyrrhonian attack, as he admits in the second paragraph of Part 12, is that he is 'less cautious on the subject of natural religion than on any other', that is, his sceptical arguments make no distinction between what is acceptable and unacceptable in Cleanthes' position. Accordingly, in Part 12, a re-evaluation of the Argument from Design and Philo's earlier sceptical objections is in order.

Philo continues by asserting that his former lack of caution in arguing against Cleanthes had a two-fold basis:

> I must confess, replied Philo, that I am less cautious on the subject of natural religion than on any other; both because I know that I can never, on that head, corrupt the principles of any man of common sense, and because no-one, I am confident, in whose eyes I appear a man of common sense, will ever mistake my intentions. (D. 172)

Each of these deserves some comment. First, Philo defends his lack of caution in argument by insisting that his procedure can never corrupt common-sense principles. Now, Cleanthes' common-sense principles in regard to causal reasoning are two in number: that experience, or observing objects constantly conjoined, is the only proper guide as to what causes what; and that causal inferences are to be guided by the principle 'like effects prove like causes'. And in regard to *natural* arguments, Cleanthes holds that, because the observation of means to ends relations and a coherence of parts leads with such forcefulness to the belief in an intelligent designer, regardless of where these features of design are observed, we ought to assent to this belief in these cases. This is an instantiation of the principle 'to assent, wherever any reasons strike him with so full a force, that he cannot, without the greatest violence, prevent it' (D. 119). We can take it, therefore, that in Part 12 Philo is admitting that no sceptical argument can so affect us that we will abandon our common-sense principles – even though we may do so momentarily. This view of Philo's appears in Part 1, where he acknowledged:

> To whatever length any-one may push his speculative principles of scepticism, he must act, I own, and live, and converse like other men; and for this conduct he is not obliged to give any other reason, than the absolute necessity he lies under of so doing. (D. 101)

The second point made by Philo in the passage under discussion is that he is less cautious on the subject of natural religion than any other, because no one who sees him as a man of common sense will ever mistake his intentions. My analysis of Philo's arguments in Part 2 and Parts 4 through 8 reveals that Philo's intention was to show that Cleanthes' principles – particularly those dealing with causal *reasoning* – cannot be applied, as Cleanthes had attempted to apply them, to natural religion. In Part 1, Philo had already warned against this effort of Cleanthes', while at the same time urging him to confine his speculations to the empirical:

> So long as we confine our speculations to trade or morals or politics or criticism, we make appeals, every moment, to common sense and experience, which strengthen our philosophical conclusions, and remove (at least, in part) the suspicion, which we so justly entertain with regard to every reasoning, that is very subtle or refined. But in theological reasonings, we have not this advantage; while at the same time we are employed upon objects, which, we must be sensible, are too large for our grasp, and of all others, require most to be familiarized to our apprehension. We are like foreigners in a strange country, to whom every thing must seem suspicious, and who are in danger every moment of transgressing against the laws and customs of the people, with whom they live and converse. We know not how far we ought to trust our vulgar methods of reasoning in such a subject; since even in common life and in that province, which is peculiarly appropriated to them, we cannot account for them, and are entirely guided by a kind of instinct or necessity in employing them. (D. 101–2)

We have yet to ask what Philo means when he says that he is 'less cautious' in natural religion than in other areas of enquiry. Our study of Philo's criticisms provides the required insight. In arguing against Cleanthes' position on God, Philo himself employs principles and utilizes data, without directly questioning whether his procedure is justified. Hence, in this respect, he violates his own position in Part 1, in which he argued against such inquiries. Nevertheless, Philo's purpose in doing so was to show Cleanthes the difficulties involved in, and the alternatives to, the Design Argument. Since Philo's aim was not to inquire into God's nature, but to show why our ordinary procedures are inadequate to such an investigation, and, therefore, ultimately to show that no system of cosmogony is defensible, Philo holds that his procedure in the earlier chapters is justified. Nevertheless, Philo's arguments sought to discredit *all* that Cleanthes had defended; no attempt was made to distinguish within Cleanthes' position those elements which are acceptable. By admitting that his scepticism possessed a certain lack of caution in argumentation, Philo is allowing for a reappraisal of Cleanthes' – as well as his own – position. Part 12 provides this reappraisal.

That the stand which Philo is about to defend is his own can be learned from the fact that, after expressing himself, he confesses: 'These, Cleanthes, are my unfeigned sentiments on this subject; and these sentiments, you know, I have ever cherished and maintained' (D. 177). Before defending his position, he makes it clear that he will be addressing, and that, therefore, his position includes, both a natural (or common-sense or instinctive) aspect and a reasoned (or analogical) aspect. In this regard, he tells Cleanthes: 'you are sensible, that, not withstanding the freedom of my conversation, and my love of singular arguments, no-one has a deeper sense of religion impressed on his mind, or pays more profound adoration to the divine Being, as he discovers himself to reason, in the inexplicable contrivance and artifice of nature' (D. 172). Accordingly, Philo will be addressing two aspects of the Design Argument (the natural or irregular argument, and the analogical argument) as these were developed by Cleanthes in the earlier Parts of the *Dialogues*.

Philo begins by elaborating on the natural or instinctive aspect of the belief in an intelligent Designer which, in Part 12, he refers to as the 'sense of religion impressed on his mind':

A purpose, an intention, a design strikes every where the most careless, the most stupid thinker; and no man can be so hardened in absurd systems, as at all times to reject it. *That nature does nothing in vain*, is a maxim established in all the schools, merely from the contemplation of the works of nature, without any religious purpose; and, from a firm conviction of its truth, an anatomist, who had observed a new organ or canal, would never be satisfied, till he had also discovered its use and intention. One great foundation of the Copernican system is the maxim, *that nature acts by the simplest methods, and chooses the most proper means to any end*; and astronomers often, without thinking of it, lay this strong foundation of piety and religion. The same thing is observable in other parts of philosophy: And thus all the sciences almost lead us insensibly to acknowledge a first intelligent author; and their authority is often so much the greater as they do not directly profess that intention.

It is with pleasure I hear Galen reason concerning the structure of the human body. The anatomy of a man, says he, discovers above 600 different muscles; and whoever duly considers these, will find, that in each of them nature must have adjusted at least ten different circumstances, in order to attain the end which she proposed; proper figure, just magnitude, right disposition of the several ends, upper and lower position of the whole, the due insertion of the several nerves, veins and arteries. So that in the muscles alone, above 6000 several views and intentions must have been formed and executed. The bones he calculates to be 284: The distinct purposes, aimed at in the structure of each above forty. What a prodigious display of artifice, even in these simple and homogeneous parts? But if we consider the skin, ligaments, vessels, glandules, humours, the several limbs and members of the body; how must our astonishment rise upon us, in proportion to the number and intricacy of the parts so artificially adjusted? The farther we advance in these researches, we discover new scenes of art and wisdom: But descry still, at a distance, farther scenes beyond our reach; in the fine internal structure of the parts, in the economy of the brain, in the fabric of the seminal vessels. All these artifices are repeated in every different species of animal, and with wonderful variety, with exact propriety, suited to the different intentions of nature, in framing each species. And if the infidelity of Galen, even when these natural sciences were still imperfect, could not withstand such striking appearances; to what pitch of pertinacious obstinacy must a philosopher in this age have attained, who can now doubt of a supreme intelligence? (D. 172–3)

Purposive design, Philo urges, strikes anyone who contemplates nature. We have already seen, and Philo repeats here, this belief in purposiveness is not identical to the observation of means to ends relations and a coherence of parts. When Philo maintains that anyone who contemplates nature is struck by purposiveness, he does not mean that the act of contemplation invariably discloses specific purposes. His point is rather that by observing the adaptation of means to ends and coherence of parts throughout nature we are struck with a belief in purposiveness. Hence, this belief in purpose is actually prior to the investigation of nature. Philo's point is that there is a causal connection between the observation of means to ends relations and a coherence of parts and a belief in purposive design: the belief in purposive design does not await an understanding of a given case of purposiveness. This explains why, in the first paragraph quoted immediately above, Philo asserts that the maxims of science, which involve a purposive view of the design of the world, can be obtained from 'the contemplation of the works of nature'. It is also important to realize that in these two paragraphs Philo is not concerned with reasoning analogically to purposiveness in design. What he is saying here does not in any way rely upon noting resemblances between the world and machines. We are, he points out, 'struck' by the machine-like or purposive nature of the world, and not reasoning to it. His point, therefore, is that science does not require a system of cosmogony which is arrived at through reason before it can obtain maxims needed for the study of nature. The observation of nature, he is saying, impresses us with the needed beliefs required to provide those maxims for science which will prove to be its most dependable guide.

I now turn to Philo's efforts to correct his former lack of caution when addressing Cleanthes' *analogical* Argument from Design. The sceptical objections which Philo has advanced in the earlier parts of the *Dialogues* when dealing with the intelligence claim stem from Cleanthes' insistence that the principle 'like effects prove like causes' can be used to establish an anthropomorphic conception of God, given the presence of means to ends relations and a coherence of parts in the design of the world and the design of machines. The cumulative effect of these sceptical objections is to show that an anthropomorphic conception of the Deity, and along with it a purposive view of design, cannot be supported; that no account based on the features of design cited by Cleanthes can, strictly speaking, be shown to be an acceptable system of cosmogony; and that a suspense of judgement on the topic of the nature of God is the only reasonable position to adopt.

But Philo's sceptical arguments also challenged certain 'common-sense' beliefs which we hold about causality. (It will be recalled that, early in Part 12, Philo emphasized that common-sense principles cannot be corrupted by the sceptic's arguments, and that he himself is a man of common sense.) His arguments (in Part 4) generated doubts as to whether causal claims can be put forth which do not lead to an infinite regress; Philo's version of the Epicurean hypothesis (in Part 8), which accounts for all design without reference to powers in objects and principles of order or design, raised doubts about the propriety of employing constant conjunction as a guide to what causes what, and about employing the principle 'like effects prove like causes' when reasoning about what causes what.

We will see that, in correcting his lack of caution when attacking the analogical Argument from Design, Philo reintroduces our common-sense beliefs regarding causality: the concern with an infinite regress disappears, principles of order and powers in objects to produce change are accepted (although never explained), and constant conjunction and the principle 'like effects prove like causes' are regarded as our only means of gaining knowledge of causes. It is only in the context of Philo's pyrrhonian attack on the Argument from Design with his admitted 'lack of caution' when advancing the sceptic's arguments that our common-sense beliefs in regard to causality come to be challenged.

Throughout his attack on the Argument from Design, Philo has insisted that the features of design in the world cited by Cleanthes cannot prove that anthropomorphism is true. Nevertheless, at no point in the first eight parts of the *Dialogues* does Philo establish what conclusion about the cause of the design of the world is supported by the means to ends relations and a coherence of parts which we find in the world and in machines. Or, what comes to the same thing, he has not yet shown the significance of the differences between the design of the world and machines, when we attempt to learn about the cause of the design of the world. As a result, Philo has again exhibited a lack of caution in his arguments. It remains for Part 12 to disclose the causal inferences which can be made about God from the similarities and differences present in the design of the world and machines.

It is in the sixth paragraph of Part 12 that Philo begins his re-evaluation of the analogical Argument from Design and his previous pyrrhonian objections against this argument.

So little, replied Philo, do I esteem this suspense of judgement in the present case to be possible, that I am apt to suspect there enters somewhat of a dispute of words into this controversy, more than is usually imagined. That the works of nature bear a great analogy to the productions of art is evident; and according to all the rules of good reasoning, we ought to infer, if we argue at all concerning them, that their causes have a proportional analogy. But as there are also considerable differences, we have reason to suppose a proportional difference in the causes; and in particular ought to attribute a much higher degree of power and energy to the supreme cause than any we have ever observed in mankind. Here then the existence of a Deity is plainly ascertained by reason; and if we make it a question, whether, on account of these analogies, we can properly call him a *mind* or *intelligence,* notwithstanding the vast difference, which may reasonably be supposed between him and human minds; what is this but a mere verbal controversy? No man can deny the analogies between the effects: To restrain ourselves from enquiring concerning the causes is scarcely possible: From this enquiry, the legitimate conclusion is, that the causes have also an analogy: And if we are not contented with calling the first and supreme cause a God or Deity, but desire to vary the expression; what can we call him but *mind* or *thought,* to which he is justly supposed to bear a considerable resemblance? (D. 174–5)

He begins the seventh paragraph by elaborating on the nature of a 'verbal dispute' – the type of dispute he claims is involved in trying to decide whether 'on account of these analogies, we can properly call him [i.e. God] a *mind* or *intelligence,* notwithstanding the vast difference, which may reasonably be supposed between him and human minds' (D. 175). He explains that the only remedy for a verbal dispute arises 'from clear definitions, from the precision of those ideas which enter into any argument, and from the strict and uniform use of those terms which are employed' (D. 175). A verbal dispute, therefore, requires that both the language and ideas employed not allow for accuracy in judgement: 'But there is a species of controversy, which, from the very nature of language and of human ideas, is involved in perpetual ambiguity, and can never, by any precaution or any definitions, be able to reach a reasonable certainty or precision' (D. 175). Philo locates verbal disputes in 'the controversies concerning the degrees of any quality or circumstance'. He offers three examples of such disputes:

Men may argue to all eternity, whether Hannibal be a great, or a very great, or a superlatively great man, what degree of beauty Cleopatra possessed, what epithet of praise Livy or Thucydides is entitled to, without bringing the controversy to any determination. (D. 175)

And he locates the difficulty in each in the fact that we have no precise measure for quantifying these qualities:

The disputants may here agree in this sense and differ in the terms, or *vice versa;* yet never be able to define their terms, so as to enter into each others meaning: Because the degrees of these qualities are not, like quantity or number, susceptible of any exact mensuration, which may be the standard in the controversy. (D. 175)

89

In other words, in regard to certain qualities, an accurate calculation of the degrees of that quality present in an object cannot be achieved.

Philo insists that 'the dispute concerning theism is of this nature, and consequently is merely verbal, or perhaps, if possible, still more incurably ambiguous' (D. 175). He shows this by addressing himself both to the theist and the atheist. His initial comments are addressed to the theist:

> I ask the theist, if he does not allow, that there is a great and immeasurable, because incomprehensible, difference between the *human* and the *divine* mind: The more pious he is, the more readily will he assent to the affirmative, and the more will he be disposed to magnify the difference: He will even assert, that the difference is of a nature, which cannot be too much magnified. (D. 175-6)

Although there is a reference in this passage to 'the *human* and the *divine* mind', the differences between them are characterized as 'great and inmeasurable, because incomprehensible'. Not only can the differences not be measured, they cannot be understood!

What, then, of the data which Cleanthes offers in the Argument from Design to support the claim of resemblance between us and God? Philo's views on the proper use of the data are expressed in his comments addressed to the atheist:

> I next turn to the atheist, who, I assert, is only nominally so, and can never possibly be in earnest; and I ask him, whether, from the coherence and apparent sympathy in all the parts of this world, there be not a certain degree of analogy among all the operations of nature, in every situation and in every age; whether the rotting of a turnip, the generation of an animal, and the structure of human thought be not energies that probably bear some remote analogy to each other: It is impossible he can deny it: He will readily acknowledge it. Having obtained this concession, I push him still farther in his retreat; and I ask him, if it be not probable, that the principle which first arranged and still maintains order in this universe, bears not also some remote inconceivable analogy to the other operations of nature, and among the rest to the economy of human mind and thought. However reluctant, he must give his assent. (D. 176)

In this passage, Philo is calling attention to the coherence of parts which Cleanthes' Argument from Design has employed. When Philo advanced competing cosmogonies in the earlier parts of the *Dialogues*, he attempted to account for the design of the whole world through a comparison with the design found in parts of the world, especially organisms. Since no system of cosmogony can be shown to be properly grounded, the sceptic urges a suspense of judgement as the only reasonable position to adopt. One of the matters which Philo's presentation of competing cosmogonies does reveal is that all sources of design are bound by the same features of design, namely, means to ends relations and a coherence of parts. Now, whereas a suspense of judgement is held by Philo to be reasonable when systems of cosmogony are compared and contrasted, Philo has not yet established what position is reasonable in natural theology, once we grant that no system of cosmogony can be accepted, and that all sources of design are bound by identical features of design. An alteration in the sceptic's position may, therefore, be in order.

Philo's argument proceeds in two stages, each engaging the principle 'like effects prove like causes'. In the first stage of his argument, he claims that the coherence of parts evident in all parts of the world countenances the conclusion that 'there is a certain degree of analogy among all the operations of nature'. In Rule 5 of the 'Rules by which to judge of causes and effects' in the *Treatise of Human Nature*, Hume writes: 'where several different objects produce the same effect, it must be by means of some quality, which we discover to be common amongst them. For as like effects imply like causes, we must always ascribe the causation to the circumstance, wherein we discover the resemblance' (T. 174). Philo's point is that the resemblance found among all the effects in the world is so general that, in applying a rule of this sort, no specificity can be achieved when we attempt to determine the particular resemblance among the operations of nature. This explains why, in comparing the rotting of a turnip, the generation of an animal, and the structure of human thought, he concludes that these are energies 'that probably bear some remote analogy to each other'.

In the second stage of the argument, Philo calls upon the atheist once again to apply the principle 'like effects prove like causes', but, in this case, the order observed throughout the world is compared to the order observed to result from the other operations of nature. The basis of comparison is coherence in design (as it was in the first stage), and once again this feature reveals no specific resemblance between the design of the world and the designs resulting from the operations of nature within the world. The comparison of the design of the whole world with specific effects in nature in terms of coherence of design yields a conclusion which seems epistemologically much weaker than the conclusion obtained in the first stage: in the first stage of the argument, 'some remote analogy' is conceded among all the operations of nature, whereas in the second stage 'some remote *inconceivable* analogy' is conceded between the principle of design of the whole world and the other operations of nature.

That the second stage is not epistemologically weaker than the first can be learned by reading several lines further when Philo reconciles the position of the theist and atheist. For, at that point, the atheist agrees that 'the original principle of order bears some remote analogy' to the operations of nature, with the term 'inconceivable' omitted. Relying on Hume's doctrine of impressions and ideas, Philo has insisted throughout the book that the operations of nature are unknown to us: 'But reason, in its internal fabric and structure, is really as little known to us as instinct or vegetation . . . .. The effects of these principles are all known to us from experience: But the principles themselves, and their manner of operation, are totally unknown' (D. 140). As such, even when natural objects are compared in terms of coherence of design, the remote analogy between their causes should be regarded as 'inconceivable'. If the principles cannot be known or understood at all, any claim of analogy between them must be inconceivable. Therefore, regardless of whether Philo includes the term 'inconceivable' or not, any claim of analogy between principles of order must be regarded as being 'inconceivable'. What Philo has shown is that this problem of 'inconceivability' is not peculiar to natural theology: in light of the fact that all principles of design and their manner of operation are totally unknown, no claim of analogy between principles of order can be thought.

What the atheist assents to is that it is probable that the principle which first arranged, and still maintains, order in this universe, bears 'some remote inconceivable analogy to the other operations of nature, and among the rest to the economy of human mind and thought'. Accordingly, thought has no primacy when a comparison is attempted between God and the operations of nature. The 'remote inconceivable analogy' which the atheist allows between the principle of design of the world and the structure of human thought is also allowed between the principle of design of the world and the other operations of nature. What directs the atheist to single out thought is nothing more than Philo's effort to contrast the atheist's position with the theist's position, which focuses on intelligence: it is not that the resemblance between God and thought can be shown to be greater than that between God and the other operations of nature. In no case can more be established between God and any operation of nature than 'some remote inconceivable analogy', and, as we have seen, no knowledge or understanding of God is contained therein.

The theist holds that the differences between God and us are 'great and immeasurable, because incomprehensible'. The atheist will allow 'some remote inconceivable analogy' between the principle of order of the world and thought. I submit, therefore, that in the end the unknowability of the divine nature is upheld.

The verbal dispute between theist and atheist can now be clearly grasped: since neither holds a position for which there are ideas which are determinate in nature, the degree of resemblance or difference between God and human intelligence cannot be ascertained:

> The theist allows, that the original intelligence is very different from human reason: The atheist allows that the original principle of order bears some remote analogy to it. Well, you quarrel, gentlemen, about the degrees, and enter into a controversy, which admits not of any precise meaning, nor consequently of any determination. If you should be so obstinate, I should not be surprised to find you insensibly change sides; while the theist on the one hand exaggerates the dissimilarity between the supreme Being, and frail, imperfect, variable, fleeting, and mortal creatures; and the atheist on the other magnifies the analogy, among all the operations of nature, in every period, every situation, and every position. Consider then, where the real point of controversy lies, and if you cannot lay aside your disputes, endeavour, at least, to cure yourselves of your animosity. (D. 176)

The sceptic's lack of caution has now been corrected. In regard to the claim that there is 'some remote inconceivable analogy' between God and human intelligence, it is obvious that no additional sceptical attack is either anticipated or offered.

Relying on the position attributed to the atheist, Philo offers the final pronouncement on the topic under discussion:

> If the whole of natural theology, as some people seem to maintain, resolves itself into one simple, though somewhat ambiguous, at least undefined proposition, *that the cause or causes of order in the universe probably bear some remote analogy to human intelligence*: If this proposition be not capable of extension,

variation, or more particular explication: If it affords no inference that affects human life, or can be the source of any action or forbearance: And if the analogy, imperfect as it is, can be carried no farther than to the human intelligence; and cannot be transferred, with any appearance of probability, to the other qualities of the mind: If this really be the case, what can the most inquisitive, contemplative, and religious man do more than give a plain, philosophical assent to the proposition, as often as it occurs; and believe, that the arguments, on which it is established, exceed the objections, which lie against it? Some astonishment indeed will naturally arise from the greatness of the object: Some melancholy from its obscurity: Some contempt of human reason; that it can give no solution more satisfactory with regard to so extraordinary and magnificent a question. (D. 184–5)

It is particularly noteworthy that the work of the sciences and the fact that 'all the sciences almost lead us insensibly to acknowledge a first intelligent Author' is not included in this final pronouncement, in which is contained all that human reason can, with justification, express about God. This confirms the point made earlier that the concern in the early paragraphs of Part 12 is not with *reasoning* about God. That the success of science can be totally ignored in offering all that human reason can say about God does make sense if the belief in an intelligent Designer which is spoken of in those early paragraphs is the result of a natural rather than a reasonable argument. In reasoning about God, the scientist can be no more successful than the atheist, and, therefore, if reasoning were the only guide to the cause of the design of the world, the scientist would not be justified in holding that all there is in nature is the product of intelligence.

When Pamphilus assesses the three speakers in the last paragraph of the book, he maintains that 'Philo's principles are more probable than Demea's; but that those of Cleanthes approach still nearer to the truth' (D. 185). In light of Philo's concern in the penultimate paragraph of the *Dialogues* that Pamphilus does not have a proper understanding of the role of scepticism (we have also seen that Cleanthes, Pamphilus' teacher, began the dialogue with a similar lack of understanding of scepticism), it is reasonable to disregard Pamphilus' assessment of the main speakers in the dialogue.

94

DIALOGUES CONCERNING NATURAL RELIGION

PAMPHILUS TO HERMIPPUS

It has been remarked, my HERMIPPUS, that, though the ancient philosophers conveyed most of their instruction in the form of dialogue, this method of composition has been little practiced in later ages, and has seldom succeeded in the hands of those, who have attempted it. Accurate and regular argument, indeed, such as is now expected of philosophical enquirers, naturally throws a man into the methodical and didactic manner; where he can immediately, without preparation, explain the point at which he aims; and thence proceed, without interruption, to deduce the proofs on which it is established. To deliver a *System* in conversation scarcely appears natural; and while the dialogue-writer desires, by departing from the direct style of composition, to give a freer air to his performance, and avoid the appearance of *author* and *reader*, he is apt to run into a worse inconvenience, and convey the image of *pedagogue* and *pupil*. Or if he carries on the dispute in the natural spirit of good company, by throwing in a variety of topics, and preserving a proper balance among the speakers; he often loses so much time in preparations and transitions, that the reader will scarcely think himself compensated, by all the graces of dialogue, for the order, brevity, and precision, which are sacrificed to them.

There are some subjects, however, to which dialogue-writing is peculiarly adapted, and where it is still preferable to the direct and simple method of composition.

Any point of doctrine, which is so *obvious*, that it scarcely admits of dispute, but at the same time so *important*, that it cannot be too often inculcated, seems to require some such method of handling it; where the novelty of the manner may compensate the triteness of the subject, where the vivacity of conversation may enforce the precepts, and where the variety of lights, presented by various personages and characters, may appear neither tedious nor redundant.

Any question of philosophy, on the other hand, which is so *obscure* and *uncertain*, that human reason can reach no fixed determination with regard to it; if it should be treated at all; seems to lead us naturally into the style of dialogue and conversation. Reasonable men may be allowed to differ, where no-one can reasonably be positive: Opposite sentiments, even without any decision, afford an agreeable amusement: And if the subject be curious and interesting, the book carries us, in a manner, into company, and unites the two greatest and purest pleasures of human life, study and society.

Happily, these circumstances are all to be found in the subject of NATURAL RELIGION. What truth so obvious, so certain, as the *Being* of a God, which the most ignorant ages have acknowledged; for which the most refined geniuses have ambitiously striven to produce new proofs and arguments? What truth so important as this, which is the ground of all our hopes, the surest foundation of morality, the firmest support of society, and the only principle, which ought never to be a moment absent from our thoughts and meditations? But in treating of this obvious and important truth; what obscure questions occur, concerning the *nature* of that divine being; his attributes, his decrees, his plan of providence? These have been always subjected to the disputations of men: Concerning these, human reason has not reached any certain determination: But these are topics so interesting, that we cannot restrain our restless enquiry with regard to them; though nothing but doubt, uncertainty and contradiction have, as yet, been the result of our most accurate researches.

This I had lately occasion to observe while I passed, as usual, part of the summer season with CLEANTHES, and was present at those conversations of his with PHILO and DEMEA, of which I gave you lately some imperfect account. Your curiosity, you then told me, was so excited, that I must of necessity enter into a more exact detail of their reasonings, and display those various systems, which they advanced with regard to so delicate a subject as that of natural religion. The remarkable contrast in their characters still farther raised your expectations; while you opposed the accurate philosophical turn of CLEANTHES to the careless scepticism of PHILO, or compared either of their dispositions with the rigid inflexible orthodoxy of DEMEA. My youth rendered me a mere auditor of their disputes; and that curiosity natural to the early season of life, has so deeply imprinted in my memory the whole chain and connexion of their arguments, that, I hope, I shall not omit or confound any considerable part of them in the recital.

PART 1

After I joined the company, whom I found sitting in CLEANTHES's library, DEMEA paid CLEANTHES some compliments, on the great care, which he took of my education, and on his unwearied perseverance and constancy in all his friendships. The father of PAMPHILUS, said he, was your intimate friend: The son is your pupil, and may indeed be regarded as your adopted son; were we to judge by the pains which you bestow in conveying to him[1] every useful branch of literature and science. You are no more wanting, I am persuaded, in prudence than in industry. I shall, therefore, communicate to you a maxim which I have observed with regard to my own children, that I may learn how far it agrees with your practice. The method I follow in their education is founded on the saying of an ancient, *that students of Philosophy ought first to learn Logics, then Ethics, next Physics, last of all, of the Nature of the Gods.*[2] This science of natural theology, according to him, being the most profound and abstruse of any, required the maturest judgement in its students; and none but a mind, enriched with all the other sciences, can safely be entrusted with it.

Are you so late, says PHILO, in teaching your children the principles of religion? Is there no danger of their neglecting or rejecting altogether those opinions of which they have heard so little, during the whole course of their education? It is only as a science, replied DEMEA, subjected to human reasoning and disputation, that I postpone the study of natural theology. To season their minds with early piety is my chief care; and by continual precept and instruction, and I hope too, by example, I imprint deeply on their tender minds an habitual reverence for all the principles of religion. While they pass through every other science, I still remark the uncertainty of each part, the eternal disputations of men, the obscurity of all philosophy, and the strange, ridiculous conclusions, which some of the greatest geniuses have derived from the principles of mere human reason. Having thus tamed their mind to a proper submission and self-diffidence, I have no longer any scruple of opening to them the greatest mysteries of religion, nor apprehend any danger from that assuming arrogance of Philosophy, which may lead them to reject the most established doctrines and opinions.

Your precaution, says PHILO, of seasoning your children's minds with

---

1 'you take, of instructing him' scored out; 'which you bestow in conveying to him' written in its place.

2 *Chrysippus apud Plut. de repug. Stoicorum.*

early piety, is certainly very reasonable; and no more than is requisite, in this profane and irreligious age. But what I chiefly admire in your plan of education is your method of drawing advantage from the very principles of philosophy and learning, which, by inspiring pride and self-sufficiency, have commonly, in all ages, been found so destructive to the principles of religion. The vulgar, indeed, we may remark, who are unacquainted with science and profound enquiry, observing the endless disputes of the learned, have commonly a thorough contempt for philosophy; and rivet themselves the faster, by that means, in the great points of theology, which have been taught them. Those, who enter a little into study and enquiry, finding many appearances of evidence in doctrines the newest and most extraordinary, think nothing too difficult for human reason; and presumptuously breaking through all fences, profane the inmost sanctuaries of the temple. But CLEANTHES will, I hope, agree with me, that after we have abandoned ignorance, the surest remedy, there is still one expedient left to prevent this profane liberty. Let DEMEA's principles be improved and cultivated[3]: Let us become thoroughly sensible of the weakness, blindness, and narrow limits of human reason: Let us duly consider its uncertainty[4] and endless contrarieties, even in subjects of common life and practice: Let the errors and deceits[5] of our very senses be set before us; the insuperable difficulties, which attend first principles in all systems,[6] the contradictions, which adhere to the very ideas of matter, cause and effect, extension, space, time, motion; and in a word, quantity of all kinds, the object of the only science, that can fairly pretend to any certainty or evidence. When these topics are displayed in their full light, as they are by some philosophers and almost all divines; who can retain such confidence in this frail faculty of reason as to pay any regard to its determinations in points so sublime, so abstruse, so remote from common life and experience[7]? When the coherence of the parts of a stone, or even that composition of parts, which renders it extended; when these familiar objects, I say, are so inexplicable, and contain circumstances so repugnant and contradictory; with what assurance can we decide concerning the origin of worlds, or trace their history from eternity to eternity?

While PHILO pronounced these words, I could observe a smile in the

3 'embraced' scored out; 'improved and cultivated' written in its place.
4 'troublesome' scored out; 'uncertainty' written in its place.
5 'uncertainty' scored out; 'deceits' written in its place.
6 'sciences' scored out; 'systems' written in its place.
7 'practice' scored out; 'experience' written in its place.

countenances both of DEMEA and CLEANTHES. That of DEMEA seemed to imply an unreserved satisfaction in the doctrines delivered: But in CLEANTHES's features I could distinguish an air of finesse; as if he perceived some raillery or artificial malice in the reasonings of PHILO.

You propose then, PHILO, said CLEANTHES, to erect religious faith on philosophical scepticism; and you think, that if certainty or evidence be expelled from every other subject of enquiry, it will all retire to these theological doctrines, and there acquire a superior force and authority. Whether your scepticism be as absolute and sincere as you pretend, we shall learn bye and bye, when the company breaks up: We shall then see, whether you go out at the door or the window; and whether you really doubt, if your body has gravity, or can be injured by its fall; according to popular opinion, derived from our fallacious senses and more fallacious experience. And this consideration, DEMEA, may, I think, fairly serve to abate our ill-will to this humorous[8] sect of the sceptics. If they be thoroughly in earnest, they will not long trouble the world with their doubts, cavils, and disputes. If they be only in jest, they are, perhaps, bad railliers, but can never be very dangerous either to the State, to Philosophy, or to Religion.

In reality, PHILO, continued he, it seems certain, that though a man in a flush of humour, after intense reflection on the many contradictions and imperfections of human reason, may entirely renounce all belief and opinion; it is impossible for him to persevere in this total scepticism, or make it appear in his conduct for a few hours. External objects press in upon him: Passions solicit him: His philosophical melancholy dissipates; and even the utmost violence upon his own temper will not be able, during any time, to preserve the poor appearance of scepticism. And for what reason impose on himself such a violence? This is a point, in which it will be impossible for him ever to satisfy himself, consistent with his sceptical principles: So that upon the whole nothing could be more ridiculous than the principles of the ancient *Pyrrhonians*; if in reality they endeavoured as is pretended, to extend throughout[9] the same scepticism, which they had learned from the declamations of their school[10] and which they ought to have confined to them.

In this view, there appears a great resemblance between the sects of the *Stoics* and *Pyrrhonians*, though perpetual antagonists. And both of

8 'pleasant' scored out; 'humorous' written in its place.
9 'introduce into common life' scored out; 'extend throughout' written in its place.
10 'from the sciences' scored out; 'from the declamations of their school' written in its place.

them seem founded on this erroneous maxim, that what a man can perform sometimes, and in some dispositions, he can perform always, and in every disposition. When the mind, by stoical reflections, is elevated into a sublime enthusiasm of virtue, and strongly smit with any *species* of honour or public good, the utmost bodily pain and sufferance will not prevail over[11] such a high sense of duty; and it is possible, perhaps, by its means, even to smile and exult in the midst of tortures. If this sometimes may be the case in fact and reality, much more may a philosopher, in his school, or even in his closet, work himself up to such an enthusiasm, and support in imagination the acutest pain or most calamitous event, which he can possibly conceive. But how shall he support this enthusiasm itself? The bent of his mind relaxes, and cannot be recalled at pleasure. Avocations lead him astray: Misfortunes attack him unawares: And the *philosopher* sinks by degrees into the *plebeian*.

I allow of your comparison between the *Stoics* and *Sceptics*, replied PHILO. But you may[12] observe, at the same time, that though the mind cannot, in Stoicism, support the highest flights of philosophy, yet even when it sinks lower, it still retains somewhat of its former disposition; and the effects of the Stoic's reasoning will appear in his conduct in common life, and through the whole tenor of his actions. The ancient schools, particularly that of ZENO, produced examples of virtue and constancy, which seem astonishing to present times.

> Vain wisdom all and false philosophy
> Yet with a pleasing sorcery could charm
> Pain, for a while, or anguish, and excite
> Fallacious hope, or arm the obdurate breast
> With stubborn patience, as with triple steel.

In like manner, if a man has accustomed himself to sceptical considerations on the uncertainty and narrow limits of reason, he will not entirely forget them when he turns his reflection on other subjects[13]; but in all his philosophical principles and reasoning, I dare not say, in his common conduct,[14] he will be found different from those, who

---

11 'will make small impression in opposition to' scored out; 'will not prevail over' written in its place.

12 'must' scored out; 'may' written in its place.

13 'leaves his closet' scored out; 'turns his reflection on other subjects' written in its place.

14 'I dare not say, in his common conduct' added to the text.

either never formed any opinions in the case, or have entertained sentiments more favourable to human reason.

[15]To whatever length any-one may push his speculative principles of scepticism, he must act, I own, and live, and converse like other men; and for this conduct he is not obliged to give any other reason, than the absolute necessity he lies under of so doing. If he ever carries his speculations farther than this necessity constrains him, and philophizes, either on natural or moral subjects, he is allured by a certain pleasure and satisfaction, which he finds in employing himself after that manner. He considers besides, that every one, even in common life, is constrained to have more or less of this philosophy; that from our earliest infancy we make continual advances in forming more general principles of conduct and reasoning; that the larger experience we acquire and the stronger reason we are endowed with, we always render our principles the more general and comprehensive; and that what we call *Philosophy* is nothing but a more regular and methodical operation of the same kind. To philosophize on such subjects is nothing essentially different from reasoning on common life; and we may only expect greater stability, if not greater truth, from our philosophy, on account of its exacter and more scrupulous method of proceeding.

But when we look beyond human affairs and the properties of the surrounding bodies: When we carry our speculations into the two eternities, before and after the present state of things; into the creation and formation of the universe; the existence and properties of spirits; the powers and operations of one universal spirit, existing without beginning and without end; omnipotent, omniscient, immutable, infinite, and incomprehensible: We must be far removed from the smallest tendency to scepticism not to be apprehensive, that we have here gone quite beyond the reach of our faculties. So long as we confine our speculations to trade or morals or politics or criticism, we make appeals, every moment, to common sense and experience, which strengthen our philosophical conclusions, and remove (at least, in part) the suspicion, which we so justly entertain with regard to every reasoning, that is very subtle or refined. But in theological reasonings, we have not this advantage; while at the same time we are employed upon objects, which, we must be sensible, are too large for our grasp, and of all others, require most to be familiarized to our apprehension. We are like foreigners in a strange country, to whom every thing must seem suspicious, and who are in danger every moment of transgressing

15 'It seems evident that', as the beginning of the paragraph, scored out.

against the laws and customs of the people, with whom they live and converse. We know not how far we ought to trust our vulgar methods of reasoning in such a subject; since, even in common life and in that province, which is peculiarly appropriated to them, we cannot account for them, and are entirely guided by a kind of instinct or necessity in employing them.[16]

All sceptics pretend, that, if reason be considered in an abstract view, it furnishes invincible arguments against itself, and that we could never retain any conviction or assurance, on any subject[17], were not the sceptical reasonings so refined and subtle, that they are not able to counterpoise the more solid and more natural arguments, derived from the senses and experience. But it is evident, whenever our arguments lose this advantage, and run wide of common life, that the most refined scepticism comes to be on a footing with them, and is able to oppose and counterbalance them. The one has no more weight than the other. The mind must remain in suspense between them; and it is that very suspense or balance, which is the triumph of scepticism.

But I observe, says CLEANTHES, with regard to you, PHILO, and all speculative sceptics, that your doctrine and practice are as much at variance in the most abstruse points of theory as in the conduct of common life. Wherever evidence discovers itself, you adhere to it, notwithstanding your pretended scepticism; and I can observe too some of your sect to be as decisive as those who make greater professions of certainty and assurance[18]. In reality, would not a man be ridiculous, who pretended to reject NEWTON's explication of the wonderful phenomenon of the rainbow, because that explication gives a minute anatomy of the rays of light; a subject, forsooth, too refined for human comprehension? And what would you say to one, who having nothing particular to object to the arguments of COPERNICUS and GALILEO for the motion of the earth, should withhold his assent, on that general principle, that these subjects were too magnificent and remote to be explained by the narrow and fallacious reason of mankind?

There is indeed a kind of brutish and ignorant scepticism, as you well observed, which gives the vulgar a general prejudice against what they do not easily understand, and makes them reject every principle, which

16 At the end of this paragraph Hume adds in the margin, and then scores out: 'A very small part of this great system, during a very small time, is very imperfectly discovered to us: And do we thus pronounce deceptively concerning the whole?' This paragraph is added to the text in Part 2 (see p. 114).
17 'even in the most common affairs of life' scored out; 'on any subject' written in its place.
18 'dogmatism' scored out; 'assurance' written in its place.

requires elaborate reasoning to prove and establish it. This species of scepticism is fatal to knowledge, not to religion, since we find, that those who make greatest profession of it, give often their assent, not only to the great truths of theism, and natural theology, but even to the most absurd tenets, which a traditional superstition has recommended to them. They firmly believe in witches; though they will not believe nor attend to the most simple proposition of EUCLID. But the refined and philosophical sceptics fall into[19] an inconsistence of an opposite nature. They push their researches into the most abstruse corners of science; and their assent attends them in every step, proportioned to the evidence, which they meet with. They are even obliged to acknowledge, that the most abstruse and remote objects are those which are best explained by philosophy. Light is in reality anatomized: The true system of the heavenly bodies is discovered and ascertained. But the nourishment of bodies by food[20] is still an inexplicable mystery. The cohesion of the parts of matter is still incomprehensible; These sceptics, therefore, are obliged, in every question, to consider each particular evidence apart, and proportion their assent to the precise degree of evidence which occurs. This is their practice in all natural, mathematical, moral, and political science. And why not the same, I ask, in the theological and religious? Why must conclusions of this nature be alone rejected on the general presumption of the insufficiency of human reason, without any particular discussion of the evidence? Is not such an unequal conduct a plain proof of prejudice and passion?

Our senses, you say, are fallacious, our understanding erroneous, our ideas even of the most familiar objects, extension, duration, motion, full of absurdities and contradictions. You defy me to solve the difficulties, or reconcile the repugnancies, which you discover in them. I have not capacity for so great an undertaking: I have not leisure for it: I perceive it to be superfluous. Your own conduct, in every circumstance, refutes your principles; and shows the firmest reliance on all the received maxims of science, morals, prudence, and behaviour.

I shall never assent to so harsh an opinion as that of a celebrated writer[21] who says that the sceptics are not a sect of philosophers: They are only a sect of liars. I may, however, affirm, (I hope, without offence) that they are a sect of jesters or railliers. But for my part, whenever I find myself disposed to mirth and amusement, I shall

19 'are guilty of' scored out; 'fall into' written in its place.
20 'falling of a stone' scored out; 'nourishment of bodies by food' written in its place.
21 *L'Art de Penser*. [The author of this work is Antoine Arnauld.]

certainly choose my entertainment of a less perplexing and abstruse nature. A comedy, a novel, or at most a history, seems a more natural recreation than such metaphysical subtleties and abstractions.

In vain would the sceptic make a distinction between science and common life, or between one science and another. The arguments, employed in all, if just, are of a similar nature, and contain the same force and evidence. Or if there be any difference among them, the advantage lies entirely on the side of theology and natural religion. Many principles of mechanics are founded on very abstruse reasoning; yet no man, who has any pretensions to science, even no speculative sceptic, pretends to entertain the least doubt with regard to them. The COPERNICAN system contains the most surprising paradox, and the most contrary to our natural conceptions, to appearances, and to our very senses: Yet even monks and inquisitors are now constrained to withdraw their opposition to it. And shall PHILO, a man of so liberal a genius, and extensive knowledge, entertain any general undistinguished scruples with regard to the religious hypothesis, which is founded on the simplest and most obvious arguments, and, unless it meet with artificial obstacles, has such easy access and admission into the mind of man?

And here we may observe, continued he, turning himself towards DEMEA, a pretty curious circumstance in the history of the sciences. After the union of philosophy with the popular religion, upon the first establishment of Christianity, nothing was more usual, among all religious teachers, than declamations against reason, against the senses, against every principle, derived merely[22] from human research and enquiry. All the topics of the ancient academics[23] were adopted by the fathers; and thence propagated for several ages in every school and pulpit throughout Christendom. The reformers embraced the same principles of reasoning, or rather declamation; and all panegyrics on the excellency of faith were sure to be interlarded with some severe strokes of satire against natural reason. A celebrated prelate[24] too, of the Romish communion, a man of the most extensive learning, who wrote a demonstration of Christianity, has also composed a treatise, which contains all the cavils of the boldest and most determined *Pyrrhonism*. LOCKE seems to have been the first Christian, who ventured openly to assert, that faith was nothing but a species of *reason*, that religion was only a branch of philosophy, and that a chain of

22 'entirely' scored out; 'merely' written in its place.
23 'and sceptics' scored out.
24 *Mons. Huet.*

arguments, similar to that which established any truth in morals, politics, or physics, was always employed in discovering all the principles of theology, natural and revealed. The ill use, which BAYLE and other libertines made of the philosophical scepticism of the fathers and first reformers, still farther propagated the judicious sentiment of Mr. LOCKE: And it is now, in a manner, avowed, by all pretenders to reasoning and philosophy, that atheist and sceptic are almost synonymous. And as it is certain, that no man is in earnest, when he professes the latter principle; I would fain hope that there are as few, who seriously maintain the former.

Don't you remember, said PHILO, the excellent saying of Lord BACON on this head. That a little philosophy, replied CLEANTHES, makes a man an atheist: A great deal converts him to religion. That is a very judicious remark too, said PHILO. But what I have in my eyes is another passage, where, having mentioned DAVID's fool, who said in his heart there is no God, this great philosopher observes, that the atheists nowadays have a double share of folly: For they are not contented to say in their hearts there is no God, but they also utter that impiety with their lips, and are thereby guilty of multiplied indiscretion and imprudence. Such people, though they were ever so much in earnest, cannot, methinks, be very formidable.

But though you should rank me in this class of fools, I cannot forbear communicating a remark, that occurs to me from the history of the religious and irreligious scepticism, with which you have entertained us. It appears to me, that there are strong symptoms of priestcraft in the whole progress of this affair. During ignorant ages, such as those which followed the dissolution of the ancient schools, the priests perceived, that atheism, deism, or heresy of any kind could only proceed from the presumptuous questioning of received opinions, and from a belief, that human reason was equal to every thing. Education had then a mighty influence over the minds of men, and was almost equal in force to those suggestions of the senses and common understanding, by which the most determined sceptic must allow himself to be governed. But at present, when the influence of education is much diminished, and men, from a more open commerce of the world, have learned to compare the popular principles of different nations and ages, our sagacious divines have changed their whole system of philosophy, and talk the language of *Stoics, Platonists*, and *Peripatetics*, not that of *Pyrrhonians* and *Academics*. If we distrust human reason, we have now no other principle to lead us into religion. Thus, sceptics in one age, dogmatists in another; whichever system best suits the purpose of these reverend gentlemen, in giving them an ascendant over mankind, they are sure to make it their favourite principle, and established tenet.

It is very natural, said CLEANTHES, for men to embrace those principles, by which they find they can best defend their doctrines; nor need we have any recourse to priestcraft to account for so reasonable an expedient. And surely, nothing can afford a stronger presumption, that any set of principles are true, and ought to be embraced, than to observe, that they tend to the confirmation of true religion, and serve to confound the cavils of atheists, libertines and freethinkers of all denominations.

PART 2

I must own, CLEANTHES, said DEMEA, that nothing can more surprise me, than the light in which you have all along, put this argument. By the whole tenor of your discourse, one would imagine that you were maintaining the being of a God, against the cavils of atheists and infidels; and were necessitated to become a champion for that fundamental principle of all religion. But this, I hope, is not, by any means, a question among us. No man; no man, at least, of common sense, I am persuaded, ever entertained a serious doubt with regard to a truth so certain and self-evident. The question is not concerning the BEING, but the NATURE of GOD. This, I affirm, from the infirmities of human understanding, to be altogether incomprehensible and unknown to us. The essence of that supreme mind, his attributes, the manner of his existence, the very nature of his duration; these and every particular, which regards so divine a being, are mysterious[1] to men. Finite, weak, and blind creatures, we ought to humble ourselves in his august presence, and, conscious of our frailties, adore in silence his infinite perfections, which eye hath not seen, ear hath not heard, neither hath it entered into the heart of man to conceive them. They are covered in a deep cloud from human curiosity: It is profaneness to attempt penetrating through these sacred obscurities: And next to the impiety of denying his existence, is the temerity of prying into his nature and essence, decrees and attributes.

But lest you should think, that my piety has here got the better of my *philosophy*, I shall support my opinion, if it needs any support, by a very great authority. I might cite all the divines almost, from the foundation of Christianity, who have ever treated of this or any other theological subject: But I shall confine myself, at present, to one equally celebrated for piety and philosophy. It is Father MALEBRANCHE, who, I remember, thus expressed himself:[2] 'One ought not so much (says he) to call God a spirit, in order to express positively what he is, as in order to signify that he is not matter. He is a being infinitely perfect: Of this we cannot doubt. But in the same manner as we ought not to imagine, even supposing him corporeal, that he is cloathed with a human body, as the *Anthropomorphites* asserted, under colour that that figure was the most perfect of any; so neither ought we to imagine, that the

---

1 'and inconceivable' scored out.
2 *Rechercher de la verite, lev 3 chap. 9.*

spirit of God has human ideas, or bears *any* resemblance to our spirit; under colour that we know nothing more perfect than a human mind. We ought rather to believe that as he comprehends the perfections of matter without being material . . . he comprehends also the perfections of created spirits, without being spirit, in the manner we conceive spirit: That his true name is *He that is*, or in other words, Being without restriction, all Being, the Being infinite and universal.'

After so great an authority, DEMEA, replied PHILO, as that which you have produced, and a thousand more, which you might produce, it would appear ridiculous in me to add my sentiment[3] or express my approbation of your doctrine. But surely, where reasonable men treat these subjects, the question can never be concerning the *being* but only the *nature* of the Deity. The former truth, as you will observe, is unquestionable and self-evident. Nothing exists without a cause, and the original cause of this universe (whatever it be) we call GOD; and piously ascribe to him every species of perfection. Whoever scruples this fundamental truth deserves every punishment, which can be inflicted among philosophers, to wit, the greatest ridicule, contempt and disapprobation. But as all perfection is entirely relative, we ought never to imagine, that we comprehend the attributes of this Divine Being, or to suppose, that his perfections have any analogy or likeness to the perfections of a human creature. Wisdom, thought, design, knowledge; these we justly ascribe to him; because these words are honourable among men, and we have no other language or other conceptions, by which we can express our adoration of him. But let us beware, lest we think, that our ideas any wise correspond to his perfections, or that his attributes have any resemblance to these qualities among men. He is infinitely superior to our limited view and comprehension; and is more the object of worship in the temple than of disputation in the schools.

In reality, CLEANTHES, continued he, there is no need of having recourse to that affected scepticism, so displeasing to you, in order to come at this determination. Our ideas reach no farther than our experience: We have no experience of divine attributes and operations; I need not conclude my syllogism; You can draw the inference yourself. And it is a pleasure to me (and I hope to you too) that just reasoning and sound piety here concur in the same conclusion, and both of them establish the adorably mysterious and incomprehensible nature of the Supreme Being.

3 'testimony' scored out; 'sentiment' written in its place.

Not to lose any time in circumlocutions, said CLEANTHES, addressing himself to DEMEA,[4] much less in replying to the pious declamations of PHILO; I shall briefly explain how I conceive this matter. Look round the world: Contemplate the whole and every part of it: You will find it to be nothing but one great machine, subdivided into an infinite number of lesser machines, which again admit of subdivisions, to a degree beyond what human senses and faculties can trace and explain. All these various machines, and even their most minute parts, are adjusted to each other with an accuracy, which ravishes into admiration all men, who have ever contemplated them. The curious adapting of means to ends, throughout all nature, resembles exactly, though it much[5] exceeds, the productions of human contrivance; of human design, thought, wisdom, and intelligence. Since therefore the effects resemble each other, we are led to infer, by all the rules of analogy, that the causes also resemble; and that the Author of Nature is somewhat similar to the mind of man; though possessed of much larger faculties, proportioned to the grandeur of the work, which he has executed. By this argument *a posteriori*, and by this argument alone, do we prove at once the existence of a Deity, and his similarity to human mind and intelligence.

I shall be so free, CLEANTHES, said DEMEA, as to tell you, that from the beginning I could not approve of your conclusion concerning the similarity of the Deity to men; still less can I approve of the mediums, by which you endeavour to establish it. What! No demonstration of the being of a God! No abstract arguments! No proofs *a priori*! Are these, which have hitherto been so much insisted on by philosophers, all fallacy, all sophism? Can we reach no farther in this subject than experience and probability? I will not say, that this is betraying the cause of a Deity: But surely, by this affected candour, you give advantages to atheists, which they never could obtain, by the mere hint of argument and reasoning.

What I chiefly scruple in this subject, said PHILO, is not so much, that all religious arguments are by CLEANTHES reduced to experience, as that they appear not to be even the most certain and irrefragable of that inferior kind. That a stone will fall, that fire will burn, that the earth has solidity, we have observed a thousand and a thousand times; and when any new instance of this nature is presented, we draw without hesitation the accustomed inference. The exact similarity of the cases

---

4 'addressing himself to DEMEA' added to the text.
5 'extremely' scored out; 'much' written in its place.

gives us a perfect assurance of a similar event; and a stronger evidence is never desired nor sought after. But wherever you depart, in the least, from the similarity of the cases, you diminish proportionably the evidence; and may at last bring it to a very weak *analogy*, which is confessedly liable to[6] error and uncertainty. After having experienced the circulation of the blood in human creatures, we make no doubt, that it takes place in TITIUS and MAEVIUS: But from its circulation in frogs and fishes, it is only a presumption, though a strong one, from analogy, that it takes place in men and other animals. The analogical reasoning[7] is much weaker, when we infer the circulation of the sap in vegetables from our experience, that the blood circulates in animals; and those, who hastily followed that imperfect analogy, are found, by more accurate experiments, to have been mistaken.

If we see a house, CLEANTHES, we conclude, with the greatest certainty, that it had an architect or builder; because this is precisely that species of effect, which we have experienced to proceed from that species of cause. But surely you will not affirm, that the universe bears such a resemblance to a house, that we can with the same certainty infer a similar cause, or that the analogy is here entire and perfect. The dissimilitude is so striking, that the utmost you can here pretend to is a guess, a conjecture, a presumption concerning a similar cause; and how that pretension will be received in the world, I leave you to consider.

It would surely be very ill received, replied CLEANTHES; and I should be deservedly blamed and detested, did I allow, that the proofs of a Deity amounted to no more than a guess or conjecture. But is the whole adjustment of means to ends in a house and in the universe so slight a resemblance? The economy of final causes? The order, proportion, and arrangement of every part? Steps of a stair are plainly contrived, that human legs may use them in mounting; and this inference is certain and infallible. Human legs are also contrived for walking and mounting; and this inference, I allow, is not altogether so certain, because of the dissimilarity which you remark; but does it, therefore, deserve the name only of presumption or conjecture?

Good God! cried DEMEA, interrupting him, where are we? Zealous defenders of religion allow, that the proofs of a deity fall short of perfect evidence! And you, PHILO, on whose assistance I depended, in proving the adorable mysteriousness of the divine nature, do you assent to all these extravagant opinions of CLEANTHES? For what other name

6 'great' scored out.
7 'analogy' scored out; 'analogical reasoning' written in its place.

can I give them? Or why spare my censure, when such principles are advanced, supported by such an authority, before so young a man as PAMPHILUS?

You seem not to apprehend, replied PHILO, that I argue with CLEANTHES in his own way; and by showing him the dangerous consequences of his tenets, hope at last to reduce him to our opinion. But what sticks most with you, I observe, is the representation which CLEANTHES has made[8] of the argument a posteriori; and finding, that that argument is likely to escape your hold and vanish into air, you think it so disguised that you can scarcely believe it to be set in its true light. Now, however much I may dissent, in other respects, from the dangerous principles of CLEANTHES, I must allow that he has fairly represented that argument; and I shall endeavour so to state the matter to you that you will entertain no farther scruples with regard to it.

Were a man to abstract from every thing which he knows or has seen, he would be altogether incapable, merely from his own ideas, to determine what kind of scene the universe must be or to give the preference to one state or situation of things above another. For as nothing, which he clearly conceives, could be esteemed impossible or implying a contradiction, every chimera of his fancy would be upon an equal footing; nor could he assign any just reason, why he adheres to one idea or system, and rejects the others, which are equally possible.

Again; after he opens his eyes, and contemplates the world, as it really is, it would be impossible for him, at first, to assign the cause of any one event; much less, of the whole of things or of the universe. He might set his fancy a rambling; and she might bring him in an infinite variety of reports and representations. These would all be possible; but being all equally possible, he would never, of himself, give a satisfactory account for his preferring one of them to the rest. Experience alone can point out to him the true cause of any phenomenon.

Now according to this method of reasoning, DEMEA, it follows (and is, indeed, tacitly allowed by CLEANTHES himself) that order, arrangement, or the adjustment of final causes is not, of itself, any proof of design; but only so far as it has been experienced to proceed from that principle[9]. For ought we can know a priori, matter may contain the source or spring[10] of order originally, within itself, as well as mind

---

8 'that you will not allow Cleanthes to have made a just' scored out; 'the representation which Cleanthes has made' written in its place.
9 'design' scored out; 'that principle' written in its place.
10 'principle' scored out; 'source or spring' written in its place.

does; and there is no more difficulty in conceiving, that the several elements, from an internal unknown cause, may fall into the most exquisite arrangement, than to conceive that their ideas, in the great, universal mind, from a like internal, unknown cause, fall into that arrangement. The equal possibility of both these suppositions is allowed. But by experience we find (according to CLEANTHES) that there is a difference between them. Throw several pieces of steel together, without shape or form; they will never arrange themselves so as to compose a watch: Stone, and mortar, and wood, without an architect, never erect a house. But the ideas in a human mind, we see, by an unknown, inexplicable economy, arrange themselves so as to form the plan of a watch or house. Experience, therefore, proves, that there is an original principle of order in mind, not in matter. From similar effects we infer similar causes. The adjustment of means to ends[11] is alike in the universe, as in a machine of human contrivance. The causes, therefore, must be resembling.

I was from the beginning scandalized, I must own, with this resemblance, which is asserted, between the Deity and human creatures; and must conceive it to imply such a degradation of the supreme Being as no sound theist could endure. With your assistance, therefore, DEMEA, I shall endeavour to defend what you justly call the adorable mysteriousness of the divine nature, and shall refute this reasoning of CLEANTHES; provided he allows, that I have made a fair representation of it.

When CLEANTHES had assented, PHILO, after a short pause, proceeded in the following manner.

That all inferences, CLEANTHES, concerning fact are founded on experience, and that all experimental reasonings are founded on the supposition, that similar causes prove similar effects, and similar effects similar causes; I shall not, at present, much dispute with you. But observe, I entreat you, with what extreme caution all just reasoners proceed in the transferring of experiments to similar cases. Unless the cases be exactly similar, they repose no perfect confidence in applying their past observation to any particular phenomenon. Every[12] alteration of circumstances occasions[13] a doubt concerning the event; and it requires new experiments to prove certainly, that the new circumstances are of no moment or importance. A change in bulk, situation,

---

11 'final cause' scored out; 'means to ends' written in its place.
12 'to any particular phenomenon' added to the text. 'Any' scored out; 'Every' written in its place.
13 'starts' scored out; 'occasions' written in its place.

arrangement, age, disposition of the air, or surrounding bodies; any of these particulars may be attended with the most unexpected consequences: And unless the objects be quite familiar to us, it is the highest temerity to expect with assurance, after any of these changes, an event similar to that which before fell under our observation. The slow and deliberate steps of philosophers here, if any where, are distinguished from the precipitate march of the vulgar, who, hurried on by the smallest similitude, are incapable of all discernment or consideration.

But can you think, CLEANTHES, that your usual phlegm and philosophy have been preserved in so wide a step as you have taken, when you compared to the universe houses, ships, furniture, machines; and from their similarity in some circumstances inferred a similarity in their causes? Thought, design, intelligence, such as we discover in men and other animals, is no more than one of the springs and principles of the universe, as well as heat or cold, attraction or repulsion, and a hundred others, which fall under daily observation. It is an active cause, by which some particular parts of nature, we find, produce alterations on other parts. But can a conclusion, with any propriety, be transferred from parts to the whole? Does not the great disproportion bar all comparison and inference? From observing the growth of a hair, can we learn anything concerning the generation of a man? Would the manner of a leaf's blowing, even though perfectly known, afford us any instruction concerning the vegetation of a tree?

But allowing that we were to take the *operations* of one part of nature upon another for the foundation of our judgement concerning the *origin* of the[14] whole (which never can be admitted) yet why select so minute, so weak, so bounded a principle as the reason and design of animals is found to be upon this planet? What peculiar privilege has this little agitation of the brain which we call thought, that we must thus make it the model of the whole universe? Our partiality in our own favour does indeed present it on all occasions: But sound philosophy ought carefully to guard against so natural an illusion.

So far from admitting, continued PHILO, that the operations of a part can afford us any just conclusion concerning the origin of the whole, I will not allow any one part to form a rule for another part, if the latter be very remote from the former. Is there any reasonable ground to conclude, that the inhabitants of other planets possess thought, intelligence, reason, or any thing similar to these faculties in men? When

14 '*origin* of the' added to the text.

nature has so extremely diversified her manner of operation in this small globe; can we imagine that she incessantly copies herself throughout so immense a universe? And if thought, as we may well suppose, be confined merely to this narrow corner, and has even there so limited a sphere of action; with what propriety can we assign it for the original cause of all things? The narrow views of a peasant, who makes his domestic economy the rule for the government of kingdoms, is in comparison a pardonable sophism.

But were we ever so much assured, that a thought and reason, resembling the human, were to be found throughout the whole universe, and were its activity elsewhere vastly greater and more commanding than it appears in this globe: Yet I cannot see, why the operations of a world, constituted, arranged, adjusted, can with any propriety be extended to a world, which is in its embryo-state, and is advancing towards that constitution and arrangement. By observation, we know somewhat of the economy, action, and nourishment of a finished animal; but we must transfer with great caution that observation to the growth of a fetus in the womb, and still more, to the formation of an animalcule in the loins of its male-parent. Nature, we find, even from our limited experience, possesses an infinite number of springs and principles, which incessantly discover themselves on every change of her position and situation. And what new and unknown principles would actuate her in so new and unknown a situation, as that of the formation of a universe, we cannot, without the utmost temerity, pretend to determine.

**[15] A very small part of this great system, during a very short time, is very imperfectly discovered to us: And do we thence pronounce decisively concerning the origin of the whole? **

Admirable conclusion! Stone, wood, brick, iron, brass, have not, at this time, in this minute globe of earth, an order or arrangement without human art and contrivance: Therefore the universe could not originally attain its order and arrangement, without something similar to human art. But is a part of nature a rule for another part, very wide of the former? Is it a rule for the whole? Is a very small part a rule for the universe? Is nature in one situation, a certain rule for[16] nature in another situation, vastly different from the former?

And can you blame me, CLEANTHES, if I here imitate the prudent reserve of SIMONIDES, who, according to the noted story, being asked by HIERO, *what God was?* desired a day to think of it, and then two days

15 This paragraph added at the margin to be a separate paragraph.
16 'precisely similar to' scored out; 'a certain rule for' written in its place.

more; and after that manner continually prolonged the term, without ever bringing in his definition or description? Could you even blame me, if I had answered at first, *that I did not know*, and was sensible that this subject lay vastly beyond the reach of my faculties? You might cry out sceptic and raillier as much as you pleased: But having found, in so many other subjects, much more familiar, the imperfections and even contradictions of human reason, I never should expect any success from its feeble conjectures, in a subject, so sublime, and so remote from the sphere of our observation. When two *species* of objects have always been observed to be conjoined together, I can *infer*, by custom, the existence of one, wherever I *see* the existence of the other: And this I call an argument from experience. But how this argument can have place, where the objects, as in the present case,[17] are single, individual, without parallel, or specific resemblance, may be difficult to explain. And will any man tell me with a serious countenance, that an orderly universe must arise from some thought and art, like the human; because we have experience of it? To ascertain this reasoning, it were requisite, that we had experience of the origin of worlds; and it is not sufficient surely, that we have seen ships and cities arise from human art and contrivance . . .

PHILO was proceeding in this vehement manner, somewhat between jest and earnest, as it appeared to me; when he observed some signs of impatience in CLEANTHES, and then immediately stopped short. What I had to suggest, said CLEANTHES, is only that you would not abuse terms, or make use of popular expressions to subvert philosophical reasonings. You know, that the vulgar often distinguish reason from experience, even where the question relates only to matter of fact and existence; though it is found, where that *reason* is properly analyzed, that it is nothing but a species of experience. To prove by experience the origin of the universe from mind is not more contrary to common speech than to prove the motion of the earth from the same principle. And a caviller might raise all the same objections to the COPERNICAN system, which you have urged against my reasonings. Have you other earths, might he say, which you have seen to move? Have . . .

Yes! cried PHILO, interrupting him, we have other earths. Is not the moon another earth, which we see to turn round its center? Is not Venus another earth, where we observe the same phenomenon? Are not the revolutions of the sun also a confirmation, from analogy, of the same theory? All the planets, are they not earths, which revolve about

17 'concerning the origin of the world' scored out.

the sun? Are not the satellites moons, which move around Jupiter and Saturn, and along with these primary planets, around the sun? These analogies and resemblances, with others, which I have not mentioned, are the sole proofs of the COPERNICAN system: And to you it belongs to consider, whether you have any analogies of the same kind to support your theory.

In reality, CLEANTHES, continued he, the modern system of astronomy is now so much received by all enquirers, and has become so essential a part even of our earliest education, that we are not commonly very scrupulous in examining the reasons, upon which it is founded. It is now become a matter of mere curiosity to study the first writers on that subject, who had the full force of prejudice to encounter, and were obliged to turn their arguments on every side, in order to render them popular and convincing. But if we peruse GALILEO's famous Dialogues Concerning the System of the World, we shall find, that that great genius, one of the sublimest that ever existed, first bent all his endeavours to prove, that there was no foundation for the distinction commonly made between elementary and celestial substances. The schools, proceeding from the illusions of sense, had carried this distinction very far; and had established the latter substances to be ingenerable, incorruptible, unalterable, impassible; and had assigned all the opposite qualities to the former. But Galileo, beginning with the moon, proved its similarity in every particular to the earth; its convex figure, its natural darkness when not illuminated, its density, its distinction into solid and liquid, the variations of its phases, the mutual illuminations of the earth and moon, their mutual eclipses, the inequalities of the lunar surface, &c. After many instances of this kind, with regard to all the planets, men plainly saw, that these bodies became proper objects of experience; and that the similarity of their nature enabled us to extend the same arguments and phenomena from one to the other.

In this cautious proceeding of the astronomers, you may read your own condemnation, CLEANTHES; or rather may see, that the subject in which you are engaged exceeds all human reason and enquiry. Can you pretend to show any such similarity between the fabric of a house and the generation of an universe? Have you ever seen nature in any such situation as resembles the first arrangement of the elements? Have worlds ever been formed under your eye? And have you had leisure to observe the whole progress of the phenomenon, from the first appearance of order to its final consummation? If you have, then cite your experience, and deliver your theory.

PART 3

How the most absurd argument, replied CLEANTHES, in the hands of a man of ingenuity and invention, may acquire an air of[1] probability! Are you not aware, PHILO, that it became necessary for COPERNICUS and his first disciples to prove the similarity of the terrestrial and celestial matter; because several philosophers, blinded by old systems, and supported by some sensible appearances[2], had denied this similarity? But that it is by no means necessary, that theists should prove the similarity of the works of nature to those of art; because this similarity is self-evident and undeniable? The same matter, a like form: What more is requisite to show[3] an analogy between their causes, and to ascertain the origin of all things from a divine purpose and intention? Your objections, I must freely tell you, are no better than the abstruse cavils of those philosophers, who denied motion; and ought to be refuted in the same manner, by illustrations, examples, and instances, rather than by serious argument and philosophy.

Suppose, therefore, that an articulate voice were heard in the clouds, much louder and more melodious than any which human art could ever reach: Suppose, that this voice were extended in the same instant over all nations, and spoke to each nation in its own language and dialect: Suppose, that the words delivered not only contain a just sense and meaning, but convey some instruction altogether worthy of a benevolent Being, superior to mankind: Could you possibly hesitate a moment concerning the cause of this voice? And must you not instantly ascribe it to some design or purpose? Yet I cannot see but all the same objections (if they merit that appellation) which lie against the system of theism, may also be produced against this inference.

Might you not say, that all conclusions concerning fact were founded on experience: That when we hear an articulate voice in the dark, and thence infer a man, it is only the resemblance of the effects, which leads us to conclude that there is a like resemblance in the cause: But that this extraordinary voice, by its loudness, extent, and flexibility to all languages, bears so little analogy to any human voice, that we have no reason to suppose any analogy in their causes: And consequently, that a rational, wise, coherent speech proceeded, you knew not whence, from some accidental whistling of the winds, not from any divine reason

1 'truth and' scored out.
2 'the illusion of sense' scored out; 'some sensible appearances' written in its place.
3 'prove' scored out; 'show' written in its place.

or intelligence? You see clearly your own objections in these cavils; and I hope too, you see clearly, that they cannot possibly have more force in the one case than in the other.

But to bring the case still nearer the present one of the universe, I shall make two suppositions, which imply not any absurdity or impossibility. Suppose, that there is a natural, universal, invariable language, common to every individual of human race; and that books are natural productions, which perpetuate themselves in the same manner with animals and vegetables, by descent and propagation. Several expressions of our passions contain a universal language: All brute animals have a natural speech, which, however limited, is very intelligible to their own species. And as there are infinitely fewer parts and less contrivance in the finest composition of eloquence than in the coarsest organized body, the propagation of an ILIAD or ANEID is an easier supposition than that of any plant or animal.

Suppose, therefore, that you enter into your library, thus peopled by natural[4] volumes, containing the most refined reason and most exquisite beauty: Could you possibly open one of them, and doubt, that its original cause bore the strongest analogy to mind and intelligence? When it reasons and discourses; when it expostulates, argues, and enforces its views and topics; when it applies sometimes to the pure intellect, sometimes to the affections; when it collects, disposes, and adorns every consideration suited to the subject: Could you persist in asserting, that all this, at the bottom, had really no meaning, and that the first formation of this volume in the loins of its original parent proceeded not from thought and design? Your obstinacy, I know, reaches not that degree of firmness: Even your sceptical play and wantonness would be abashed at so glaring an absurdity.

But if there be any difference, PHILO, between this supposed case and the real one of the universe, it is all to the advantage of the latter. The anatomy of an animal affords many stronger instances of design than the perusal of LIVY or TACITUS: And any objection which you start in the former case, by carrying me back to so unusual and extraordinary a scene as the first formation of worlds, the same objection has place on the supposition of our vegetating library. Choose, then, your party, PHILO, without ambiguity or evasion: Assert either that a rational volume is no proof of a rational cause, or admit of a similar cause to all the works of nature.

4 'vegetating animal' scored out.

Let me here observe too, continued CLEANTHES, that this religious[5] argument, instead of being weakened by that scepticism, so much affected by you, rather acquires force from it, and becomes more firm and undisputed. To exclude all argument or reasoning of every kind is either affectation or madness. The declared profession of every reasonable sceptic is only to reject abstruse, remote and refined arguments; to adhere to common sense and the plain instincts of nature; and to assent, wherever any reasons strike him with so full a force, that he cannot, without the greatest violence, prevent it. Now the arguments for natural religion are plainly of this kind; nothing but the most perverse, obstinate metaphysics can reject them. Consider, anatomize the eye: survey its structure and contrivance; and tell me, from your own feeling, if the idea of a contriver does not immediately flow in upon you with a force like that of sensation. The most obvious conclusion surely is in favour of design; and it requires time, reflection and study to summon up those frivolous, though abstruse, objections, which can support infidelity. Who can behold the male and female of each species, the correspondence of their parts and instincts, their passions and whole course of life before and after generation, but must be sensible, that the propagation of the species is intended by nature? Millions and millions of such instances present themselves through every part of the universe; and no language can convey a more intelligible, irresistible meaning, than the curious adjustment of final causes. To what degree, therefore, of blind dogmatism must one have attained, to reject such natural and such convincing arguments?

[6] Some beauties in writing we may meet with, which seem contrary to rules, and which gain the affections, and animate the imagination, in opposition to all the precepts of criticism and to the authority of the established masters of art. And if the argument for theism be, as you pretend, contradictory to the principles of logic; its universal, its irresistible influence proves clearly, that there may be arguments of a like irregular nature. Whatever cavils may be urged; an orderly world, as well as a coherent, articulate speech, will still be received as an incontestable proof of design and intention.

It sometimes happens, I own, that the religious arguments have not their due influence on an ignorant savage and barbarian; not because

---

5 'theological' scored out; 'religious' written in its place.
6 This paragraph appears at the end of Part 3, with instructions to insert at this point in the text.

they are obscure and difficult, but because he never asks himself any question with regard to them. Whence arises the curious structure of an animal? From the copulation of its parents. And these whence? From *their* parents? A few removes set the objects at such a distance, that to him they are lost in darkness and confusion; nor is he actuated by any curiosity to trace them farther. But this is neither dogmatism nor scepticism, but stupidity; a state of mind very different from your sifting, inquisitive disposition, my ingenious friend. You can trace causes from effects: You can compare the most distant and remote objects: And your greatest errors proceed not from barrenness of thought and invention, but from too luxuriant a fertility, which suppresses your natural good sense, by a profusion of unnecessary scruples and objections.

Here I could observe, HERMIPPUS, that PHILO was a little embarrassed and confounded: But while he hesitated in delivering an answer, luckily for him, DEMEA broke in upon the discourse, and saved his countenance.

Your instance, CLEANTHES, said he, drawn from books and language, being familiar, has, I confess, so much more force on that account; but is there not some danger too in this very circumstance, and may it not render us presumptuous, by making us imagine we comprehend the Deity, and have some adequate idea of his nature and attributes. When, I read a volume, I enter into the mind and intention of the author: I become him, in a manner, for the instant; and have an immediate feeling and conception of those ideas, which revolved in his imagination, while employed in that composition. But so near an approach we never surely can make to the Deity. His ways are not our ways. His attributes are perfect, but incomprehensible. And this volume of nature contains a great and inexplicable riddle, more than any intelligible discourse or reasoning.

The ancient *Platonists*, you know, were the most religious and devout of all the pagan philosophers: Yet many of them, particularly PLOTINUS, expressly declare, that intellect or understanding is not to be ascribed to the Deity, and that our most perfect worship of him consists, not in acts of veneration, reverence, gratitude or love; but in a certain mysterious self annihilation or total extinction of all our faculties. These ideas are, perhaps, too far stretched; but still it must be acknowledged, that, by representing the Deity as so intelligible, and comprehensible, and so similar to a human mind, we are guilty of the grossest and most narrow partiality, and make ourselves the model of the whole universe.

[7] All the *sentiments* of the human mind, gratitude, resentment, love, friendship, approbation, blame, pity, emulation, envy, have a plain reference to the state and situation of man, and are calculated for preserving the existence, and promoting the activity of such a being in such circumstances. It seems therefore unreasonable to transfer such sentiments to a supreme existence, or to suppose him actuated by them; and the phenomena, besides, of the universe will not support us in such a theory. All our *ideas*, derived from the senses, are confessedly false and illusive; and cannot, therefore, be supposed to have place in a supreme intelligence: And as the ideas of internal sentiment, added to those of the external senses, compose the whole furniture of human understanding, we may conclude, that none of the *materials* of thought are in any respect similar in the human and in the divine intelligence. Now as to the *manner* of thinking; how can we make any comparison between them, or suppose them any wise resembling? Our thought is fluctuating, uncertain, fleeting, successive, and compounded; and were we to remove these circumstances, we absolutely annihilate its essence, and it would, in such a case, be an abuse of terms to apply to it the name of thought or reason. At least, if it appear more pious and respectful (as it really is) still to retain those terms, when we mention the supreme Being, we ought to acknowledge, that their meaning, in that case, is totally incomprehensible; and that the infirmities of our nature do not permit us to reach any ideas, which in the least[8] correspond to the ineffable sublimity of the divine attributes.

---

7 This paragraph appears at the end of the Part 3, with instructions to insert at this point in the text.
8 'in the least' added to the text.

PART 4

It seems strange to me, said CLEANTHES, that you, DEMEA, who are so
sincere in the cause of religion, should still maintain the mysterious,
incomprehensible nature of the Deity, and should insist so strenuously,
that he has no manner of likeness or resemblance to human creatures.[1]
The Deity, I can readily allow, possesses many powers and attributes,
of which we can have no comprehension: But if our ideas, so far as they
go, be not just, and adequate, and correspondent to his real nature, I
know not what there is in this subject worth insisting on. Is the name,
without any meaning, of such mighty importance? Or how do you
mystics, who maintain the absolute incomprehensibility of the deity,
differ from sceptics or atheists, who assert, that the first cause of all is
unknown and unintelligible? Their temerity must be very great, if,
after rejecting the production by a mind; I mean, a mind, resembling
the human (for I know of no other) they pretend to assign, with
certainty, any other specific, intelligible cause[2]: And their conscience
must be very scrupulous indeed, if they refuse to call the universal,
unknown cause a God or Deity; and to bestow on him as many sublime
eulogies and unmeaning epithets, as you shall please to require of them.

Who could imagine, replied DEMEA, that CLEANTHES, the calm,
philosophical CLEANTHES, would attempt to refute his antagonists, by
affixing a nick-name to them; and like the common bigots and
inquisitors of the age, have recourse to invective and declamation,
instead of reasoning? Or does he not perceive, that these topics are
easily retorted, and that *anthropomorphite* is an appellation as invidious,
and implies as dangerous consequences, as the epithet of *Mystic*, with
which he has honoured us? In reality, CLEANTHES, consider what it is
you assert, when you represent the Deity as similar to a human mind
and understanding. What is the soul of man? A composition of various
faculties, passions, sentiments, ideas; united, indeed, into one self or
person but still distinct from each other. When it reasons, the ideas,
which are the parts of its discourse, arrange themselves in a certain
form or order; which is not preserved entire for a moment, but
immediately gives place to another arrangement. New opinions, new
passions, new affections, new feelings arise, which continually diver-

---

1 The following sentence appears after the first sentence in Part 4, and is then scored out:
   'Are you unacquainted with that principle of philosophy that we have no idea of
   anything, which has no likeness to ourselves, or to those objects, that have been
   exposed to our senses and experience?'
2 'distinct from it' scored out.

sify the mental scene, and produce in it the greatest variety, and most rapid succession imaginable. How is this compatible, with that perfect immutability and simplicity, which all true theists ascribe[3] to the Deity? By the same act, say they, he sees past, present, and future: His love and his hatred, his mercy and his justice are one individual operation: He is entire in every point of space; and complete in every instant of duration. No succession, no change, no acquisition, no diminution. What he is implies not in it any shadow of distinction or diversity. And what he is, this moment, he ever has been, and ever will be, without any new judgement, sentiment, or operation. He stands fixed in one simple, perfect state; nor can you ever say, with any propriety, that this act of his is different from that other, or that this judgement[4] or idea has been lately formed, and will give place, by succession, to any different judgement or idea.

I can readily allow, said CLEANTHES, that those who maintain the perfect simplicity of the supreme Being, to the extent in which you have explained it, are complete *mystics*, and chargeable with all the consequences which I have drawn from their opinion. They are, in a word, atheists, without knowing it. For though it be allowed, that the Deity possesses attributes, of which we have no comprehension; yet ought we never to ascribe to him any attributes, which are absolutely incompatible with that intelligent nature, essential to him. A mind, whose acts and sentiments and ideas are not distinct and successive; one that is wholly[5] simple, and totally immutable;[6] is a mind, which has no thought, no reason, no will, no sentiment, no love, no hatred; or in a word, is no mind at all. It is an abuse of terms to give it that appellation; and we may as well speak of limited extension without figure, or of number without composition.

Pray consider, said PHILO, whom you are at present inveighing against. You are honouring with the appellation of atheist all the sound, orthodox divines almost, who have treated of this subject; and you will, at last, be, yourself, found, according to your reckoning, the only sound theist in the world. But if idolaters be atheists, as I think, may justly be asserted, and Christian theologians the same; what becomes of the argument, so much celebrated, derived from the universal consent of mankind?

But because I know you are not much swayed by names and

3 'agree to belong' scored out; 'ascribe' written in its place.
4 'opinion' scored out; 'judgement' written in its place.
5 'perfectly' scored out; 'wholly' written in its place.
6 'inalterable' scored out; 'immutable' written in its place.

authorities, I shall endeavour to show you, a little more distinctly, the inconveniences of that anthropomorphism, which you have embraced; and shall prove, that there is no ground to suppose a plan of the world to be formed in the divine mind, consisting of distinct ideas, differently arranged; in the same manner as an architect forms in his head the plan of a house which he intends to execute.

[7] It is not easy, I own, to see, what is gained by this supposition, whether we judge of the matter by *reason* or by *experience*. We are still obliged to mount higher, in order to find the cause of this cause, which you had assigned as satisfactory and conclusive.

[8] If *reason* (I mean abstract reason, derived from enquiries *a priori*) be not alike mute with regard to all questions concerning cause and effect; this sentence at least it will venture to pronounce, that a mental world or universe of ideas requires a cause as much as does a material world or universe of objects; and if similar in its arrangement must require a similar cause. For what is there in this subject, which should occasion a different conclusion or inference? In an abstract view, they are entirely alike; and no difficulty attends the one supposition, which is not common to both of them.

Again, when we will needs force *experience* to pronounce some sentence, even on these subjects, which lie beyond her sphere; neither can she perceive any material difference in this particular, between these two kinds of worlds, but finds them to be governed by similar

---

7 The following sentence is scored out by Hume. It would have formed the first sentence in the paragraph: 'Tis evident, CLEANTHES, when you assert, that the world arose from a design, similar to the human, you do nothing but present us with a mind or ideal world, consisting of similar parts with the universe or material world, and affirm the former to be the cause of the latter.'

8 This paragraph, written at the end of Part 4 with instructions to insert at this point, replaces the following paragraph which had been scored out. Also scored out were two instructions to 'Print these Lines, tho' eraz'd': 'When we consult *reason*, all causes and effects seem equally explicable *a priori*; nor is it possible to assign either of them, by the mere abstract contemplation of their nature, without consulting *experience*, or considering what we have found to result from the operation of objects. And if this proposition be true in general, that *reason, judging a priori, finds all causes and effects alike explicable*; it must appear more so, when we compare the external world of objects with that world of thought, which is represented as its cause. If *reason* tells us, that the world of objects requires a cause, it must give us the same information concerning that world of thought: And if the one seems to reason to require a cause of any particular kind, the other must require a cause of a like kind. Any proposition, therefore, which we can form concerning the cause of the former, if it be consistent, or intelligible, or necessary, must also appear to reason consistent or intelligible or necessary, when applied to the latter, such as you have described it; and *vice versa*. 'Tis evident, then, that as far as abstract reason can judge, 'tis perfectly indifferent, whether we rest on the universe of matter or on that of thought; nor do we gain any thing by tracing the one into the other.'

principles, and to depend upon an equal variety of causes in their operations. We have specimens in miniature of both of them. Our own mind resembles the one: A vegetable or animal body the other. Let experience, therefore, judge from these samples. Nothing seems more delicate with regard to its causes than thought; and as these causes never operate in two persons after the same manner, so we never find two persons, who think exactly alike. Nor indeed does the same person think exactly alike at any two different periods of time. A difference of age, of the disposition of his body, of weather, of food, of company, of books, of passions; any of these particulars or others more minute, are sufficient to alter the curious machinery of thought, and communicate to it very different movements and operations. As far as we can judge, vegetables and animal bodies are not more delicate in their motions, nor depend upon a greater variety or more curious adjustment of springs and principles.

How therefore shall we satisfy ourselves concerning the cause of that Being[9] whom you suppose the Author of Nature, or, according to your system of anthropomorphism, the ideal world, into which you trace the material? Have we not the same reason to trace that ideal world into another ideal world, or new intelligent principle? But if we stop, and go no farther; why go so far? Why not stop at the material world? How can we satisfy ourselves without going on *in infinitum*? And after all, what satisfaction is there in that infinite progression? Let us remember the story of the *Indian* philosopher and his elephant. It was never more applicable than to the present subject. If the material world rests upon a similar ideal world, this ideal world must rest upon some other; and so on, without end. It were better, therefore, never to look beyond the present material world. By supposing it to contain the principle of its order within itself, we really assert it to be God; and the sooner we arrive at that divine Being so much the better. When you go one step beyond the mundane system[10], you only excite an inquisitive humour, which it is impossible ever to satisfy.

To say, that the different ideas, which compose the reason of the supreme Being, fall into order, of themselves, and by their own nature, is really to talk without any precise meaning. If it has a meaning, I would fain know, why it is not as good sense to say, that the parts of the material world fall into order, of themselves, and by their own nature? Can the one opinion be intelligible, while the other is not so?

9 'Deity' scored out; 'Being' written in its place.
10 'universe' scored out; 'mundane system' written in its place.

We have, indeed, experience of ideas, which fall into order, of themselves, and without any *known* cause: But, I am sure, we have a much larger experience of matter, which does the same; as in all instances of generation and vegetation, where the accurate analysis of the cause exceeds all human comprehension[11]. We have also experience of particular systems of thought and of matter, which have no order; of the first, in madness, of the second, in corruption. Why then should we think, that order is more essential to one than the other? And if it requires a cause in both, what do we gain by your system, in tracing the universe of objects into a similar universe of ideas? The first step, which we make, leads us on for ever. It were, therefore, wise in us, to limit all our enquiries to the present world, without looking farther. No satisfaction can ever be attained by these speculations, which so far exceed the narrow bounds of human understanding.

It was usual with the *Peripatetics*, you know, Cleanthes, when the cause of any phenomenon was demanded, to have recourse to their *faculties* or *occult qualities*, and to say, for instance, that bread nourished by its nutritive faculty, and senna purged by its purgative: But it has been discovered, that this subterfuge was nothing but the disguise of ignorance; and that these philosophers, though less ingenuous, really said the same thing with the sceptics or the vulgar, who fairly confessed, that they knew not the cause of these phenomena. In like manner, when it is asked, what cause produces order in the ideas of the supreme Being, can any other reason be assigned by you, anthropomorphites, than that it is a *rational* faculty, and that such is the nature of the Deity? But why a similar answer will not be equally satisfactory in accounting for the order of the world, without having recourse to any such intelligent Creator, as you insist on, may be difficult to determine. It is only to say, that *such* is the nature of material objects, and that they are all originally possessed of a *faculty* of order and proportion. These are only more learned and elaborate ways of confessing our ignorance; nor has the one hypothesis any real advantage above the other, except in its greater conformity to vulgar prejudices.

You have displayed this argument with great emphasis, replied Cleanthes: You seem not sensible, how easy it is to answer it. Even in common life, if I assign a cause for any event; is it any objection, Philo, that I cannot assign the cause of that cause, and answer every new question, which may incessantly be started? And what philosophers could possibly submit to so rigid a rule? philosophers, who

11 The phrase 'where the accurate analysis . . . comprehension' is added to the text.

confess ultimate causes to be totally unknown, and are sensible, that the most refined principles, into which they trace the phenomena, are still to them as inexplicable as these phenomena themselves are to the vulgar. The order and arrangement of nature, the curious adjustment of final causes, the plain use and intention of every part and organ; all these bespeak in the clearest language an intelligent cause or author. The heavens and the earth join in the same testimony: The whole chorus of nature raises one hymn to the praises of its Creator: You alone, or almost alone, disturb this general harmony. You start abstruse doubts, cavils, and objections: You ask me, what is the cause of this cause? I know not; I care not; that concerns not me. I have found a Deity, and here I stop my enquiry. Let those go farther, who are wiser or more enterprising.

[12] I pretend to be neither, replied PHILO: And for that very reason, I should never perhaps have attempted to go so far; especially when I am sensible, that I must at last be contended to sit down with the same answer, which, without further trouble, might have satisfied me from the beginning. If I am still to remain in utter ignorance of causes, and can absolutely give an explication of nothing, I shall never esteem it any advantage to shove off for a moment a difficulty, which, you acknowledge, must immediately, in its full force, recur upon me. Naturalists indeed very justly explain particular effects by more general causes; though these general causes themselves should remain in the end totally inexplicable: But they never surely thought it satisfactory to explain a particular effect by a particular cause, which was no more to be accounted for than the effect itself. An ideal system, arranged of itself, without a precedent design, is not a whit more explicable than a material one, which attains its order in a like manner; nor is there any more difficulty in the latter supposition than in the former.

12 This passage is written at the end of the Part 4 with instructions to be inserted here, in place of the following: 'Your answer may, perhaps, be good, said Philo, upon your principles, that the religious system can be proved by experience, and by experience alone; and that the Deity arose from some external cause. But these opinions, you know, will be adopted by very few. And as to all those, who reason upon other principles, and yet deny the mysterious simplicity of the divine nature, my objection still remains good.'

PART 5

But to show you still more inconveniences, continued PHILO, in your anthropomorphism; please to take a new survey of your principles. *Like effects prove like causes.* This is the experimental argument; and this, you say too, is the sole theological[1] argument. Now it is certain, that the liker the effects are, which are seen, and the liker the causes, which are inferred, the stronger is the argument. Every departure on either side diminishes the probability, and renders the experiment less conclusive. You cannot doubt[2] of this principle: Neither ought you to reject[3] its consequences.

All the new discoveries in astronomy, which prove the immense grandeur and magnificence of the works of nature, are so many additional arguments for a deity, according to the true system of theism: But according to your hypothesis of experimental theism[4] they become so many objections, by removing the effect still farther from all resemblance to the effects of human art and contrivance. For if LUCRETIUS,[5] even following the old system of the world, could exclaim

> *Quis regere immensi summam, quis habere profundi*
> *Indu manu validas potis est moderanter habenas?*
> *Quis pariter cœlos omnes convertere? & omnes*
> *Ignibus ætheriis terras suffire feraces?*
> *Omnibus inque locis esse omni tempore præsto?*

If TULLY[6] esteemed this reasoning so natural as to put it into the mouth of his EPICUREAN. *Quibus enim oculis animi intueri potuit vester Plato fabricam illam tanti operis, qua construi a deo atque ædificari mundum facit? quæ molitio? quæ ferramenta? qui vectes? quæ machinæ? qui ministri tanti muneris fuerunt? quemadmodum autem obedire & parere voluntati architecti aer, ignis, aqua, terra*

---

1 'religious' scored out; 'theological' written in its place.
2 'deny' scored out; 'doubt' written in its place.
3 'refuse' scored out: 'reject' written in its place.
4 'of experimental theism' added to the text.
5 *Lib. II, 1094.* [Lucretius, *De Rerum Natura*, trans. C. Bailey (Clarendon Press, 1947, p. 295): 'Who can avail to rule the whole sum of the boundless, who to hold in his guiding hand the mighty reins of the deep, who to turn round all firmaments at once, and warm all fruitful lands with heavenly fires, or to be at all times present in all places.']
6 *De nat. deor. lib. 1.* [Cicero, *The Nature of the Gods*, trans. H. C. P. McGregor (Penguin Books, 1972, p. 77): 'How could your friend Plato in his mind's eye comprehend so vast a piece of architecture as the building of a universe, and how God laboured to create it? How did he think God went about it? What tools did he use? What levers? What machines? Who assisted him in so vast an enterprise? And how came air and fire and water to serve and obey the will of this creator?']

potuerunt? If this argument, I say, had any force in former ages; how much greater must it have at present; when the bounds of nature are so infinitely enlarged[7], and such a magnificent scene is opened to us? It is still more unreasonable[8] to form our idea of so unlimited a cause from our experience of[9] the narrow productions[10] of human design and invention.

The discoveries by microscopes, as they open a new universe in miniature, are still objections, according to you; arguments, according to me. The farther we push our researches of this kind, we are still led to infer the universal cause of all to be vastly different from mankind, or from any object of human experience and observation.

And what say you to the discoveries in anatomy, chemistry, botany? — These surely are no objections, replied CLEANTHES: They only discover new instances of art and contrivance. It is still the image of mind reflected on us from innumerable objects. Add, a mind *like the human*, said PHILO. I know of no other, replied CLEANTHES. And the liker the better, insisted PHILO. To be sure, said CLEANTHES.

Now, CLEANTHES, said PHILO, with an air of alacrity and triumph. Mark the consequences. *First.* By this method of reasoning, you renounce all claim[11] to infinity in any of the attributes of the Deity. For as the cause ought only to be proportioned to the effect, and the effect, so far as it falls under our cognizance, is not infinite; What pretensions, have we, upon your suppositions,[12] to ascribe that attribute[13] to the divine Being? You will still insist, that, by[14] removing him so much from all similarity to human creatures, we give into the most arbitrary hypothesis,[15] and at the same time, weaken[16] all proofs of his existence.

Secondly. You have no reason, on your theory[17], for ascribing perfection to the deity, even in his finite capacity; or for supposing him free from every error, mistake, or incoherence[18] in his undertakings. There are many inexplicable difficulties in the works of nature, which, if we allow a perfect author to be proved *a priori*, are easily solved, and

7 'extended' scored out; 'enlarged' written in its place.
8 'We ought still less' scored out: 'It is still more unreasonable' written in its place.
9 'our experience of' added to the text.
10 'effects' scored out; 'production' written in its place.
11 'pretension' scored out; 'claim' written in its place.
12 'upon your suppositions' added to the text.
13 'epithet' scored out; 'attribute' written in its place.
14 'You will still insist, that, by' added to the text.
15 'give into the most arbitrary ['supposition' scored out] hypothesis' added to the text.
16 'destroy' scored out; 'weaken' written in its place.
17 'according to your hypothesis' scored out; 'on your theory' added in its place.
18 'blunder' scored out; 'incoherence' written in its place.

become only seeming difficulties, from the narrow capacity of man, who cannot trace infinite relations. But, according to your method of reasoning, these difficulties become all real; and perhaps will be insisted on[19], as new instances of likeness to human art and contrivance. At least, you must acknowledge, that it is impossible for us to tell, from our limited views, whether this system contains any great faults, or deserves any considerable praise, if compared to other possible, and even real systems. Could a peasant, if the *Aenid* were read to him, pronounce that poem to be absolutely faultless, or even assign to it its proper rank among the productions of human wit; he, who had never seen any other production?

**[20] But were this world ever so perfect a production, it must still remain uncertain, whether all the excellencies of the work can justly be ascribed to the workman. If we survey a ship, what an exalted idea must we form of the ingenuity of the carpenter, who framed so complicated useful and beautiful a machine? And what surprise must we entertain, when we find him a stupid mechanic, who imitated others, and copied an art, which, through a long succession of ages, after multiplied trials, mistakes, corrections, deliberations, and controversies, had been gradually improving? Many worlds might have, been botched and bungled, throughout an eternity, 'ere this system was struck out: Much labour lost: Many fruitless trials made: And a slow, but continued improvement carried on during infinite ages in the art of world-making. In such subjects, who can determine, where the truth; nay, who can conjecture where the probability, lies; amidst a great number of hypotheses which may be proposed, and a still greater number, which may be imagined? **

And what shadow of an argument, continued PHILO, can you produce, from your hypothesis, to prove the unity of the Deity? A great number of men join in building a house or ship, in rearing a city, in framing a commonwealth: Why may not several deities combine in contriving and framing a world? This is only so much greater similarity to human affairs. By sharing the work among several, we may so much farther limit the attributes of each, and get rid of that extensive power and knowledge, which must be supposed in one deity, and which, according to you, can only serve to weaken the proof of his existence. And if such foolish, such vicious creatures as man can yet often unite in framing and executing one plan; how much more those deities or

19 'by you' deleted from the text.
20 This passage is written at the end of Part 5, with instructions for insertion at this point.

demons, whom we may suppose several degrees more perfect?

[21] To multiply causes without necessity is indeed contrary to true philosophy: But this principle applies not to the present case. Were one deity antecedently proved by your theory, who were possessed of every attribute, requisite to the production of the universe; it would be needless, I own (though not absurd) to suppose any other deity existent. But while it is still a question, whether all these attributes are united in one subject, or dispersed among several independent beings: By what phenomena in nature can we pretend to decide the controversy? Where we see a body raised in a scale, we are sure that there is in the opposite scale, however concealed from sight, some counterpoising weight equal to it: But it is still allowed to doubt, whether that weight be an aggregate of several distinct bodies, or one uniform united mass. And if the weight requisite very much exceeds any thing which we have ever seen conjoined in any single body, the former supposition becomes still more probable and natural. An intelligent being of such vast power and capacity, as is necessary to produce the universe, or to speak in the language of ancient philosophy, so prodigious an animal, exceeds all analogy and even comprehension.

But farther, CLEANTHES; men are mortal, and renew their species by generation; and this is common to all living creatures. The two great sexes of male and female, says MILTON, animate the world. Why must this circumstance, so universal, so essential, be excluded from those numerous and limited deities? Behold then the theogony of ancient times brought back upon us.

And why not become a perfect anthropomorphite? Why not assert the deity or deities to be corporeal, and to have eyes, a nose, mouth, ears, &c. EPICURUS maintained, that no man had ever seen reason but in a human figure; therefore the gods must have a human figure. And this argument, which is deservedly so much ridiculed by CICERO, becomes, according to you, solid and philosophical.

In a word, CLEANTHES, a man, who follows your hypothesis, is able, perhaps, to assert, or conjecture, that the universe, some time, arose from some thing like[22] design: But beyond that position he cannot ascertain one single circumstance, and is left afterwards to fix every point of his theology, by the utmost licence of fancy and hypothesis[23]. This world, for aught he knows, is very faulty and imperfect, compared

---

21 This passage is written at the end of Part 5, with instructions for insertion at this point.
22 'kind of' scored out; 'thing like' written in its place.
23 'conjecture' scored out; 'hypothesis' written in its place.

to a superior standard; and was only the first rude essay of some infant deity, who afterwards abandoned it, ashamed of his lame performance: It is the work only of some dependent, inferior deity; and is the object of derision to his superiors: It is the production of old age and dotage in some superannuated deity; and ever since his death, has run on at adventures, from the first impulse and active force, which it received from him . . . You justly give signs of horror, DEMEA, at these strange suppositions: But these, and a thousand more of the same kind, are CLEANTHES's suppositions, not mine. From the moment the attributes of the Deity are supposed finite, all these have place. And I cannot, for my part, think, that so wild and unsettled a system of theology is, in any respect, preferable to none at all.

These suppositions I absolutely disown; cried CLEANTHES. They strike me, however, with no horror; especially when proposed in that rambling way, in which they drop from you. On the contrary, they give me pleasure, when I see, that, by the utmost indulgence of your imagination, you never get rid of the hypothesis of design in the universe; but are obliged, at every turn, to have recourse to it. To this concession I adhere steadily; and this I regard as a sufficient foundation for religion.

PART 6

It must be a slight fabric, indeed, said DEMEA, which can be erected on so tottering a foundation. While we are uncertain, whether there is one deity or many; whether the deity or deities, to whom we owe our existence, be perfect or imperfect, subordinate or supreme, dead or alive; what trust or confidence can we repose in them? What devotion or worship address to them? What veneration or obedience pay them? To all the purposes of life, the theory of religion becomes altogether useless: And even with regard to speculative consequences, its uncertainty, according to you, must render it totally precarious and unsatisfactory.

To render it still more unsatisfactory, said PHILO, there occurs to me another hypothesis, which must acquire an air of probability from the method of reasoning so much insisted on by CLEANTHES. That like effects arise from like causes: This principle he supposes the foundation of all religion. But there is another principle of the same kind, no less certain, and derived from the same source of [1] experience; that where several known circumstances are *observed* to be similar, the unknown will[2] also be *found* similar. Thus, if we see the limbs of a human body, we conclude that it is also attended with a human head, though hid from us. Thus, if we[3] see, through a chink in a wall a small part of the sun, we conclude, that, were the wall removed, we should see the whole body. In short, this method of reasoning is so obvious and familiar, that no scruple can ever be made with regard to its solidity.

Now if we survey the universe, so far as it falls under our knowledge, it bears a great resemblance to an animal or organized body, and seems actuated with a like principle of life and motion. A continual circulation of matter in it produces no disorder: A continual waste in every part is incessantly repaired: The closest sympathy is perceived throughout the entire system: And each part or member, in performing its proper offices, operates both to its own preservation and to that of the whole. The world, therefore, I infer, is an animal, and the Deity is the SOUL of the world, actuating it, and actuated by it.

You have too much learning, CLEANTHES, to be at all surprised at this

---

1 'practice and' scored out.
2 'must' scored out; 'will' written in its place.
3 'hear, in the dark, reason and sense delivered in an articulate voice, we infer, that there is also present a human figure, which we shall discover on the return of light' scored out; 'see, through a chink in a wall, a small part of the sun, we conclude, that, were the wall removed, we should see the whole body' written in its place.

opinion, which, you know, was maintained by almost all the theists of antiquity, and chiefly prevails in their discourses and reasonings. For though sometimes the ancient philosophers reason from final causes, as if they thought the world the workmanship of God; yet it appears rather their favourite notion to consider it as his body, whose organization renders it subservient to him. And it must be confessed, that as the universe resembles more a human body than it does the works of human art and contrivance; if our limited analogy could ever, with any propriety, be extended to the whole of nature, the inference seems juster in favour of the ancient than the modern theory.

There are many other advantages too, in the former theory, which recommended it to the ancient theologians. Nothing more repugnant to all their notions, because nothing more repugnant to common experience, than mind without body; a mere spiritual substance, which fell not under their senses nor comprehension, and of which they had not observed one single instance throughout all nature. Mind and body they knew, because they felt both: An order, arrangement, organization, or internal machinery in both they likewise knew, after the same manner: And it could not but seem reasonable to transfer this experience to the universe, and to suppose the divine mind and body to be also co-eval, and to have, both of them, order and arrangement naturally inherent in them, and inseparable from them.

Here therefore is a new species of anthropomorphism, CLEANTHES, on which you may deliberate; and a theory, which seems not liable to any considerable difficulties. You are too much superior surely to *systematical prejudices*, to find any more difficulty in supposing an animal body to be, originally, of itself, or from unknown causes, possessed of order and organization, than in supposing a similar order to belong[4] to mind. But the *vulgar prejudice*, that body and mind ought always to accompany each other, ought not, one should think, to be entirely neglected; since it is founded on *vulgar experience*, the only guide which you profess to follow in all these theological enquiries. And if you assert, that our limited experience is an unequal standard, by which to judge of the unlimited extent of nature; you entirely abandon your own hypothesis, and must thenceforward adopt our mysticism, as you call it, and admit of the absolute incomprehensibility of the divine nature.[5]

This theory, I own, replied CLEANTHES, has never before occurred to me, though a pretty natural one; and I cannot readily, upon so short an

4 'principle belonging' scored out; 'order to belong' added in its place.
5 The sentence 'And if you assert . . . divine nature' is scored out, but a margin note indicates that it is to be printed.

examination and reflection, deliver any opinion with regard to it. You are very scrupulous, indeed, said PHILO; were I to examine any system of yours, I should not have acted with half that caution and reserve, in starting objections and difficulties to it. However, if anything occur to you, you will oblige us by proposing it.

Why then, replied CLEANTHES, it seems to me, that, though the world does, in many circumstances, resemble an animal body, yet is the analogy also defective in many circumstances, the most material:[6] No organs of sense; no seat of thought or reason; no-one precise origin of motion and action. In short, it seems to bear a[7] stronger resemblance to a vegetable than to an animal; and your inference would be so far inconclusive in favour of the soul of the world.

But in the next place, your theory seems to imply the eternity of the world; and that is a principle which, I think, can be refuted by the strongest reasons and probabilities. I shall suggest an argument to this purpose, which, I believe, has not been insisted on by any writer. Those, who reason from the late origin of arts and sciences, though their inference[8] wants not force, may perhaps be refuted by considerations, derived from the nature of human society, which is in continual revolution[9], between ignorance and knowledge, liberty and slavery, riches and poverty; so that it is impossible for us, from our limited experience, to foretell with assurance what events may or may not be expected. Ancient learning and history seem to have been in great danger of entirely perishing after the inundation of the barbarous nations; and had these convulsions continued a little longer or been a little more violent, we should not probably have now known what passed in the world a few centuries before us. Nay, were it not for the superstition of the Popes, who preserved a little jargon of LATIN, in order to support the appearance of an ancient and universal church, that tongue must have been utterly lost: In which case, the western world, being totally barbarous, would not have been in a fit disposition for receiving the GREEK language and learning, which was conveyed to them after the sacking of CONSTANTINOPLE. When learning and books had been extinguished, even the mechanical arts would have fallen considerably to decay; and it is easily imagined, that fable or tradition might ascribe to them a much later origin than the true one[10]. This

6 'the most material:' added to the text.
7 'much' scored out.
8 'argument' scored out; 'inference' written in its place.
9 'and uncertainty' scored out.
10 'what it was supposed' scored out; 'the true one' written in its place.

vulgar argument, therefore, against the eternity of the world, seems a little precarious.

But here appears to be the foundation of a better argument. LUCULLUS was the first that brought cherry-trees from ASIA to EUROPE; though that tree thrives so well in many European climates, that it grows in the woods without any culture. Is it possible, that throughout a whole eternity, no European had ever passed into ASIA, and thought of transplanting so delicious a fruit into his own country? Or if the tree was once transplanted and propagated, how could it ever afterwards perish? Empires may rise and fall; liberty and slavery succeed alternately; ignorance and knowledge give place to each other; but the cherry-tree will still remain in the woods of GREECE, SPAIN and ITALY, and will never be affected by the revolutions of human society.

It is not two thousand years, since vines were transplanted into FRANCE; though there is no climate in the world more favourable to them. It is not three centuries since horses, cows, sheep, swine, dogs, corn were known in AMERICA. Is it possible, that, during the revolutions of a whole eternity, there never arose a COLUMBUS, who might open the communication between EUROPE and that continent? We may as well imagine, that all men would wear stockings for ten thousand years, and never have the sense to think of garters to tie them. All these seem convincing proofs of the youth, or rather infancy, of the world; as being founded on the operation of principles more constant and steady, than those by which human society is governed and directed. Nothing less than a total convulsion of the elements will ever destroy all the European animals and vegetables, which are now to be found in the western world.

And what argument have you against such convulsions? replied PHILO. Strong and almost incontestable proofs may be traced over the whole earth, that every part of this globe has continued for many ages entirely covered with water. And though order were supposed inseparable from matter, and inherent in it; yet may matter be susceptible of many and great revolutions, through the endless periods of eternal duration. The incessant changes, to which every part of it is subject, seem to intimate some such general transformations; though at the same time, it is observable, that all the changes, and corruptions, of which we have ever had experience, are but passages from one state of order to another; nor can matter ever rest in total deformity and confusion. What we see in the parts, we may infer in the whole; at least, that is the method of reasoning, on which you rest your whole theory. And were I obliged to defend any particular system of this nature (which I never willingly should do) I esteem none more plausible, than that which ascribes an eternal, inherent principle of order to the world[11]; though attended with great and continual revolutions and alterations. This at once solves all difficulties[12]; and if the solution, by being so general, is[13] not entirely complete and satisfactory, it is, at least, a theory, that we must, sooner or later, have recourse to, whatever system we embrace. How could things have been as they are, were there not an original, inherent principle of order somewhere, in thought or in matter? And it is very indifferent to which of these we give the preference. Chance has no place, on any hypothesis, sceptical or religious.[14] Every thing is surely governed by steady, inviolable laws. And were the inmost essence of things laid open to us, we should then discover a scene, of which, at present, we can have no idea. Instead of admiring the order of natural beings, we should clearly see, that it was absolutely impossible for them, in the smallest article, ever to admit of any other disposition.

Were any one inclined to revive the ancient pagan theology, which maintained, as we learn from HESIOD[15], that this globe was governed by 30,000 deities, who arose from the unknown powers of nature: You would naturally object, CLEANTHES, that nothing is gained by this hypothesis, and that it is as easy to suppose all men and animals, beings more numerous, but less perfect, to have sprung immediately from a like origin. Push the same inference a step farther; and you will find a numerous society of deities as explicable as one universal deity, who possesses, within himself, the powers and perfections of the whole society. All these systems, then, of scepticism, polytheism, and theism you must allow, on your principles, to be on a like footing[16], and that no-one of them has any advantages over the others. You may thence learn the fallacy of your principles.

---

11 'as matter' scored out; 'to the world' written in its place.
12 'answers all questions' scored out; 'solves all difficulties' written in its place.
13 'by being so general, is' added to the text.
14 Originally written as: 'Chance it is ridiculous to maintain on any hypothesis.' Then altered to: 'Chance, or what is the same thing liberty, seems not to have place on any hypothesis, sceptical or religious.' Then revised to the text above.
15 'mentioned by Varro' scored out; 'which maintained, as we learn from HESIOD' written in its place.
16 'alike explicable' scored out; 'on a like footing' written in its place.

PART 7

But here, continued PHILO, in examining this ancient system of the soul of the world, there strikes me, all on a sudden, a new idea, which, if just, must go near to subvert all your reasoning, and destroy even your first inferences, on which you repose such confidence. If the universe bears a greater likeness to animal bodies and to vegetables than to the works of human art, it is more probable, that its cause resembles the cause of the former than that of the latter, and its origin ought rather to be ascribed to generation or vegetation than to reason or design. Your conclusion, even according to your own principles, is therefore lame and defective.

Pray open up this argument a little farther, said DEMEA. For I do not rightly apprehend it, in that concise manner, in which you have expressed it.

Our friend, CLEANTHES, replied PHILO, as you have heard, asserts, that since no question of fact can be proved otherwise than by experience, the existence of a deity admits not of proof from any other medium. The world, says he, resembles the works of human contrivance: Therefore, its cause must also resemble that of the other. Here we may remark, that the operation of one very small part of nature, to wit man, upon another very small part, to wit that inanimate matter lying within his reach, is the rule, by which CLEANTHES judges of the origin of the whole; and he measures objects, so widely disproportioned, by the same individual standard. But to waive all objections, drawn from this topic; I affirm, that there are other parts of the universe (besides the machines of human invention) which bear still a greater resemblance to the fabric of the world, and which therefore afford a better conjecture concerning the universal origin of this system[1]. These parts are animals and vegetables. The world plainly resembles more an animal or vegetable than it does a watch or a knitting loom. Its cause, therefore, it is more probable, resembles the cause of the former. The cause of the former is generation or vegetation. The cause, therefore, of the world, we may infer to be something similar or analogous to generation or vegetation.

But how is it conceivable, said DEMEA, that the world can arise from any thing similar to vegetation or generation?

Very easily, replied PHILO. In like manner as a tree sheds its seed

---

1 'the whole of nature' scored out; 'this system' written in its place.

into the neighbouring fields, and produces other trees; so the great vegetable, the world, or this planetary system,[2] produces within itself certain seeds, which, being scattered into the surrounding chaos, vegetate into new worlds. A comet, for instance, is the seed of a world; and after it has been fully ripened, by passing from sun to sun, and star to star, it is at last lost into the unformed elements, which every where surround this universe, and immediately sprouts up into a new system.

Or if, for the sake of variety (for I see no other advantage) we should[3] suppose this world to be an animal; a comet is the egg of this animal; and in like manner as an ostrich lays its egg in the sand, which, without any farther care, hatches the egg, and produces a new animal; so . . .

I understand you, says DEMEA: But what wild, arbitrary suppositions are these? What *data* have you for such extraordinary conclusions? And is the slight, imaginary resemblance of the world to a vegetable or an animal sufficient to establish the same inference with regard to both? Objects, which are in general so widely different; ought they to be a standard for each other?

Right, cries PHILO: This is the topic on which I have all along insisted. I have still asserted that we have no *data* to establish any system of cosmogony. Our experience, so imperfect in itself, and so limited both in extent and duration, can afford us no probable conjecture concerning the whole of things. But if we must needs fix on some hypothesis; by what rule, pray, ought we to determine our choice? Is there any other rule than the greater similarity of the objects compared? And does not a plant or an animal, which springs from vegetation or generation, bear a stronger resemblance to the world, than does any artificial machine, which arises from reason and design?

But what is this vegetation and generation, of which you talk, said DEMEA? Can you explain their operations, and anatomize that fine internal structure, on which they depend?

As much, at least, replied PHILO, as CLEANTHES can explain the operations of reason, or anatomize that internal structure, on which *it* depends. But without any such elaborate disquisitions, when I see an animal, I infer, that it sprang from generation; and that with as great

---

2 'or this planetary system' added to the text.
3 'will' scored out; 'should' written in its place.

certainty as you conclude a house to have been reared by[4] design. These words, *generation, reason,*[5] mark only certain powers and energies in nature, whose effects are known, but whose essence is incomprehensible; and one of these principles, more than the other, has no privilege for being made a standard to the whole of nature.

In reality, DEMEA, it may reasonably be expected, that the larger the views are which we take of things, the better will they[6] conduct us in our conclusions concerning such extraordinary and such magnificent subjects. In this little corner of the world alone, there are four principles, *reason, instinct, generation, vegetation,* which are similar to each other, and are the causes of similar effects. What a number of other principles may we naturally suppose in the immense extent and variety of the universe, could we travel from planet to planet and from system to system, in order to examine each part of this mighty fabric? Any one of these four principles above mentioned (and a hundred others, which lie open to our conjecture) may afford us a theory[7], by which to judge of the origin of the world; and it is a palpable and egregious[8] partiality to confine our view entirely to that principle, by which our own minds operate. Were this principle more intelligible on that account, such a partiality, might be somewhat excusable: But reason, in its internal fabric and structure, is really as little known to us as instinct or vegetation; and perhaps even that vague, undeterminate word, nature, to which the vulgar refer every thing, is not at the bottom more inexplicable. The effects of these principles are all known to us from experience: But the principles themselves, and their manner of operation are totally unknown: Nor is it less intelligible, or less conformable to experience to say, that the world arose by vegetation from a seed shed by another world, than to say that it arose from a divine reason or contrivance, according to the sense in which CLEANTHES understands it.

But methinks, said DEMEA, if the world had a vegetative quality, and could sow the seeds of new worlds into the infinite chaos, this power would be still an additional argument for design in its author. For whence could arise so wonderful a faculty but from design? Or how can order spring from any thing, which perceives not that order which it bestows?

You need only look around you, replied PHILO, to satisfy yourself

---

4 'reason and' scored out.
5 *'generation, reason'* added to the text.
6 'will probably' scored out; 'the better will they' added in its place.
7 'standard' scored out; 'theory' written in its place.
8 'and egregious' added to the text.

with regard to this question. A tree bestows order and organization on that tree, which springs from it, without knowing the order: An animal, in the same manner, on its offspring: A bird on its nest. And instances of this kind are even more frequent in the world, than those of order, which arise from reason and contrivance[9]. To say that all this order in animals and vegetables proceeds ultimately from design is begging the question; nor can that great point be ascertained otherwise than by proving *a priori*, both that order is, from its nature, inseparably attached to thought[10], and that it can never, of itself, or from original unknown principles, belong to matter.

But farther, DEMEA; this objection, which you urge, can never be made use of by CLEANTHES, without renouncing a defence, which he has already made against one of my objections. When I enquired concerning the cause of that supreme reason and intelligence, into which he resolves every thing; he told me, that the impossibility of satisfying such enquiries could never be admitted as an objection in any species of philosophy. *We must stop somewhere, says he; nor is it ever within the reach of human capacity to explain ultimate causes, or show the last connections of any objects. It is sufficient, if the steps, so far as we go, are supported by experience and observation.* Now that vegetation and generation, as well as reason, are experienced to be principles of order in nature, is undeniable. If I rest my system of cosmogony on the former, preferably to the latter, it is at my choice. The matter seems entirely arbitrary. And when CLEANTHES asks me what is the cause of my great vegetative or generative faculty, I am equally entitled to ask him the cause of his great reasoning principle. These questions we have agreed to forbear on both sides; and it is chiefly his interest on the present occasion to stick to this agreement. Judging by our limited and imperfect[11] experience, generation has some privileges above reason: For we see every day the latter arise from the former, never the former from the latter.

Compare, I beseech you, the consequences on both sides. The world, say I, resembles an animal, therefore it is an animal, therefore it arose from generation. The steps, I confess, are wide; yet there is some small[12] appearance of analogy in each step. The world, says CLEANTHES, resembles a machine, therefore it is a machine, therefore it arose from design. The steps here are equally wide, and the analogy less striking. And if he pretends to carry on *my* hypothesis a step farther,

9 'perception' scored out; 'contrivance' written in its place.
10 'perception' scored out; 'thought' written in its place.
11 'and imperfect' added to the text.
12 'small' added to the text.

and to infer design or reason from the great principle of generation on which I insist; I may, with better authority, use the same freedom to push farther his hypothesis, and infer a divine generation or theogony from his principle of reason. I have at least some faint shadow of experience, which is the utmost, that can ever be attained in the present subject. Reason, in innumerable instances, is observed to arise from the principle of generation, and never to arise from any other principle.

[13] HESIOD and all the ancient mythologists, were so struck with this analogy, that they universally explained the origin of nature from an animal birth, and copulation. PLATO, too, so far as he is intelligible, seems to have adopted some such notion in his TIMEUS.

[14] The BRAMINS assert, that the world arose from an infinite spider, who spun this whole complicated mass from his bowels, and annihilates afterwards the whole or any part of it, by absorbing it again, and resolving it into his own essence. Here is a species of cosmogony, which appears to us ridiculous; because a spider is a little contemptible animal, whose operations we are never likely to take for a model of the whole universe. But still here is a new species of analogy even in our globe. And were there a planet, wholly inhabited by spiders (which is very possible)[15], this inference would there appear as natural and irrefragable as that which in our planet ascribes the origin of all things to design and intelligence, as explained by CLEANTHES. Why an orderly system may not be spun from the belly as well as from the brain, it will be difficult for him to give a satisfactory reason.

I must confess, PHILO, replied CLEANTHES, that, of all men living, the task which you have undertaken, of raising doubts and objections, suits you best, and seems, in a manner, natural and unavoidable to you. So great is your fertility of invention, that I am not ashamed to acknowledge myself unable, on a sudden, to solve regularly such out-of-the-way difficulties as you incessantly start upon me: Though I clearly see, in general, their fallacy and error. And I question not, but you are yourself, at present, in the same case, and have not the solution so ready as the objection; while you must be sensible, that common sense and reason is entirely against you, and that such whimsies, as you have delivered, may puzzle, but never can convince us.

13 This passage is written in the margin with indications for insertion at this point in the text.
14 This paragraph is written at the end of part 7 with indications to insert it at this point in the text.
15 The bracketed portion is an addition to the text.

PART 8

What you ascribe to the fertility of my invention, replied PHILO, is entirely owing to the nature of the subject. In subjects, adapted to the narrow compass of human reason, there is commonly but one determination, which carries probability or conviction with it; and to a man of sound judgement, all other suppositions, but that one, appear entirely absurd and chimerical. But in such questions, as the present, a hundred contradictory views may preserve a kind of imperfect analogy; and invention has here full scope to exert itself. Without any great effort of thought, I believe that I could, in an instant, propose other systems of cosmogony, which would have some faint appearance of truth; though it is a thousand, a million to one, if either yours or[1] any one of mine be the true system.

For instance; what if I should revive the old EPICUREAN hypothesis? This is commonly, and I believe, justly, esteemed the most absurd system, that has yet been proposed; yet, I know not, whether, with a few alterations, it might not be brought to bear a faint appearance of probability. Instead of supposing matter infinite, as EPICURUS did; let us suppose it finite. A finite number of particles is only susceptible of finite transpositions: And it must happen, in an eternal duration, that every possible order or position must be tried an infinite number of times. This world, therefore, with all its events, even the most minute, has before been produced and destroyed, and will again be produced and destroyed, without any bounds and limitations. No-one, who has a conception of the powers of infinite, in comparison of finite, will ever scruple this determination.

But this supposes, said DEMEA, that matter can acquire motion, without any voluntary agent or first mover.

And where is the difficulty, replied PHILO, of that supposition? Every event, before experience, is equally difficult and incomprehensible; and every event, after experience, is equally easy and intelligible. Motion, in many instances, from gravity, from elasticity, from electricity, begins in matter, without any known voluntary agent; and to suppose always, in these cases, an unknown voluntary agent is mere hypothesis; and hypothesis attended with no advantages. The beginning of motion in matter itself is as conceivable *a priori* as its communication from mind and intelligence.

---

1 'either yours or' added to the text.

Besides; why may not motion have been propagated by impulse through all eternity, and the same stock of it, or nearly the same, be still upheld in the universe? As much as is lost by the composition of motion, as much is gained by its resolution. And whatever the causes are, the fact is certain, that matter is, and always has been in continual agitation, as far as human experience or tradition reaches. There is not probably, at present, in the whole universe, one particle of matter at absolute rest.

And this very consideration too, continued PHILO, which we have stumbled on in the course of the argument, suggests a new hypothesis[2] of cosmogony, that is not absolutely absurd and improbable. Is there a system, an order, an economy of things, by which matter can preserve that perpetual agitation, which seems essential to it, and yet maintain a constancy[3] in the forms, which it produces? There certainly is such an economy: For this is actually the case with the present world. The continual motion of matter, therefore, in less than infinite transpositions, must produce this economy or order; and by its very nature, that order, when once established, supports itself[4], for many ages, if not to eternity. But wherever matter is so poised, arranged, and adjusted as to continue in perpetual motion, and yet preserve a constancy in the forms, its situation[5] must of necessity have all the same appearance of art[6] and contrivance, which we observe at present. All the parts of each form must have a relation to each other, and to the whole: And the whole itself must have a relation to the other parts of the universe; to the element, in which the form subsists; to the materials, with which it repairs its waste and decay; and to every other form, which is hostile or friendly. A defect in any of these particulars destroys the form; and the matter, of which it is composed, is again set loose, and is thrown into irregular motions and fermentations, till it unite itself to some other regular form. If no such form be prepared to receive it, and if there be a great quantity of this corrupted matter in the universe, the universe itself is entirely disordered; whether it be the feeble embryo of a world in its first beginnings, that is thus destroyed, or the rotten

2 'system' scored out; 'hypothesis' written in its place.
3 'uniformity' scored out; 'constancy' written in its place.
4 'supports itself' scored out; 'that order, which once established, supports itself' written in its place.
5 'its situation' added to the text.
6 This word altered from 'artifice' to 'art'.

carcass of one, languishing in old age and infirmity. In either case, a chaos ensues; till finite, though[7] innumerable revolutions[8] produce at last some forms, whose parts and organs are so adjusted as to support the forms amidst a continued succession of matter.

**[9] Suppose, (for we shall endeavour to vary the expression)[10] that matter were thrown into any position, by a blind, unguided force; it is evident that this first position must in all probability be the most confused and most disorderly imaginable, without any resemblance to those works of human contrivance, which, along with a symmetry of parts, discover an adjustment of means to ends and a tendency to self-preservation. If the actuating force cease after this operation, matter must remain for ever in disorder, and continue an immense chaos, without any proportion or activity. But suppose, that this actuating force, whatever it be, still continues in matter, this first position will immediately give place to a second, which will likewise in all probability be as disorderly as the first, and so on, through many successions of changes and revolutions. No particular order or position ever continues a moment unaltered. The original force, still remaining in activity, gives a perpetual restlessness to matter. Every possible situation is produced, and instantly destroyed. If a glimpse or dawn of order appears for a moment, it is instantly hurried away and confounded, by that never-ceasing force, which actuates every part of matter.

Thus the universe goes on for many ages in a continued succession of chaos and disorder. But is it not possible that it may settle at last, so as not to lose its motion and active force (for that we have supposed inherent in it) yet so as to preserve an uniformity of appearance, amidst the continual motion and fluctuation of its parts? This we find to be the case with the universe at present. Every individual is perpetually changing, and every part of every individual and yet the whole remains, in appearance, the same. May we not hope for such a position, or rather be assured of it,[11] from the eternal revolutions of unguided matter, and may not this account for all the appearing wisdom and contrivance, which is in the universe? Let us contemplate the subject a

---

7 'finite, though' added to the text.
8 'succession of forms and changes' scored out; 'revolutions' written in its place.
9 The following passage is added at the end of Part 8 with indications for insertion at this point.
10 '(for we shall endeavour to vary the expression)' added to the text.
11 'or rather be assured of it' added to the text.

little, and we shall find, that this adjustment, if attained by matter, of a seeming stability in the forms, with a real and perpetual revolution or motion of parts, affords a plausible, if not a true solution of the difficulty.**

It is in vain, therefore, to insist upon the uses of the parts in animals or vegetables and their curious adjustment to each other. I would fain know how an animal could subsist, unless its parts were so adjusted? Do we not find, that it immediately perishes whenever this adjustment ceases, and that its matter corrupting tries some new form? It happens, indeed, that the parts of the world are so well adjusted, that some regular form immediately lays claim to this corrupted matter: And if it were not so, could the world subsist? Must it not dissolve as well as the animal, and pass through new positions and situations; till in a great, but finite succession, it fall at last into the present or some such order?

It is well, replied CLEANTHES, you told us, that this hypothesis was suggested on a sudden in the course of the argument. Had you had leisure to examine it, you would soon have perceived the insuperable objections, to which it is exposed. No form, you say, can subsist, unless it possess those powers and organs, requisite for its subsistence: Some new order or economy must be tried, and so on, without intermission; till at last some order, which can support and maintain itself, is fallen upon. But according to this hypothesis, whence arise the many conveniencies and advantages, which men and all animals possess? Two eyes, two ears are not absolutely necessary for the subsistence of the species. Human race might have been propagated and preserved, without horses, dogs, cows, sheep, and those innumerable fruits and products, which serve to our satisfaction and enjoyment. If no camels had been created for the use of man in the sandy deserts of AFRICA and ARABIA, would the world have been dissolved? If no loadstone had been framed to give that wonderful and useful[12] direction to the needle, would human society and the human kind have been immediately extinguished? Though the maxims of nature be in general very frugal, yet instances of this kind are far from being rare; and any one of them is a sufficient proof of design, and of a benevolent design, which gave rise to the order and arrangement of the universe.

At least, you may safely infer, said PHILO, that the foregoing hypothesis is so far incomplete and imperfect; which I shall not scruple to allow. But can we ever reasonably expect greater success in any attempts of this nature? Or can we ever hope to erect a system of

12 'and useful' added to the text.

cosmogony, that will be liable to no exceptions, and will contain no circumstance repugnant to our limited and imperfect experience of the[13] analogy of nature? Your theory itself cannot surely pretend to any such advantage; even though you have run into *anthropomorphism*, the better to preserve a conformity to common experience. Let us once more put it to trial.[14] In all instances which we have ever seen, ideas are copied from real objects, and are ectypal, not archetypal, to express myself in learned terms: You reverse this order, and give thought the precedence. In all instances which we have ever seen, thought has no influence upon matter, except where that matter is so conjoined with it, as to have an equal reciprocal influence upon it. No animal can move immediately any thing but the members of its own body; and indeed, the equality of action and re-action seems to be an universal law of nature: But your theory implies a contradiction to this experience. These instances, with many more, which it were easy to collect (particularly the supposition of a mind or system of thought that is eternal, or in other words, an animal ingenerable and immortal) these instances, I say,[15] may teach, all of us, sobriety in condemning each other, and let us see, that as no system of this kind ought ever to be received from a slight analogy, so neither ought any to be rejected on account of a small incongruity. For that is an inconvenience, from which we can justly pronounce no-one to be exempted.

All religious systems, it is confessed, are subject to great and insuperable difficulties. Each disputant triumphs in his turn; while he carries on an offensive war, and exposes the absurdities, barbarities, and pernicious tenets[16] of his antagonist. But all of them, on the whole, prepare a complete triumph for the sceptic, who tells them, that no system ought ever to be embraced with regard to such subjects: For this plain reason, that no absurdity ought ever to be assented to with regard to any subject. A total suspense of judgement is here our only reasonable resource.[17] And if every attack, as is commonly observed, and no defence, among theologians, is successful; how complete must be *his* victory, who remains always, with all mankind, on the offensive, and has himself no fixed station or abiding city, which he is ever, on any occasion,[18] obliged to defend?

13 'the usual' scored out; 'our limited and imperfect experience of the' written in its place.
14 This sentence 'Let us . . . trial.' is an addition to the text.
15 'the creation from nothing' scored out; 'the supposition of a mind or system of thought . . . these instance, I say,' added in the margin to be inserted in its place.
16 'consequences' scored out; 'tenets' written in its place.
17 'expedient' scored out; 'resource' written in its place.
18 'on any occasion' added to the text.

PART 9

But if so many difficulties attend the argument *a posteriori*, said DEMEA; had we not better adhere to that simple and sublime argument *a priori*, which by offering to us infallible demonstration, cuts off at once all doubt and difficulty? By this argument too, we may prove the INFINITY of the divine attributes, which, I am afraid, can never be ascertained with certainty from any other topic. For how can an effect, which either is finite, or, for aught we know, may be so; how can such an effect, I say, prove an infinite cause? The unity too of the divine nature, it is very difficult, if not absolutely impossible, to deduce merely from contemplating the works of nature; nor will the uniformity alone of the plan, even were it allowed, give us any assurance of that attribute. Whereas the argument *a priori* . . .

You seem to reason, DEMEA, interposed CLEANTHES, as if those advantages and conveniencies in the abstract argument were full proofs of its solidity. But it is first proper, in my opinion, to determine what argument of this nature you choose to insist on; and we shall afterwards, from itself, better than from its *useful* consequences, endeavour to determine what value we ought to put upon it.

The argument, replied DEMEA, which I would insist on is the common one. Whatever exists must have a cause or reason of its existence; it being absolutely impossible for any thing to produce itself, or be the cause of its own existence. In mounting up, therefore, from effects to causes, we must either go on in tracing an infinite succession, without any ultimate cause at all, or must at last have recourse to some ultimate cause, that is *necessarily* existent: Now that the first supposition is absurd may be thus proved. In the infinite chain or succession of causes and effects, each single effect is determined to exist by the power and efficacy of that cause, which immediately preceded; but the whole eternal chain or succession, taken together, is not determined or caused by any thing: And yet it is evident that it requires a cause or reason, as much as any particular object, which begins to exist in time. The question is still reasonable, why this particular succession of causes existed from eternity, and not any other succession, or no succession at all. If there be no necessarily existent Being, any supposition, which can be formed, is equally possible; nor is there any more absurdity in nothing's having existed from eternity, than there is in that succession of causes, which constitutes the universe. What was it then, which determined something to exist rather than nothing, and bestowed being on a particular possibility, exclusive of the rest? *External causes*, there are supposed to be none. *Chance* is a word without a meaning. Was it *nothing*? But that can never produce any thing. We must, therefore, have recourse to a necessarily existent Being, who carries the REASON of his existence in himself; and who cannot be supposed not to exist without an express contradiction. There is consequently such a Being, that is, there is a Deity.

I shall not leave it to PHILO, said CLEANTHES, (though I know that the starting objections is his chief delight) to point out the weakness of this metaphysical reasoning. It seems to me so obviously ill-grounded, and at the same time of so little consequence to the cause of true piety and religion, that I shall myself venture to show the fallacy of it.

I shall begin with observing, that there is an evident absurdity in pretending to demonstrate a matter of fact, or to prove it by any arguments *a priori*[1]. Nothing is demonstrable, unless the contrary implies a contradiction. Nothing, that is distinctly conceivable, implies a contradiction. Whatever we conceive as existent, we can also conceive as non-existent. There is no Being, therefore, whose non-existence implies a contradiction. Consequently there is no Being, whose existence is demonstrable. I propose this argument as entirely decisive, and am willing to rest the whole controversy upon it.

It is pretended, that the Deity is a necessarily existent Being, and this necessity of his existence is attempted to be explained by asserting, that, if we knew his whole essence or nature, we should perceive it to be as impossible for him not to exist as for twice two not to be four. But it is evident, that this can never happen, while our faculties remain the same as at present: It will still be possible for us, at any time, to conceive the non-existence of what we formerly conceived to exist; nor can the mind ever lie under a necessity of supposing any object to remain always in being; in the same manner as we lie under a necessity of always conceiving twice two to be four. The words, therefore, *necessary existence* have no meaning; or which is the same thing, none that is consistent.

But farther; why may not the material universe be the necessarily existent Being, according to this pretended[2] explication of necessity? We dare not affirm that we[3] know all the qualities of matter; and for aught we can determine, it may contain some qualities, which, were they known, would make its non-existence appear as great a contradiction as that twice two is five. I find only one argument employed to

1 The phrase, 'or to prove it by any arguments *a priori*', is an addition to the text.
2 'pretended' added to the text.
3 'pretend not to' scored out; 'dare not affirm that we' written in its place.

prove, that the material world is not the necessarily existent Being; and this argument is derived from the contingency both of the matter and the form of the world. 'Any particle of matter', it is said,[4] 'may be *conceived* to be annihilated; and any form may be *conceived* to be altered. Such an annihilation or alteration, therefore, is not impossible.' But it seems a great partiality not to perceive, that the same argument extends equally to the Deity, so far as we have any conception of him; and that the mind can at least imagine him to be non-existent, or his attributes to be altered. It must be some unknown, inconceivable qualities, which can make his non-existence appear impossible, or his attributes unalterable: And no reason can be assigned[5], why these qualities may not belong to matter. As they are altogether unknown and inconceivable, they can never be proved incompatible with it.

Add to this, that in tracing an eternal succession of objects, it seems absurd to enquire for a general cause or first author. How can any thing, that exists from eternity, have a cause; since that relation implies a priority in time and a beginning of existence?

In such a chain too, or succession of objects, each part is caused by that which preceded it, and causes that which succeeds it. Where then is the difficulty? But the WHOLE, you say, wants a cause. I answer, that the uniting of these parts into a whole, like the uniting of several distinct counties into one kingdom, or several distinct members into one body, is performed merely by an arbitrary act of the mind, and has no influence on the nature of things. Did I show you the particular causes of each individual in a collection of twenty particles of matter, I should think it very unreasonable, should you afterwards ask me, what was the cause of the whole twenty. That is sufficiently explained in explaining the cause of the parts.

**[6] Though the reasonings, which you have urged, CLEANTHES, may well excuse me, said PHILO, from starting any farther difficulties; yet I cannot forbear insisting still upon another topic. It is observed by arithmeticians, that the products of 9 compose always either 9 or some lesser product of 9; if you add together all the characters, of which any of the former products is composed. Thus, of 18, 27, 36, which are products of 9, you make 9 by adding 1 to 8, 2 to 7, 3 to 6. Thus 369 is a product also of nine; and if you add 3, 6, and 9 you make 18, a lesser

---

4 *Dr. Clarke.*

5 'shown' scored out; 'assigned' written in its place.

6 This passage is written at the end of Part 9 with indications for insertion at this point; it is scored out, but a note, 'Print this Passage' is written in the margin.

product of 9.[7] To a superficial observer, so wonderful a regularity may be admired as the effect of either chance or design; but a skillful algebraist immediately concludes it to be the work of necessity, and demonstrates, that it must for ever result from the nature of these numbers. Is it not probable, I ask, that the whole economy of the universe is conducted by a like necessity, though no human algebra can furnish a key, which solves the difficulty? And instead of admiring the order of natural beings, may it not happen, that, could we penetrate into the intimate nature of bodies, we should clearly see why it was absolutely impossible, they could ever admit of any other disposition? So dangerous is it to introduce this idea of necessity into the present question! And so naturally does it afford an inference directly opposite to the religious hypothesis!

But dropping all these abstractions, continued PHILO; and confining ourselves to more familiar topics; I shall venture to add an observation,**[8] that the argument *a priori* has seldom been found very convincing, except to people of a metaphysical head, who have accustomed themselves to abstract reasoning, and who finding from mathematics, that the understanding frequently leads to truth, through obscurity and contrary to first appearances, have transferred the same habit of thinking to subjects, where it ought not to have place. Other people, even of good sense and best inclined to religion, feel always some deficiency in such arguments, though they are not perhaps able to explain distinctly where it lies. A certain proof, that men ever did and ever will derive their religion from other sources than from this species of reasoning.

7 '*Republique des Lettres Aout 1685*', written in the margin.
8 'I shall venture, said Philo, to add to these reasonings of Cleanthes' scored out in the text; 'I shall venture, said Philo, to address these reasonings of Cleanthes' written in the margin with indications for insertion and then scored out. The paragraph then begins with 'But dropping . . . observation' as indicated in the insertion.

PART 10

It is my opinion, I own, replied DEMEA, that each man feels, in a manner, the truth of religion within his own breast; and from a consciousness of his imbecility and misery, rather than from any reasoning, is led to seek protection from that Being, on whom he and all nature is dependent. So anxious or so tedious are even the best scenes of life, that futurity is still the object of all our hopes and fears. We incessantly look forward, and endeavour, by prayers, adoration, and sacrifice, to appease those unknown powers, whom we find, by experience, so able to afflict and oppress us. Wretched creatures that we are! What resource for us amidst the innumerable ills of life, did not religion suggest some methods of atonement, and appease those terrors, with which we are incessantly agitated and tormented?

I am indeed persuaded, said PHILO, that the best and indeed the only method of bringing every one to a due sense of religion is by just representations of the misery and wickedness of men. And for that purpose a talent of eloquence and strong imagery is more requisite than that of reasoning and argument. For is it necessary to prove, what every one feels within himself? It is only necessary to make us feel it, if possible,[1] more intimately and sensibly.

The people, indeed, replied DEMEA, are sufficiently convinced of this great and melancholy truth. The miseries of life, the unhappiness of man, the general corruptions of our nature, the unsatisfactory enjoyment of pleasures, riches, honours; these phrases have become almost proverbial in all languages. And who can doubt of what all men declare from their own immediate feeling and experience?

In this point, said PHILO, the learned are perfectly agreed with the vulgar; and in all letters, *sacred* and *profane*, the topic of human misery has been insisted on with the most pathetic eloquence, that sorrow and melancholy could inspire. The poets, who speak from sentiment, without a system, and whose testimony has therefore the more authority, abound in images of this nature. From HOMER down to DR. YOUNG, the whole inspired tribe have ever been sensible, that no other representation of things would suit the feeling and observation of each individual.

---

1 'if possible' added to the text.

As to authorities, replied DEMEA, you need not seek them. Look round this library of CLEANTHES. I shall venture to affirm, that, except authors of particular sciences, such as chemistry or botany, who have no occasion to treat of human life, there scarce is one of those innumerable writers, from whom the sense of human misery has not, in some passage or other, extorted a complaint and confession of it. At least, the chance is entirely on that side; and no one author has ever, so far as I can recollect, been so extravagant as to deny it.

There you must excuse me, said PHILO: LEIBNITZ has denied it; and is perhaps the first,[2] who ventured upon so bold and paradoxical an opinion; at least, the first, who made it essential to his philosophical system.[3]

And by being the first, replied DEMEA, might he not have been sensible of his error. For is this a subject, in which philosophers can propose to make discoveries, especially in so late an age? And can any man hope by a simple denial (for the subject scarcely admits of reasoning) to bear down the united testimony of mankind, founded on sense and consciousness?

And why should man, added he, pretend to an exemption from the lot of all other animals? The whole earth, believe me, PHILO, is cursed and polluted. A perpetual war is kindled amongst all living creatures. Necessity, hunger, want stimulate the strong and courageous: Fear, anxiety, terror agitate the weak and infirm. The first entrance into life gives anguish to the new-born infant and to its wretched parent. Weakness, impotence, distress attend each stage of that life: And it is at last finished in agony and horror.

Observe too, says PHILO, the curious artifices of nature in order to imbitter the life of every living being. The stronger prey upon the weaker, and keep them in perpetual terror and anxiety. The weaker too, in their turn, often prey upon the stronger, and vex and molest them without relaxation. Consider that innumerable race of insects, which either are bred on the body of each animal, or flying about infix their stings in him. These insects have others still less than themselves, which torment them. And thus on each hand, before and behind, above and below, every animal is surrounded with enemies, which incessantly seek his misery and destruction.

Man alone, said DEMEA, seems to be, in part, an exception to this

---

2 The following is added in the margin with the instruction that it be placed as a footnote at the bottom of the page: '*That sentiment had been maintained by Dr. King and some few others before Leibnitz, though by none of so great fame as that German philosopher.*'
3 'to his philosophical system' added to the text.

rule. For by combination in society, he can easily master lions, tigers, and bears, whose greater strength and agility naturally enable them to prey upon him.

On the contrary, it is here chiefly, cried PHILO, that the uniform and equal maxims of nature are most apparent. Man, it is true, can, by combination, surmount all his *real* enemies, and become master of the whole animal creation: But does he not immediately raise up to himself *imaginary* enemies, the demons of his fancy, who haunt him with superstitious terrors, and blast every enjoyment of life? His pleasure, as he imagines, becomes, in their eyes, a crime: His food and repose give them umbrage and offence: His very sleep and dreams furnish new materials to anxious fear: And even death, his refuge from every other ill, presents only the dread of endless and innumerable woes. Nor does the wolf molest more the timid flock, than superstition does the anxious breast of wretched mortals.

Besides, consider, DEMEA; this very society, by which we surmount those wild beasts, our natural enemies; what new enemies does it not raise to us? What woe and misery does it not occasion? Man is the greatest enemy of man. Oppression, injustice, contempt, contumely, violence, sedition, war, calumny, treachery, fraud; by these they mutually torment each other: And they would soon dissolve that society which they had formed, were it not for the dread of still greater ills, which must attend their separation.

But though these external insults, said DEMEA, from animals, from men, from all the elements, which assault us, form a frightful catalogue of woes, they are nothing in comparison of those, which arise within ourselves, from the distempered condition of our mind and body. How many lie under the lingering torment of diseases. Hear the pathetic enumeration of the great poet.

> Intestine stone and ulcer, colic pangs,
> Daemoniac frenzy, moaping melancholy,
> And moon-struck madness, pining atrophy,
> Marasmus and wide wasting pestilence.
> Dire was the tossing, deep the groans: DESPAIR
> Tended the sick, busiest from couch to couch.
> And over them triumphant DEATH his dart
> Shook, but delay'd to strike, tho oft invok'd
> With vows, as their chief good and final hope.

The disorders of the mind, continued DEMEA, though more secret, are not perhaps less dismal and vexatious. Remorse, shame, anguish, rage, disappointment, anxiety, fear, dejection, despair; who has ever passed through life without cruel inroads from these tormentors? How many have scarcely ever felt any better sensations? Labour and poverty, so abhorred by every one, are the certain lot of the far greater number: And those few privileged persons, who enjoy ease and opulence, never reach contentment or true felicity. All the goods of life united would not make a very happy man: But all the ills united would make a wretch indeed; and any one of them almost (and who can be free from every one) nay often the absence of one good (and who can possess all) is sufficient to render life ineligible.

Were a stranger to drop, on a sudden, into the world, I would show him, as a specimen of its ills, an hospital full of diseases, a prison crowded with malefactors and debtors, a field of battle strowed with carcasses, a fleet foundering in the ocean, a nation languishing under tyranny, famine, or pestilence. To turn the gay side of life to him, and give him a notion of its pleasures; wither should I conduct him? to a ball, to an opera, to court? He might justly think, that I was only showing him a diversity of distress and sorrow.

There is no evading such striking instances, said PHILO, but by apologies, which still farther aggravate the charge. Why have all men, I ask, in all ages, complained incessantly of the miseries of life? . . . They have no just reason, says one: These complaints proceed only from their discontented, repining, anxious disposition. . . . And can there possibly, I reply, be a more certain foundation of misery, than such a wretched temper?

But if they were really as unhappy as they pretend, says my antagonist, why do they remain in life . . . not satisfied with life, afraid of death. This is the secret chain, say I, that holds us. We are terrified, not bribed to the continuance of our existence.

It is only a false delicacy, he may insist, which a few refined spirits indulge, and which has spread these complaints among the whole race of mankind. . . . And what is this delicacy, I ask, which you blame? Is it any thing but a greater sensibility to all the pleasures and pains of life? And if the man of a delicate, refined temper, by being so much more alive than the rest of the world, is only so much more unhappy; what judgement must we form in general of human life?

Let men remain at rest, says our adversary; and they will be easy. They are willing artificers of their own misery. . . . No! reply I; an anxious languor follows their repose: Disappointment, vexation, trouble, their activity and ambition.

I can observe something like what you mention in some others, replied CLEANTHES: But I confess, I feel little or nothing of it in myself; and hope that it is not so common as you represent it.

If you feel not human misery yourself, cried DEMEA, I congratulate \ you on so happy a singularity. Others, seemingly the most prosperous, have not been ashamed to vent their complaints in the most melancholy strains. Let us attend to the great, the fortunate Emperor, CHARLES the fifth, when, tired with human grandeur, he resigned all his extensive dominions into the hands of his son. In the last harangue, which he made on that memorable occasion, he publicly avowed, *that the greatest prosperities which he had ever enjoyed, had been mixed with so many adversities, that he might truly say he had never enjoyed any satisfaction or contentment.* But did the retired life, in which he sought for shelter, afford him any greater happiness? If we may credit his son's account, his repentance commenced the very day of his resignation.

CICERO's fortune, from small beginnings, rose to the greatest lustre and renown; yet what pathetic complaints of the ills of life do his familiar letters, as well as philosophical discourses, contain? And suitably to his own experience, he introduces CATO, the great, the fortunate CATO, protesting in his old age, that, had he a new life in his offer, he would reject the present.

Ask yourself, ask any of your acquaintance, whether they would live over again the last ten or twenty years of their life. No! But the next twenty, they say, will be better.

> And from the dregs of life; hope to receive
> What the first sprightly running could not give.

Thus at last they find (such is the greatness of human misery; it reconciles even contradictions) that they complain, at once, of the shortness of life, and of its vanity and sorrow.

And is it possible, CLEANTHES, said PHILO, that after all these reflections, and infinitely more, which might be suggested, you can still persevere in your anthropomorphism, and assert the moral attributes of the Deity, his justice, benevolence, mercy, and rectitude, to be of the same nature with these virtues in human creatures? His power we allow infinite: Whatever he wills is executed: But neither man nor any other animal are happy: Therefore he does not will their happiness. His wisdom is infinite: He is never mistaken in choosing the means to any end: But the course of nature tends not to human or animal felicity: Therefore it is not established for that purpose. Through the whole compass of human knowledge, there are no inferences more certain and infallible than these. In what respect, then, do his benevolence and mercy resemble the benevolence and mercy of men?

EPICURUS's old questions are yet unanswered. Is he willing to prevent evil, but not able? then is he impotent. Is he able, but not willing? then is he malevolent. Is he both able and willing? whence then is evil?

You ascribe CLEANTHES, (and I believe justly) a purpose and intention to nature. But what, I beseech you, is the object of that curious artifice and machinery, which she has displayed in all animals? The preservation alone of individuals and propagation of the species. It seems enough for her purpose, if such a rank be barely upheld in the universe, without any care or concern for the happiness of the members that compose it. No resource for this purpose: No machinery, in order merely to give pleasure or ease: No fund of pure joy and contentment: No indulgence without some want or necessity, accompanying it. At least, the few phenomena of this nature are over-balanced by opposite phenomena of still greater importance.

Our sense of music, harmony, and indeed beauty of all kinds gives satisfaction, without being absolutely necessary to the preservation and propagation of the species. But what racking pains, on the other hand, arise from gouts, gravels, megrims, toothaches, rheumatisms; where the injury to the animal-machinery is either small or incurable? Mirth, laughter, play, frolic seem gratuitous satisfactions, which have no farther tendency: Spleen, melancholy, discontent, superstition are pains of the same nature. How then does the divine benevolence display itself, in the sense of you anthropomorphites? None but we mystics, as you were pleased to call us,[4] can account for this strange mixture of phenomena, by deriving it from attributes, infinitely perfect, but incomprehensible.

And have you at last, said CLEANTHES, smiling, betrayed your intentions, PHILO? Your long agreement with DEMEA did indeed a little surprise me; but I find you were all the while erecting a concealed battery against me. And I must confess, that you have now fallen upon a subject worthy of your noble spirit of opposition and controversy. If you can make out the present point, and prove mankind to be unhappy or corrupted, there is an end at once of all religion. For to what purpose establish the natural attributes of the Deity, while the moral are still doubtful and uncertain?

You take umbrage very easily, replied DEMEA, at opinions the most innocent, and the most generally received even amongst the religious

---

4 'as you were pleased to call us' added to the text.

and devout themselves: And nothing can be more surprising than to find a topic like this, concerning the wickedness and misery of man, charged with no less than atheism and profaneness. Have not all pious divines and preachers, who have indulged their rhetoric on so fertile a subject; have they not easily, I say, given a solution of any difficulties, which may attend it? This world is but a point in comparison of the universe: This life but a moment in comparison of eternity. The present evil phenomena, therefore, are rectified in other regions, and in some future period of existence. And the eyes of men, being then opened to larger views of things, see the whole connection of general laws, and trace, with adoration, the benevolence and rectitude of the Deity, through all the mazes and intricacies of his providence.

No! replied CLEANTHES, No! These arbitrary suppositions can never be admitted, contrary to matter of fact, visible and uncontroverted. Whence can any cause be known but from its known effects? Whence can any hypothesis be proved but from the apparent phenomena? To establish one hypothesis upon another is building entirely in the air; and the utmost we ever attain, by these conjectures and fictions, is to ascertain the bare possibility of our opinion; but never can we, upon such terms, establish its reality.

The only method of supporting divine benevolence (and it is what I willingly embrace) is to deny absolutely the misery and wickedness of man. Your representations are exaggerated: Your melancholy views mostly fictitious: Your inferences contrary to fact and experience. Health is more common than sickness: Pleasure than pain: Happiness than misery. And for one vexation, which we meet with, we attain, upon computation, a hundred enjoyments.

Admitting your position, replied PHILO, which yet is extremely doubtful; you must, at the same time, allow, that, if pain be less frequent than pleasure, it is infinitely more violent and durable. One hour of it is often able to outweigh a day, a week, a month of our common insipid enjoyments: And how many days, weeks, and months are past by several in the most acute torments? Pleasure, scarcely in one instance, is ever able to reach ecstasy and rapture: And in no one instance can it continue for any time at its highest pitch and altitude. The spirits evaporate; the nerves relax; the fabric is disordered; and the enjoyment quickly degenerates into fatigue and uneasiness. But pain often, Good God, how often! rises to torture and agony; and the longer it continues, it becomes still more genuine agony and torture. Patience is exhausted; courage languishes; melancholy seizes us; and nothing terminates our misery but the removal of its cause, or another event, which is the sole cure of all evil, but which, from our natural folly, we regard with still greater horror and consternation.

But not to insist upon these topics, continued PHILO, though most obvious, certain and important; I must use the freedom to admonish you, CLEANTHES, that you have put this controversy upon a most dangerous issue, and are unawares[5] introducing a total scepticism into the most essential articles of natural and revealed theology. What! no method of fixing[6] a just foundation for religion, unless we allow the happiness of human life, and maintain a continued existence even in this world, with all our present pains, infirmities, vexations, and follies, to be eligible and desirable! But this is contrary to every one's feeling and experience: It is contrary to an authority so established as nothing can subvert: No decisive proofs can ever be produced against this authority; nor is it possible for you to compute, estimate, and compare all the pains and all the pleasures in the lives of all men and of all animals: And thus by your[7] resting the whole system of religion on a point, which, from its very nature, must for ever be uncertain, you tacitly confess, that that system is equally uncertain.

But allowing you, what never will be believed; at least, what you never possibly[8] can prove, that animal, or at least,[9] human happiness in this life exceeds its misery; you have yet done nothing: For this is not, by any means, what we expect from infinite power, infinite wisdom, and infinite goodness. Why is there any misery at all in the world? Not by chance surely. From some cause then. Is it from the intention of the Deity? But he is perfectly benevolent. Is it contrary to his intention? But he is almighty. Nothing can shake the solidity of this reasoning, so short, so clear, so decisive; except we assert, that these subjects exceed all human capacity, and that our common measures of truth and falsehood are not applicable to them; a topic, which I have all along insisted on, but which you have, from the beginning, rejected with scorn and indignation.

But I will be contented to retire still from this retrenchment[10] For I deny that you can ever force me in it: I will allow, that pain or misery in man is *compatible* with infinite power and goodness in the Deity, even in your sense of these attributes: What are you advanced by all these

---

5 'unawares' added to the text.
6 'ascertaining' scored out; 'fixing' written in its place.
7 'your' added to the text.
8 'possibly' scored out, then added to the text.
9 'animal, or at least,' added to the text.
10 'defence' scored out; 'retrenchment' written in its place.

concessions? A mere possible compatibility is not sufficient. You must *prove* these pure, unmixed, and uncontrollable attributes from the present mixed and confused phenomena, and from these alone. A hopeful[11] undertaking! Were the phenomena ever so pure and unmixed, yet being finite, they would be insufficient for that purpose. How much more, when they are also so jarring and discordant?

Here, CLEANTHES, I find myself at ease in my argument. Here I triumph. Formerly, when we argued concerning the natural attributes of intelligence and design, I needed all my sceptical and metaphysical subtlety to elude your grasp. In many views of the universe, and of its parts, particularly the latter, the beauty and fitness of final causes strike us with such irresistible force, that all objections appear (what I believe[12] they really are) mere cavils and sophisms; nor can we then imagine how it was ever possible for us to repose any weight on them. But there is no view of human life or of the condition of mankind, from which, without the greatest violence, we can infer the moral attributes, or learn that infinite benevolence, conjoined with infinite power and infinite wisdom, which we must discover by the eyes of faith alone. It is your turn now to tug the labouring oar, and to support your philosophical subtleties against the dictates of plain reason and experience.

11 'strange' scored out; 'hopeful' written in its place.
12 'perhaps' scored out; 'I believe' written in its place.

PART 11

I scruple not to allow, said CLEANTHES, that I have been apt to suspect the frequent repetition of the word, infinite, which we meet with in all theological writers, to savour more of panegyric than of philosophy, and that any purposes of reasoning, and even of religion, would be better served, were we to rest contented with more accurate and more moderate expressions. The terms, *admirable, excellent, superlatively great, wise,* and *holy*; these sufficiently fill the imaginations of men; and any thing beyond, besides that it leads into absurdities, has no influence on the affections or sentiments. Thus, in the present subject, if we abandon all human analogy, as seems your intention, DEMEA, I am afraid we abandon all religion, and retain no conception of the great object of our adoration. If we preserve human analogy, we must for ever find it impossible to reconcile any mixture of evil in the universe with infinite attributes; much less, can we ever prove the latter from the former. But supposing the Author of Nature to be finitely perfect, though far exceeding mankind; a satisfactory account may then be given of natural and moral evil, and every untoward phenomenon be explained and adjusted. A less evil may then be chosen, in order to avoid a greater: Inconveniences be submitted to, in order to reach a desirable end: And in a word, benevolence, regulated by wisdom, and limited by necessity, may produce just such a world as the present. You, PHILO, who are so prompt at starting views, and reflections, and analogies; I would gladly hear, at length, without interruption, your opinion of this new theory; and if it deserve our attention, we may afterwards, at more leisure, reduce it into form.

My sentiments, replied PHILO, are not worth being made a mystery of; and therefore, without any ceremony, I shall deliver what occurs to me, with regard to the present subject. It must, I think, be allowed, that, if a very limited intelligence, whom we shall suppose utterly unacquainted with the universe, were assured, that it were the production of a very good, wise, and powerful Being, however finite,[1] he would, from his conjectures, form *beforehand* a different notion of it from what we find it to be by experience; nor would he ever imagine, merely from these attributes of the cause, of which he is informed, that the effect[2] could be so full of vice and misery and disorder, as it appears in this life. Supposing now, that this person were brought into the

1 'however finite' added to the text.
2 'that it' scored out; 'merely from these attributes of the cause, of which he is informed, that the effect' written in the margin with indication to insert.

world, still assured, that it was the workmanship of such a sublime and benevolent[3] Being; he might, perhaps, be surprised at the disappointment; but would never retract his former belief, if founded on any very solid argument; since such a limited intelligence must be sensible of his own blindness and ignorance, and must allow, that there may be[4] many solutions of those phenomena, which will forever escape his comprehension. But supposing, which is the real case with regard to man, that this creature is not antecedently convinced of a supreme intelligence, benevolent,[5] and powerful, but is left to gather such a belief from the appearances of things: this entirely alters the case, nor will he ever find any reason for such a conclusion. He may be fully convinced of the narrow limits of his understanding; but this will not help him in forming an inference concerning the goodness of superior powers, since he must form that inference from what he knows, not from what he is ignorant of. The more you exaggerate his weakness and ignorance, the more diffident you render him, and give him the greater suspicion, that such subjects are beyond the reach of his faculties. You are obliged, therefore, to reason with him merely from the known phenomena, and to drop every arbitrary supposition or conjecture.

Did I show you a house or palace, where there was not one apartment convenient or agreeable; where the windows, doors, fires, passages, stairs, and the whole economy of the building were the source of noise, confusion, fatigue, darkness, and the extremes of heat and cold; you would certainly blame the contrivance, without any farther examination. The architect would in vain display his subtlety, and prove to you, that if this door or that window were altered, greater ills would ensue. What he says, may be strictly true: The alteration of one particular, while the other parts of the building remain, may only augment the inconveniences. But still you would assert, in general,[6] that, if the architect had had skill and good intentions, he might have formed such a plan of the whole, and might have adjusted the parts in such a manner, as would have remedied all or most of[7] these inconveniences. His ignorance, or even your own ignorance of such a plan, will never convince you of the impossibility of it. If you find many inconveniences and deformities in the building, you will always, without entering into any detail, condemn the architect.

3 'perfect' scored out; 'sublime and benevolent' written in its place.
4 'are' scored out; 'may be' written in its place.
5 'good, wise' scored out; 'benevolent' written in its place.
6 'in general' added to the text.
7 'or most of' added to the text.

In short, I repeat the question: Is the world, considered in general, and as it appears to us in this life[8], different from what a man or such a limited being would, *beforehand*, expect from a very powerful, wise, and benevolent Deity? It must be strange prejudice to assert the contrary. And from thence I conclude, that, however consistent the world may be, allowing certain suppositions and conjectures, with the idea of such a Deity[9], it can never afford us an inference concerning his existence. The consistence is not absolutely denied, only the inference. Conjectures, especially where infinity is excluded from the divine attributes, may, perhaps, be sufficient to prove a consistence; but can never be foundations for any inference.

There seem to be *four* circumstances, on which depend all, or the greater part of the ills, that molest sensible creatures; and it is not impossible but all these circumstances may be necessary and unavoidable. We know so little beyond common life, or even of common life, that, with regard to the economy of a universe, there is no conjecture, however wild, which may not be just; nor any one, however plausible, which may not be erroneous. All that belongs to human understanding, in this deep ignorance and obscurity, is to be sceptical, or at least cautious; and not to admit of any hypothesis, whatever; much less, of any which is supported by no appearance of probability. Now this I assert to be the case with regard to all the causes of evil, and the circumstances on which it depends. None of them appear to human reason, in the least degree, necessary or unavoidable; nor can we suppose them such, without the utmost licence of imagination.

The *first* circumstance, which introduces evil, is that contrivance or economy of the animal creation, by which pains, as well as pleasures, are employed to excite all creatures to action, and make them vigilant in the great work of self-preservation. Now pleasure alone, in its various degrees, seems to human understanding sufficient for this purpose. All animals might be constantly in a state of enjoyment; but when urged by any of the necessities of nature, such as thirst, hunger, weariness; instead of pain, they might feel a diminution of pleasure, by which they might be prompted to seek that object, which is necessary to their subsistence. Men pursue pleasure as eagerly as they avoid pain; at least, might have been so constituted. It seems, therefore, plainly possible to carry on the business of life without any pain. Why then is any animal ever rendered susceptible of such a sensation? If animals can

8 'in this life' added to the text.
9 'such a perfect Being' scored out; 'such a Deity' written in its place.

be free from it an hour, they might enjoy a perpetual exemption from it; and it required as particular a contrivance of their organs to produce that feeling, as to endow them with sight, hearing, or any of the senses. Shall we conjecture, that such a contrivance was necessary, without any appearance of reason? And shall we build on that conjecture as on the most certain truth?

But a capacity of pain would not alone produce pain, were it not for the *second* circumstance, *viz.* the conducting of the world by general laws; and this seems no wise necessary to a very perfect Being. It is true; if every thing were conducted by particular volitions, the course of nature would be perpetually broken, and no man could employ his reason in the conduct of life. But might not other particular volitions remedy this inconvenience? In short, might not the Deity exterminate all ill, wherever it were to be found; and produce all good, without any preparation or long progress of causes and effects?

Besides, we must consider, that, according to the present economy of the world, the course of nature, though supposed exactly regular, yet to us appears not so, and many events are uncertain, and many disappoint our expectations. Health and sickness, calm and tempest, with an infinite number of other accidents, whose causes are unknown and variable, have a great influence both on the fortunes of particular persons and on the prosperity of public societies: And indeed all human life, in a manner, depends on such accidents. A Being, therefore, who knows the secret springs of the universe, might easily, by particular volitions, turn all these accidents to the good of mankind, and render the whole world happy, without discovering himself in any operation. A fleet, whose purposes were salutary to society, might always meet with a fair wind: Good princes enjoy sound health and long life: Persons, born to power and authority, be framed with good tempers and virtuous dispositions. A few such events as these, regularly and wisely conducted, would change the face of the world; and yet would no more seem to disturb the course of nature or confound human conduct, than the present economy of things, where the causes are secret, and variable, and compounded. Some small touches, given to CALIGULA's brain in his infancy, might have converted him into a TRAJAN: One wave, a little higher than the rest, by burying CAESAR and his fortune in the bottom of the ocean, might have restored liberty to a considerable part of mankind. There may, for aught we know, be good reasons, why providence interposes not in this manner; but they are unknown to us: And though the mere supposition, that such reasons exist, may be sufficient to *save* the conclusion concerning the divine attributes, yet surely it can never be sufficient to *establish* that conclusion.

If every thing in the universe be conducted by general laws, and if animals be rendered susceptible of pain, it scarcely seems possible but some ill must arise in the various shocks of matter, and the various concurrence and opposition of general laws: But this ill would be very rare, were it not for the *third* circumstance, which I proposed to mention, *viz.* the great frugality, with which all powers and faculties are distributed to every particular being. So well adjusted are the organs and capacities of all animals, and so well fitted to their preservation, that, as far as history or tradition reaches, there appears not to be any single species, which has yet been extinguished in the universe.[10] Every animal has the requisite endowments; but these endowments are bestowed with so scrupulous an economy, that any considerable diminution must entirely destroy the creature. Wherever one power is increased, there is a proportional abatement in the others. Animals, which excel in swiftness, are commonly defective in force. Those, which possess both, are either imperfect in some of their senses, or are oppressed with the most craving wants. The human species, whose chief excellency is reason and sagacity, is of all others the most necessitous, and the most deficient in bodily advantages; without clothes, without arms, without food, without lodging, without any convenience of life, except what they owe to their own skill and industry. In short, nature seems to have formed an exact calculation of the necessities of her creatures; and like a *rigid master*, has afforded them little[11] more powers or endowments[12] than what are strictly sufficient to supply those necessities. An *indulgent parent* would have bestowed a large stock, in order to guard against accidents, and secure the happiness and welfare of the creature, in the most unfortunate concurrence of circumstances. Every course of life would not have been so surrounded with precipices, that the least departure from the true path, by mistake or necessity, must involve us in misery and ruin. Some reserve, some fund would have been provided to ensure happiness; nor would the powers and the necessities have been adjusted

10 This footnote is written in the margin, but scored out: '*Caesar, speaking of the woods in Germany, mentions some animals as subsisting there, which are now utterly extinct. De bello Gall. Lib. 6. These, and some few more instances, may be exceptions to the proposition here delivered. Strabo [Lib.4] quotes from Polybius an account of an animal about the Tyrol, which is not now to be found. If Polybius was not deceived, which is possible, the animal must have been then very rare, since Strabo cites but one authority and speaks doubtfully.*'

11 'no' scored out; 'little' written in its place.

12 'capacities' scored out; 'endownments' written in its place.

with so rigid an economy. The Author of Nature is inconceivably powerful: His force is supposed great, if not altogether inexhaustible. Nor is there any reason, as far as we can judge, to make him observe this strict frugality in his dealings with his creatures. **[13] It would have been better, were his power extremely limited, to have created fewer animals, and to have endowed them with more faculties for their happiness and preservation. A builder is never esteemed prudent, who undertakes a plan, beyond what his stock will enable him to finish.

In order to cure most of the ills of human life, I require not that man should have the wings of the eagle, the swiftness of the stag, the force of the ox, the arms of the lion, the scales of the crocodile or rhinoceros; much less do I demand the sagacity of an angel or cherubim. I am contented to take an increase in one single power or faculty of his soul. Let him be endowed with a greater propensity to industry and labor; a more vigorous spring and activity of mind; a more constant bent to business and application. Let the whole species possess naturally an equal diligence with that which many individuals are able to attain by habit and reflection; and the most beneficial consequences, without any allay of ill, is the immediate and necessary result of this endowment. Almost all the moral, as well as natural evils of human life arise from idleness, and were our species, by the original constitution of their frame, exempt from this vice or infirmity, the perfect cultivation of land, the improvement of arts and manufactures, the exact execution of every office and duty, immediately follow; and men at once may fully reach that state of society, which is so imperfectly attained by the best regulated government. But as industry is a power, and the most valuable of any, nature seems determined, suitably to her usual maxims, to bestow it on men with a very sparing hand; and rather to punish him severely for his deficiency in it, than to reward him for his attainments. She has so contrived his frame, that nothing but the most violent necessity can oblige him to labor; and she employs all his other wants to overcome, at least in part, the want of diligence, and to endow him with some share of a faculty, of which she has thought fit naturally to bereave him. Here our demands may be allowed very humble, and therefore the more reasonable[14]. If we required the endowments of superior penetration and judgement, of a more delicate taste of beauty, of a nicer sensibility to benevolence and friendship; we

13 'It would have been better . . . will enable him to finish' is written in the margin and then scored out. It is then written on Hume's page 76 with instructions to insert this passage and the following paragraph at this point in the text.
14 'legitimate' scored out; 'reasonable' written in its place.

might be told, that we impiously pretend to break the order of nature, that we want to exalt ourselves into a higher rank of being, that the presents which we require, not being suitable to our state and condition, would only be pernicious to us. But it is hard; I dare to repeat it, it is hard, that being placed in a world so full of wants and necessities; where almost every being and element is either our foe or refuses us their assistance; we should also have our own temper to struggle with, and should be deprived of that faculty, which can alone fence against these multiplied evils.**

The *fourth* circumstance, whence arises the misery and ill of the universe, is the inaccurate workmanship of all the springs and principles of the great machine of nature. It must be acknowledged, that there are few parts of the universe, which seem not to serve some purpose, and whose removal would not produce a visible defect and disorder in the whole. The parts hang all together; nor can one be touched without affecting the rest, in a greater or less degree. But at the same time, it must be observed, that none of these parts or principles, however useful, are so accurately adjusted, as to keep precisely within those bounds, in which their utility consists; but they are, all of them, apt, on every occasion, to run into the one extreme or the other. One would imagine, that this grand production had not received the last hand of the maker; so little finished is every part, and so coarse are the strokes, with which it is executed. Thus, the winds are requisite to convey the vapours along the surface of the globe, and to assist men in navigation: But how oft, rising up to tempests and hurricanes, do they become pernicious? Rains are necessary to nourish all the plants and animals of the earth: But how often are they defective? how often excessive? Heat is requisite to all life and vegetation, but is not always found in the due[15] proportion. On the mixture and secretion of the humours and juices of the body depend the health and prosperity of the animal: But the parts perform not regularly their proper function. What more useful than all the passions of the mind, ambition, vanity, love, anger? But how often do they break their bounds, and cause the greatest convulsions[16] in society? There is nothing so advantageous in the universe, but what frequently becomes pernicious, by its excess or defect; nor has nature guarded, with the requisite accuracy, against all disorder or confusion. The

15 'just' scored out; 'due' written in its place.
16 'utmost confusion' scored out; 'greatest convulsions' written in its place.

irregularity is never, perhaps,[17] so great as to destroy any species; but is often sufficient to involve the individuals in ruin and misery.

On the concurrence, then of these *four* circumstances does all, or the greatest part of natural evil depend. Were all living creatures incapable of pain, or were the world administered by particular volitions, evil never could have found access into the universe: And were animals endowed with a large stock of powers and faculties, beyond what strict necessity requires; or were the several springs and principles of the universe so accurately framed as to preserve always the just temperament and medium; there must have been very little ill in comparison of what we feel at present. What then shall we pronounce on this occasion? Shall we say, that these circumstances are not necessary, and that they might easily have been altered in the contrivance of the universe? This decision seems too presumptuous for creatures, so blind and ignorant. Let us be more modest in our conclusions. Let us allow, that, if the goodness of the Deity (I mean a goodness like the human) could be established on any tolerable reasons[18] *a priori*, these phenomena, however untoward, would not be sufficient to subvert that principle; but might easily, in some unknown manner, be reconcilable to it. But let us still assert, that as this goodness is not antecedently established, but must be inferred from the phenomena, there can be no grounds for such an inference, while there are so many ills in the universe, and while these ills might so easily have been remedied, as far as human understanding can be allowed to judge on such a subject. I am sceptic enough to allow, that the bad appearances, notwithstanding all my reasonings may[19] be compatible with such attributes as you suppose. But surely they can never prove these attributes. Such a conclusion cannot result from scepticism; but must arise from the phenomena, and from our confidence in the reasonings which we deduce from these phenomena.

**[20] Look round this universe. What an immense profusion of beings, animated and organized, sensible and active! You admire this prodigious variety and fecundity. But inspect a little more narrowly these living existences, the only beings worth regarding. How hostile and destructive to each other! How insufficient all of them for their own happiness! How contemptible or odious to the spectator! The whole presents nothing but the idea of a blind nature, impregnated by a

17 'perhaps' added to the text.
18 'on any tolerable reasons' added to the text.
19 'possibly' scored out.
20 This passage is written at the conclusion of this Part, with instructions for insertion at this point in the text.

great[21] vivifying principle; and pouring forth from her lap, without discernment or parental care, her maimed and abortive children.**

Here the *Manichaean* system[22] occurs as a proper hypothesis to solve the difficulty: And no doubt, in some respects, it is very specious, and has more probability than the common hypothesis, by giving a plausible account of the strange mixture of good and ill, which appears in life. But if we consider, on the other hand, the perfect uniformity and agreement of the parts of the universe, we shall not discover in it any marks of the combat of a malevolent with a benevolent Being. There is indeed an opposition of pains and pleasures in the feelings of sensible creatures: But are not all the operations of nature carried on by an opposition of principles, of hot and cold, moist and dry, light and heavy? The true conclusion is, that the original source[23] of all things is entirely indifferent to all these principles, and has no more regard to good above ill than to heat above cold, or to drought above moisture, or to light above heavy.

There may *four* hypotheses be framed concerning the first causes of the universe: *that* they are endowed with perfect goodness, *that* they have perfect malice, *that* they are opposite and have both goodness and malice, *that* they have neither goodness nor malice. Mixed phenomena can never prove the two former unmixed principles. And the uniformity and steadiness of general laws seems to oppose the third. The fourth, therefore, seems by far[24] the most probable.

What I have said concerning natural evil will apply to moral, with little or no variation; and we have no more[25] reason to infer, that the rectitude of the supreme Being[26] resembles human rectitude than that his benevolence resembles the human. Nay, it will be thought, that we have still greater cause[27] to exclude from him moral sentiments, such as we feel them; since moral evil, in the opinion of many, is much more predominant above moral good than natural evil above natural good.

But even though this should not be allowed, and though the virtue, which is in mankind, should be acknowledged much superior to the vice; yet so long as there is any vice at all in the universe, it will very much puzzle you anthropomorphites, how to account for it. You must

21 'an infinitely' scored out; 'a great' written in its place.
22 'of true principles' deleted from the text.
23 'cause' scored out; 'source' written in its place.
24 'by far' added to the text.
25 'the same' scored out; 'no more' written in its place.
26 'First Cause' scored out; 'supreme Being' written in its place.
27 'more reason' scored out; 'greater cause' written in its place.

assign a cause for it, without having recourse to the first cause. But as every effect must have a cause, and that cause another; you must either carry on the progression *in infinitum*, or rest on that original principle, who is the ultimate cause of all things. . . .

Hold! Hold! cried DEMEA. Whither does your imagination hurry you? I joined in alliance with you, in order to prove the incomprehensible nature of the divine being, and refute the principles of CLEANTHES, who would measure every thing by a human rule and standard. But I now find you running into all the topics of the greatest libertines and infidels;[28] and betraying that holy cause, which you seemingly espoused. Are you secretly, then, a more dangerous enemy than CLEANTHES himself?

And are you so late in perceiving it? replied CLEANTHES. Believe me, DEMEA; your friend,[29] PHILO, from the beginning, has been amusing himself at both our expense; and it must be confessed, that the injudicious reasoning of our vulgar theology has given him but too just a handle of ridicule. The total infirmity of human reason, the absolute incomprehensibility of the divine nature, the great and universal misery and still greater wickedness of men; these are strange topics surely to be so fondly cherished by orthodox divines and doctors. In ages of stupidity and ignorance, indeed, these principles[30] may safely be espoused; and perhaps, no views of things are more proper to promote superstition, than such as encourage the blind amazement, the diffidence, and melancholy of mankind. But at present. . . .

Blame not so much, interposed PHILO, the ignorance of these reverend gentlemen. They know how to change their style with the times. Formerly it was a most popular theological topic to maintain, that human life was vanity and misery, and to exaggerate all the ills and pains, which are incident to men. But of late years, divines, we find, begin to retract this position, and maintain, though still with some hesitation, that there are more goods than evils, more pleasures than pains, even in this life. When religion stood entirely upon temper and education, it was thought proper to encourage melancholy; as indeed, mankind never have recourse to superior powers so readily as in that disposition. But as men have now learned to form principles, and to draw consequences, it is necessary to change the batteries, and to make use of such arguments as will endure, at least some scrutiny and

---

28 'sceptics' scored out; 'infidels' written in its place.
29 'Believe me, DEMEA; your friend,' added to the text.
30 'arguments' written in and scored out; 'doctrines' written in and scored out; 'principles' written in their place.

examination. This variation is the same (and from the same causes) with that which I formerly remarked with regard to scepticism.

Thus PHILO continued to the last his spirit of opposition, and his censure of established opinions. But I could observe, that DEMEA did not at all relish the latter part of the discourse; and he took occasion soon after, on some pretense or other, to leave the company.

PART 12

After DEMEA's departure, CLEANTHES and PHILO continued the conversation, in the following manner. Our friend, I am afraid, said
CLEANTHES, will have little inclination to revive this topic of discourse,
while you are in company; and to tell truth, PHILO, I should rather wish
to reason with either of you apart on a subject, so sublime and
interesting. Your spirit of controversy, joined to your abhorrence of
vulgar superstition, carries you strange lengths, when engaged in an
argument[1]; and there is nothing so sacred and venerable, even in your
own eyes, which you spare on that occasion.

I must confess, replied PHILO, that I am less cautious on the subject
of natural religion than on any other; both because I know that I can
never, on that head, corrupt the principles of any man of common
sense, and because no-one, I am confident, in whose eyes I appear a
man of common sense, will ever mistake my intentions. You in
particular, CLEANTHES, with whom I live in unreserved intimacy; you
are sensible, that, notwithstanding the freedom of my conversation,
and my love of singular arguments[2], no-one has a deeper sense of
religion impressed on his mind, or pays more profound adoration to
the divine Being, as he discovers himself to reason, in the inexplicable
contrivance and artifice of nature. A purpose, an intention, a design
strikes every where the most careless, the most stupid thinker; and no
man can be so hardened in absurd systems, as at all times to reject it.
That nature does nothing in vain, is a maxim established in all the schools,
merely from the contemplation of the works of nature, without any
religious purpose; and, from a firm conviction of its[3] truth, an
anatomist, who had observed[4] a new organ or canal, would never be
satisfied, till he had also discovered its use and intention. One great
foundation of the COPERNICAN system is the maxim, *that nature acts by
the simplest methods, and chooses the most proper means to any end*; and
astronomers often, without thinking of it, lay this strong foundation
of piety and religion. **[5] The same thing is observable in other
parts of philosophy: And ** thus all the sciences almost lead us
insensibly to acknowledge a first intelligent author; and their

1 'when engaged in an argument' added to the text.
2 'opinions' scored out; 'arguments' written in its place.
3 'this' scored out; 'its' written in its place.
4 'discovered' scored out: 'observed' written in its place.
5 'The same thing is observable in other parts of Philosophy: And' is added in the
margin with instruction for insertion.

authority is often so much the greater as they do not directly profess that intention.

It is with pleasure I hear GALEN reason concerning the structure of the human body. The anatomy of a man, says he,[6] discovers above 600 different muscles; and whoever duly considers these, will find, that in each of them nature must have adjusted at least ten different circumstances, in order to attain the end which she proposed; proper figure, just magnitude, right disposition of the several ends, upper and lower position of the whole, the due insertion of the several nerves, veins, and arteries: So that in the muscles alone, above 6000 several views and intentions must have been formed and executed. The bones he calculates to be 284: The distinct purposes, aimed at in the structure of each, above forty. What a prodigious display of artifice, even in these simple and homogeneous parts? But if we consider the skin, ligaments, vessels, glandules, humours, the several limbs and members of the body; how must our astonishment rise upon us, in proportion to the number and intricacy of the parts so artificially adjusted? The farther we advance in these researches, we discover new scenes of art and wisdom: But descry still, at a distance, farther scenes beyond our reach; in the fine internal structure of the parts, in the economy of the brain, in the fabric of the seminal vessels. All these artifices are repeated in every different species of animal, with wonderful variety, and with exact propriety, suited to the different intentions of nature, in framing each species. And if the infidelity of Galen, even when these natural sciences were still imperfect, could not withstand such striking appearances; to what pitch of pertinacious obstinacy must a philosopher in this age have attained, who can now doubt of a supreme intelligence?

Could I meet with one of these species (who, I thank God, are very rare) I would ask him: Supposing there were a God, who did not discover himself immediately to our senses; were it possible for him to give stronger proofs of his existence, than what appear on the whole face of nature? What indeed could such a divine being do, but copy the present economy of things; render many of his artifices so plain, that no stupidity could mistake them; afford glimpses of still greater artifices, which demonstrate his prodigious superiority above our narrow apprehensions; and conceal altogether a great many from such imperfect creatures? Now according to all rules of just reasoning, every[7] fact must pass for undisputed, when it is supported by all the

---

6 *De formatione foetus.*
7 'any' scored out; 'every' written in its place.

arguments, which its nature admits of, even though these arguments be not, in themselves, very numerous or forcible: How much more, in the present case, where no human imagination can compute their number, and no understanding[8] estimate their cogency?

I shall farther add, said CLEANTHES, to what you have so well urged, that one great advantage of the principle[9] of theism, is, that it is the only system of cosmogony which can be rendered intelligible and complete, and yet can throughout preserve a strong analogy to what we every day see and experience in the world. The comparison of the universe to a machine of human contrivance is so obvious and natural, and is justified by so many instances of order and design in nature[10], that it must immediately strike all[11] unprejudiced apprehensions, and procure universal approbation. Whoever attempts to weaken this theory, cannot pretend to succeed by establishing in its place any other, that is precise and determinate: It is sufficient for him, if he start doubts and difficulties; and by remote and abstract views of things, reach that suspense of judgement, which is here the utmost boundary of his wishes. But besides, that this state of mind is in itself unsatisfactory, it can never be steadily maintained against such striking appearances, as continually engage us into the religious hypothesis[12] A false, absurd system, human nature, from the force of prejudice, is capable of adhering to, with obstinacy and perseverance: But no system at all, in opposition to a theory, supported by strong and obvious[13] reason, by natural propensity, and by early education, I think it absolutely impossible to maintain or defend.

So little, replied PHILO, do I esteem this suspense of judgement in the present case to be possible, that I am apt to suspect there enters somewhat of a dispute of words into this controversy, more than is usually imagined. That the works of nature bear a great analogy to the productions of art is evident; and according to all the rules of good reasoning, we ought to infer, if we argue[14] at all concerning them, that their causes have a proportional analogy. But as there are also considerable differences, we have reason to suppose a proportional difference in the causes; and in particular ought to attribute a much

8 'and no understanding' added to the text.
9 'system' scored out; 'principle' inserted in its place.
10 'contrivance' scored out; 'design in nature' written in its place.
11 'the most' scored out; 'all' written in its place.
12 'theory' scored out; 'hypothesis' written in its place.
13 'and obvious' added to the text.
14 'reason' scored out; 'argue' written in its place.

higher degree of power and energy to the supreme cause than any we have ever observed in mankind. Here then the existence of a DEITY is plainly ascertained by reason; and if we make it a question, whether, on account of these analogies, we can properly call him a *mind* or *intelligence*, notwithstanding the vast difference, which may reasonably be supposed between him and human minds; what is this but a mere verbal controversy? No man can deny the analogies between the effects: To restrain ourselves from enquiring concerning the causes is scarcely possible: From this enquiry, the legitimate conclusion is, that the causes also have an analogy: And if we are not contented with calling the first and supreme cause a GOD or DEITY, but desire to vary the expression; what can we call him but *mind* or *thought*, to which he is justly supposed to bear a considerable resemblance[15]?

**[16]All men of sound reason are disgusted with verbal disputes, which abound so much in philosophical and theological enquiries; and it is found, that the only remedy for this abuse must arise from clear definitions, from the precision of those ideas which enter into any argument, and from the strict and uniform use of those terms which are employed. But there is a species of controversy, which, from the very nature of language and of human ideas, is involved in perpetual ambiguity, and can never, by any precaution or any definitions, be able to reach a reasonable certainty or precision. These are the controversies concerning the degrees of any quality or circumstance. Men may argue to all eternity, whether Hannibal be a great, or a very great, or a superlatively great man, what degree of beauty Cleopatra possessed, what epithet of praise Livy or Thucydides is entitled to, without bringing the controversy to any determination. The disputants may here agree in their sense and differ in the terms, or *vice versa*; yet never be able to define their terms, so as to enter into each others meaning: Because the degrees of these qualities are not, like quantity or number, susceptible of any exact mensuration, which may be the standard in the controversy. That the dispute concerning theism is of this nature, and consequently is merely verbal, or perhaps, if possible, still more incurably ambiguous, will appear upon the slightest enquiry. I ask the theist, if he does not allow, that there is a great and immeasurable, because incomprehensible, difference between the *human* and the *divine* mind: The more pious he is, the more readily will he assent to the affirmative, and the more will he be disposed to

15 'analogy' scored out; 'resemblance' written in its place.
16 This passage is written at the end of Part 12, with instructions for insertion at this point in the text.

magnify the difference: He will even assert, that the difference is of a nature, which cannot be too much magnified. I next turn to the atheist, who, I assert, is only nominally so, and can never possibly be in earnest; and I ask him, whether, from the coherence and apparent sympathy in all the parts of this world, there be not a certain degree of analogy among all the operations of nature, in every situation and in every age; whether the rotting of a turnip, the generation of an animal, and the structure of human thought be not energies that probably bear some remote analogy to each other: It is impossible he can deny it: He will readily acknowledge it. Having obtained this concession, I push him still farther in his retreat; and I ask him, if it be not probable, that the principle which first arranged and still maintains order in this universe, bears not also some remote inconceivable[17] analogy to the other operations of nature, and among the rest to the economy of human mind and thought. However reluctant, he must give his assent. Where then, cry I to both these antagonists, is the subject of your dispute: The theist allows, that the original intelligence is very different from human reason: The atheist allows that the original principle of order bears some remote analogy to it. Well, you quarrel, gentlemen, about the degrees, and enter into a controversy, which admits not of any precise meaning, nor consequently of any determination. If you should be so obstinate, I should not be surprised to find you insensibly change sides; while the theist on the one hand exaggerates the dissimilarity between the supreme Being, and frail, imperfect, variable, fleeting, and mortal creatures; and the atheist on the other magnifies the analogy, among all the operations of nature, in every period, every situation, and every position. Consider then, where the real point of controversy lies, and if you cannot lay aside your disputes, endeavour, at least, to cure yourselves of your animosity.**

And here I must also acknowledge, CLEANTHES, that, as the works of nature have a much greater analogy to the effects of *our* art and contrivance, than to those of *our* benevolence and justice; we have reason to infer that the natural attributes of the Deity have a greater resemblance to those of man, than his moral have to human virtues. But what is the consequence? Nothing but this, that the moral qualities of man are more defective in their kind then his natural abilities. For as the supreme Being is allowed to be absolutely and entirely perfect,

17 'inconceivable' added to the text.

whatever differs most from him departs the farthest from the supreme standard of rectitude and perfection.[18]

These, CLEANTHES, are my unfeigned sentiments on this subject; and these sentiments, you know, I have ever cherished and maintained. But in proportion to my veneration for true religion, is my abhorrence of vulgar superstitions; and I indulge a peculiar pleasure, I confess,[19] in pushing such principles, sometimes into absurdity, sometimes into impiety. And you are sensible, that all bigots, notwithstanding their great aversion to the latter above the former, are commonly equally guilty of both.

My inclination, replied CLEANTHES, lies, I own, a contrary way. Religion, however corrupted, is still better than no religion at all. The doctrine of[20] a future state is so strong and necessary a security to morals, that we never ought to abandon or neglect it. For if finite and temporary rewards and punishments have so great an effect, as we daily find: How much greater must be expected from such as are infinite and eternal?

How happens it then, said PHILO, if vulgar superstition[21] be so salutary to society, that all history abounds so much with accounts of its pernicious consequences on public affairs? Factions, civil wars, persecutions, subversions of government, oppression, slavery; these are the dismal consequences which always attend its prevalency over the minds of men. If the religious spirit be ever mentioned in any historical narration, we are sure to meet afterwards with a detail of the miseries which attend it. And no period of time can be happier or more prosperous, than those in which it is never regarded, or heard of.

The reason of this observation, replied CLEANTHES, is obvious. The proper office of religion is to regulate the heart of men, humanize their conduct, infuse the spirit of temperance, order, and obedience; and as its operation is silent, and only enforces the motives of morality and justice, it is in danger of being overlooked, and confounded with these other motives. When it distinguishes itself, and acts as a separate

18 The following passage written at the end of Part 12 with instructions for insertion as a footnote. ** *It seems evident, that the dispute between the sceptics and dogmatists is entirely verbal, or at least regards only the degrees of doubt and assurance, which we ought to indulge with regard to all reasoning: And such disputes are commonly, at the bottom, verbal, and admit not of any precise determination. No philosophical dogmatist denies, that there are difficulties both with regard to the senses and to all science, and that these difficulties are in a regular, logical method, absolutely insolvable. No sceptic denies, that we lie under an absolute necessity, notwithstanding these difficulties, of thinking, and believing, and reasoning with regard to all kind of subjects, and even of frequently assenting with confidence and security. The only difference, then, between these sects, if they merit that name, is, that the sceptic, from habit, caprice, or inclination, insists most on the difficulties; the dogmatist, for like reasons, on the necessity.* ***
19 'I confess' added to the text.
20 'The doctrine of' added to the text.
21 'religion' scored out; 'superstition' written in its place.

principle over men, it has departed from its proper sphere, and has become only a cover to faction and ambition.

And so will all religion, said PHILO, except the philosophical and rational kind. Your reasonings are more easily eluded than my facts. The inference is not just, because finite and temporary rewards and punishments have so great influence, that therefore such as are infinite and eternal must have so much greater.[22] Consider, I beseech you, the attachment, which we have to present things, and the little concern which we discover for objects, so remote and uncertain. When divines are declaiming against the common behaviour and conduct of the world, they always represent this principle as the strongest imaginable (which indeed it is) and describe almost all human kind as lying under the influence of it, and sink into the deepest lethargy and unconcern about their religious interests. Yet these same divines, when they refute their speculative antagonists, suppose the motives of religion to be so powerful, that, without them, it were impossible for civil society to subsist; nor are they ashamed of so palpable a contradiction. It is certain, from experience, that the smallest grain of natural honesty and benevolence has more effect on men's conduct, than the most pompous views, suggested by theological theories and systems. A man's natural inclination works incessantly upon him; it is for ever present to the mind; and mingles itself with every view and consideration: Whereas religious motives, where they act at all, operate only by starts and bounds; and it is scarcely possible for them to become altogether habitual to the mind. The force of the greatest gravity, say the philosophers, is infinitely small, in comparison of that of the least impulse; yet it is certain, that the smallest gravity will, in the end, prevail above a great impulse; because no strokes or blows can be repeated with such constancy as attraction and gravitation.

Another advantage of inclination: It engages on its side all the wit and ingenuity of the mind; and when set in opposition to religious principles, seeks every method and art of eluding them: In which it is almost always successful. Who can explain the heart of man, or

22 The following passage was scored out: 'If indeed we consider the matter merely in an abstract light: If we compare only the importance of the motives, and then reflect on the natural self-love of mankind; we shall not only look for a great effect from religious considerations, but we must really esteem them absolutely irresistible and infallible in their operation. For what other motive can reasonably counterbalance them even for a moment? But this is not found to hold in reality ['fact' scored out; 'reality' written in its place]; and therefore, we may be certain that there is some other principle of human nature, which we have here overlooked, and which diminishes, at least, the force of these motives. This principle is'.

account for those strange salvos and excuses, with which people satisfy themselves, when they follow their inclinations, in opposition to their religious duty? This is well understood in the world; and none but fools ever repose less trust in a man, because they hear, that, from study and philosophy, he has entertained some speculative doubts with regard to theological subjects. And when we have to do with a man, who makes a great profession of religion and devotion; has this any other effect upon several, who[23] pass for prudent, than to put them on their guard, lest they be cheated and deceived by him?

We must farther consider, that philosophers, who cultivate reason and reflection, stand less[24] in need of such motives to keep them under the restraint of morals: And that the vulgar, who alone may need them, are utterly incapable of so pure a religion, as represents the Deity to be pleased with nothing but virtue in human behaviour. The recommendations to the Divinity are generally[25] supposed to be either frivolous observances, or rapturous ecstasies, or a bigoted credulity, **[26]and though there may be exceptions to this rule with regard to particular persons, yet these compose much the smaller number. We need not run back into antiquity, or wander into remote regions, to find instances of this degeneracy. Amongst ourselves, some have been guilty of that atrociousness, unknown to the EGYPTIAN and GRECIAN superstitions, of declaiming, in express terms, against morality, and representing it as a sure forfeiture of the divine favour, if the least trust or reliance be laid upon it.**

But even though superstition or enthusiasm[27] should not put itself in direct opposition to morality; the very diverting of the attention[28], the raising up a new and frivolous species of merit, the preposterous distribution, which it makes of praise and blame; must have the most pernicious consequences, and weaken extremely men's attachment to the natural motives of justice and humanity.

---

23 'justly' is added, then stroked out.
24 'and men of education stand little' scored out; 'who cultivate reason and reflection, stand less' added in its place.
25 'generally' added to the text.
26 This passage is scored out in the text, but a margin note indicates that it is to be printed. The first phrase of the scored-out text – 'and though there may be exceptions to this rule with regard to particular persons, yet these compose much the smaller number.' – is scored out using a horizontal line through the words. The remainder – 'We need not run back into antiquity . . . if the least trust or reliance be laid upon it.' – is scored out using four diagonal strokes. This edition has interpreted Hume's note to 'Print this passage' to mean the *entire* passage is to be printed.
27 'or enthusiasm' added to the text.
28 'of the mind' scored out.

Such a principle of action likewise, not being any of the[29] familiar motives of human conduct, acts only by intervals on the temper, and must be roused by continual efforts, in order to render the pious zealot satisfied with his own conduct, and make him fulfil his devotional task. Many religious exercises are entered into with seeming fervour, where the heart, at the time, feels cold and languid: A habit of dissimulation is by degrees contracted: And fraud and falsehood become the predominant principle. Hence the reason of that vulgar observation[30], that the highest zeal in religion and the deepest hypocrisy, so far from being inconsistent, are often or commonly[31] united in the same individual character.

The bad effects of such habits, even in common life, are easily imagined. But where the interests of religion are concerned, no morality can be forcible enough to bind the enthusiastic zealot. The sacredness of the cause sanctifies every measure, which can be made use of to promote it.

The steady attention alone to so important an interest as that of eternal salvation is apt to extinguish the benevolent affections, and beget a narrow, contracted selfishness. And when such a temper is encouraged, it easily eludes all the general percepts of charity and benevolence.

Thus the motives of vulgar superstition have no great influence on general conduct; nor is their operation very[32] favourable to morality, in the[33] instances, where they predominate.

Is there any maxim in politics more certain and infallible, than that both the number and authority of priests should be[34] confined within very narrow limits, and that the civil magistrate ought, for ever, to keep his *fasces* and *axes* from such dangerous hands? But if the spirit of popular religion were so salutary to society, a contrary maxim ought to prevail. The greater number of priests, and their greater authority and riches will always augment the religious spirit. And though the priests have the guidance of this spirit;[35] why may we not expect a superior sanctity of life, and greater[36] benevolence and moderation, from persons, who are set apart for religion, who are continually inculcating

29 'natural or' scored out.
30 'common phenomena' scored out; 'vulgar observation' written in its place.
31 'or commonly' added to the text.
32 'very' added to the text.
33 'few' scored out.
34 'might not be' scored out; 'should be' written in its place.
35 'of this spirit;' added to the text.
36 'greater' added to the text.

it upon others, and who must themselves imbibe a greater share of it? Whence comes it then,[37] that, in fact,[38] the utmost a wise magistrate can propose with regard to popular religions, is, as far as possible,[39] to make a saving game of it, and to prevent their pernicious consequences with regard to society. Every expedient which he tries for so humble a purpose is surrounded with inconveniences. If he admits only one religion among his subjects, he must sacrifice, to an uncertain prospect of tranquillity, every consideration of public liberty, science, reason, industry, and even his own independency. If he gives indulgence to several sects, which is the wiser maxim, he must preserve a very philosophical indifference to all of them, and carefully restrain the pretensions of the prevailing sect; otherwise he can expect nothing but endless disputes, quarrels, factions, persecutions, and civil commotions.

True religion, I allow, has no such pernicious consequences: But we must treat of religion, as it has commonly[40] been found in the world; nor have I any thing to do with that speculative tenet[41] of[42] theism, which, as it is a species of philosophy, must partake of the beneficial influence, of that principle, and at the same time must lie under a like inconvenience, of being always confined to very few persons.[43]

Oaths are requisite in all courts of judicature; but it is a question whether their authority arises from any popular religion. It is the solemnity and importance of the occasion, the regard to reputation, and the reflecting on the general interests of society, which are the chief restraints upon mankind. Custom-house oaths and political oaths are but little regarded even[44] by some who pretend to principles of honesty and religion: And a Quaker's asseveration is with us[45] justly put upon the same footing with the oath of any other person. I know, that POLYBIUS[46] ascribes the infamy of GREEK faith to the prevalency of the

37 'But so it is, we find' scored out: 'Whence comes it then' written in its place.
38 'in fact' added to the text.
39 'as far as possible' added to the text.
40 'always' scored out; 'commonly' written in its place.
41 'principle' scored out; 'tenet' written in its place.
42 'refined' scored out.
43 The following passage is written in the margin with instructions that it be a separate paragraph, but then is scored out: 'Since government, reason, learning, friendship, love and every human advantage are attended with inconveniences, as we daily find, what may be expected in all the various models of superstition; a quality, composed of whatever is the most absurd, corrupted, and barbarous of our nature? Were there any one exception to that universal mixture of good and ill, which is found in life, this might be pronounced thoroughly and entirely ill.'
44 'even' added to the text.
45 'with us' added to the text.
46 *Lib. 6 Cap. 54.*

EPICUREAN philosophy; but I know also, that PUNIC faith[47] had as bad a reputation in ancient[48] times, as IRISH evidence has in modern;[49] though we cannot account for these vulgar observations[50] by the same reason. Not to mention, that GREEK faith was infamous before the rise of the EPICUREAN philosophy; and EURIPIDES;[51] in a passage which I shall point out to you,[52] has gleaned a remarkable stroke of satire against his nation, with regard to this circumstance.

Take care, PHILO, replied CLEANTHES, take care: Push not matters too far: Allow not your zeal against false religion to undermine your veneration for the true. Forfeit not this principle, the chief, the only great comfort in life; and our principal support amidst all the attacks of adverse fortune. The most agreeable reflection, which it is possible for human imagination to suggest, is that of genuine theism, which represents us as the workmanship of a Being perfectly good, wise, and powerful; who created us for happiness, and who, having implanted in us immeasurable desires of good, will prolong our existence to all eternity, and will transfer us into an infinite variety of scenes, in order to satisfy those desires, and render our felicity complete and durable. Next to such a Being himself (if the comparison be allowed) the happiest lot which we can imagine, is that of being under his guardianship and protection.

These appearances, said PHILO, are most engaging and alluring; and with regard to the true philosopher, they are more than appearances. But it happens here, as in the former case, that, with regard to the greater part of mankind, the appearances are deceitful, and that the terrors of religion commonly prevail above its comforts.

It is allowed, that men never have recourse to devotion so readily as when dejected with grief or depressed with sickness. Is not this a proof, that the religious spirit is not so nearly allied to joy as to sorrow?

But men, when afflicted, find consolation in religion, replied CLEANTHES. Sometimes, said PHILO: But it is natural to imagine, that they will form a notion of those unknown beings, suitably to the present gloom and melancholy of their temper, when they betake themselves to the contemplation of them.[53] Accordingly, we find the tremendous images to predominate in all[54] religions; and we ourselves,

---

47 'IRISH evidence' scored out; 'PUNIC faith' written in its place.
48 'modern' scored out; 'ancient' written in its place.
49 'IRISH evidence in modern' added to the text.
50 'it' scored out; 'these vulgar observations' written in its place.
51 *Iphigenia in Tauride.*
52 'when you please' deleted from the text.
53 'when they betake themselves to the contemplation of them' added to the text.
54 'most' scored out: 'all' written in its place.

after having employed[55] the most exalted expression in our descriptions of the Deity, fall into the flattest contradiction, in affirming, that the damned are infinitely superior in number to the elect.

I shall venture to affirm, that there never was a popular religion,[56] which represented the state of departed souls in such a light, as would render it eligible for human kind, that there should be such a state. These fine models of religion are the mere product of philosophy. For as death lies between the eye and the prospect of futurity, that event is so shocking to nature, that it must throw a gloom on all the regions, which lie beyond it; and suggest to the generality of mankind the idea of CERBERUS and furies; devils, and torrents of fire and brimstone.

It is true; both fear and hope enter into religion; because both these passions, at different times, agitate the human mind, and each of them forms a species of divinity, suitable to itself. But when a man is in a cheerful disposition, he is fit for business or company or entertainment of any kind; and he naturally applies himself to these, and thinks not of religion. When melancholy, and dejected, he has nothing to do but brood upon the terrors of the invisible world, and to plunge himself still deeper in affliction. It may, indeed, happen, that after he has, in this manner, ingraved the religious opinions deep into his thought and imagination, there may arrive a change of health or circumstances which may restore his good humour, and raising cheerful prospects of futurity, make him run into the other extreme of joy and triumph. But still it must be acknowledged, that, as terror is the primary principle of religion, it is the passion, which always[57] predominates in it, and admits but of short intervals of pleasure.

Not to mention, that these fits of excessive, enthusiastic joy, by exhausting the spirits, always prepare the way for equal fits of superstitious terror and dejection; nor is there any state of mind so happy as the calm and equable. But this state, it is impossible to support, where a man thinks, that he lies, in such profound darkness and uncertainty, between an eternity of happiness and an eternity of misery. No wonder, that such an opinion disjoints the ordinary frame of the mind, and throws it into the utmost confusion. And though that opinion is seldom so steady in its operation as to influence all the actions; yet is it apt to make a considerable breach in the temper, and to produce that gloom and melancholy, so remarkable in all devout people.

55 'all' deleted from the text.
56 'in the world' scored out.
57 'must' scored out.

It is contrary to common sense to entertain apprehensions or terrors, upon account of any opinion whatsoever, or to imagine that we run any risk hereafter, by the freest use of our reason. Such a sentiment implies both an *absurdity* and an *inconsistency*. It is an absurdity to believe the Deity has human passions, and one of the lowest of human passions, a restless appetite for[58] applause. It is an inconsistency to believe, that, since the Deity has this human passion, he has not others also; and in particular, a disregard to the opinions of creatures, so much inferior.[59]

To know God, says SENECA, *is to worship him*. All other worship is indeed absurd, superstitious, and even impious. It degrades him to the low condition of mankind, who are delighted with entreaty, solicitation, presents, and flattery. Yet is this impiety the smallest of which superstition is guilty. Commonly, it depresses the Deity far below the condition of mankind; and represents him as a capricious demon, who exercises his power without reason and without humanity. And were that Divine Being disposed to be offended at the vices and follies of silly mortals, who are his own workmanship; ill would it surely fare with the votaries of most[60] popular superstitions. Nor would any of human race merit his *favour*, but a very few, the philosophical theists, who entertain or rather indeed endeavour to entertain, suitable notions of his divine perfections. As the only persons, intitled to his *compassion* and *indulgence*, would be the philosophical sceptics, a sect almost equally rare, who, from a natural diffidence of their own capacity, suspend, or endeavour to suspend all judgement with regard to such sublime and such extraordinary subjects.

If the whole of natural theology, as some people seem to maintain, resolves itself into one simple, though somewhat ambiguous, at least undefined proposition, *that the cause or causes of order in the universe probably*[61] *bear some remote analogy to human intelligence*: If this proposition be

58 'vulgar' scored out.
59 The text originally ends on this page, but three paragraphs are scored out and instructions (not in Hume's hand) indicate that the text is to continue on the next page. The scored-out portions of this page consist of a margin paragraph, 'To know God . . . such extraordinary subjects', the footnote regarding the dispute between the sceptics and the dogmatists, '*It seems evident, that the dispute between the sceptics and dogmatists . . . the dogmatist, for like reasons, on the necessity*', and the final paragraph of the text where Pamphilus gives his assessment of the argument, 'CLEANTHES and PHILO pursued not this conversation . . . those of CLEANTHES approach still nearer to the truth.' (This paragraph constitutes the final paragraph of the text before the changes.) The margin paragraph is rewritten on the following page along with more text, the footnote rewritten with instructions for insertion at the earlier point, and the final paragraph rewritten as the new conclusion of the text.
60 'all' scored out: 'most' written in its place.
61 '*probably*' added to the text.

not capable of extension, variation, or more particular explication: If it affords no inference that affects human life, or can be the source of any action[62] or forbearance:[63] And if the analogy, imperfect as it is, can be carried no farther than to the human intelligence; and cannot be transferred,[64] with any appearance of[65] probability, to the other qualities of the mind: If this really be the case,[66] what can the most inquisitive, contemplative, and religious man do more than give a plain, philosophical assent to the proposition, as often as it occurs; and believe, that the arguments, on which it is established, exceed the objections, which lie against it? Some astonishment indeed will naturally arise from the greatness of the object: Some melancholy from its obscurity: Some contempt of human reason, that it can give no solution more satisfactory with regard to so extraordinary and magnificent a question. But believe me, CLEANTHES, the most natural sentiment, which a well disposed mind will feel on this occasion, is a longing desire and expectation, that heaven would be pleased to dissipate, at least alleviate this profound ignorance, by affording some more particular revelation to mankind, and making discoveries of the nature, attributes, and operations of the divine object of our faith. A person, seasoned with a just sense of the imperfections of natural reason, will fly to revealed truth with the greatest avidity: While the haughty dogmatist, persuaded, that he can erect a complete system of theology by the mere help of Philosophy, disdains any further aid and rejects this adventitious instructor. To be a philosophical sceptic is, in a man of letters, the first and most essential step towards being a sound, believing Christian; a proposition, which I would willingly recommend to the attention of PAMPHILUS: And I hope CLEANTHES will forgive me for interposing so far in the education and instruction of his pupil.

CLEANTHES and PHILO pursued not this conversation much farther; and as nothing ever made greater impression on me, than all the reasonings of that day; so, I confess, that, upon a serious review of the whole, I cannot but think, that PHILO's principles are more probable than DEMEA's; but that those of CLEANTHES approach still nearer to the truth.**

FINIS

62 'steady sentiment' scored out; 'action' written in its place.
63 'forbearance' scored out and restored.
64 'extended' scored out; 'transferred' written in its place.
65 'appearance of' added to the text.
66 'If this really be the case' added to the text.

HUME'S DIALOGUES ON EVIL

Stanley Tweyman

Only two sections of Hume's *Dialogues Concerning Natural Religion* are concerned with the topic of the benevolence of the Designer of the world (Parts 10 and 11), and the conclusion reached is stated by Philo in an unambiguous manner:

> The true conclusion is, that the original source of all things is entirely indifferent to all these principles, and has no more regard to good above ill than to heat above cold, or to drought above moisture, or to light above heavy. (D. 169)[1]

In light of the fact that much of the *Dialogues* is concerned with setting out sceptical or pyrrhonian objections to positions in natural theology which reveal our ignorance in this area, it is important for an understanding of Parts 10 and 11 to ask whether we are meant to take Philo's conclusion seriously; that is, does Hume intend Philo's conclusion in Part 11 to be a truth in natural theology? Nelson Pike answers this negatively:

> Philo claims that *there is* an 'original Source of all things' and that this source is indifferent with respect to matters of good and evil. He pretends to be inferring this conclusion from observed data. This represents a departure from Philo's much professed skepticism in the *Dialogues*. . . . I think the center of Philo's remarks in this passage must be located in their skeptical rather than their metaphysical import. Philo has proposed a hypothesis which is counter to the one offered by Cleanthes. And he claims

This and the following papers were originally presented as a symposium at the Edinburgh Hume Conference, August 25–30, 1986, and subsequently appeared in *Hume Studies*, 13, 1987.
1 All page references to the *Dialogues* refer to the version in this volume.

that this hypothesis is the 'true conclusion' to be drawn from the observed data. But the point is not, I think, that Philo's new hypothesis is true, or even probable. The conclusion is, rather, that the hypothesis advanced by Cleanthes is false, or very improbable. When claiming that evil in the world *supports* a hypothesis which is counter to the one offered by Cleanthes, I think Philo simply means to be calling attention to the fact that evil in the world provides *evidence against* Cleanthes' theological position.[2]

It is true that at certain points in the *Dialogues* Philo does profess to be a sceptic (Pyrrhonian), and he often attempts to show Cleanthes that his hypothesis is false by generating a hypothesis from the available data which is as plausible as Cleanthes' hypothesis (e.g. Part 4, where they debate Cleanthes' view that God is external to the world which He has designed), or which has greater plausibility than Cleanthes' hypothesis (e.g. Parts 6 and 7, where Philo argues against Cleanthes' claim that the available data support the hypothesis of an intelligent designer for the world). However, whenever Philo proceeds in this manner, he makes it clear that he has no hypothesis on the matter under discussion (e.g. D. 127) which he is willing to defend, and that he has proceeded in this manner, not to argue for a position – he maintains that the available data are not adequate to do so – but to argue against the position Cleanthes is defending (see, for example, D. 138). In fact, at one stage in the discussion, Philo urges against embracing any religious system, because of the victory which awaits the sceptic:

> All religious systems, it is confessed, are subject to great and insuperable difficulties. Each disputant triumphs in his turn; while he carries on an offensive war, and exposes the absurdities, barbarities, and pernicious tenets of his antagonist. But all of them, on the whole, prepare a complete triumph for the sceptic; who tells them, that no system ought ever to be embraced with regard to such subjects: For this plain reason, that no absurdity ought ever to be assented to with regard to any subject. A total suspense of judgment is here our only reasonable resource. (D. 147)

This passage, which appears toward the end of Part 8, is reminiscent of the point Philo made in Part 1, when he warned of arguments which 'run wide of common life'. In the case of such arguments, 'the most refined scepticism comes to be upon a footing with them, and is able to

2 Nelson Pike, 'Hume on Evil', in *God and Evil*, edited by Nelson Pike (Englewood Cliffs, New Jersey, Prentice-Hall, 1964), p. 100.

188

oppose and counterbalance them. The one has no more weight than the other. The mind must remain in suspense between them; and it is that very suspense or balance which is the triumph of scepticism' (D. 102).

There is, therefore, much in the *Dialogues* which shows that Philo frequently argues for a position in order to show that the hypothesis advanced by Cleanthes is false. However, this does not establish that Philo is a Pyrrhonian throughout the *Dialogues,* and that he *always* supports positions in order to argue against the hypothesis advanced by Cleanthes. Accordingly, we must now examine those passages which give insight into Philo's mode of argumentation in Parts 10 and 11.

The first passage in this regard occurs at the end of Part 8:

And if every attack, as is commonly observed, and no defence, among theologians, is successful; how complete must be *his* victory, who remains always, with all mankind, on the offensive, and has himself no fixed station or abiding city, which he is ever, on any occasion, obliged to defend? (D. 147)

What is noteworthy in this passage is that Philo speaks of the triumph of scepticism over all religious systems in the third person, rather than (what we should have expected) in the first person. It was Philo, who, as sceptic, argued against Cleanthes; therefore, it is Philo who has scored the victory. That he speaks in the third person at the end of Part 8 is a clear signal to the reader – and, perhaps, to Cleanthes – that his pyrrhonism, which proved so effective when arguing against Cleanthes' hypothesis that the cause of the design of the world is an intelligent being, has now been abandoned.

Philo's argument against Cleanthes in Part 10 is distinctly unpyrrhonian. Cleanthes urges that the hypothesis of an infinite benevolent Deity can explain the design of the world. When Philo argues against Cleanthes' hypothesis, he does so not (as we should expect if Pike's account is correct) by generating alternative hypotheses which are as plausible as, or even more plausible than, Cleanthes' hypothesis, but by showing that the design of the world fails to confirm Cleanthes' hypothesis:

And is it possible, Cleanthes, said Philo, that after all these reflections, and infinitely more, which might be suggested, you can still persevere in your anthropomorphism, and assert the moral attributes of the Deity, his justice, benevolence, mercy, and recitutde, to be of the same nature with these virtues in human creatures? His power we allow infinite: Whatever he wills is executed: But neither man nor any other animal are happy: Therefore, he does not will their happiness. His wisdom is infinite: He is never mistaken in choosing the means to any end: But the course of nature tends not to human or animal felicity: Therefore it is not established for that purpose. Through the whole compass of human knowledge, there are no inferences more certain and infallible than these. (D. 156-7)

Philo is not arguing as a sceptic; rather he is employing the hypo-thetico-deductive method for testing Cleanthes' hypothesis.

What accounts for this shift in Philo's procedure? When Cleanthes argued by analogy that the Designer of the world is an intelligent being, he emphasized the resemblances between the world and machines in terms of means to ends relations and a coherence of parts.[3] Philo argued that these features are present not only in those cases where intelligence is the cause of design, but also when non-intelligent causes (e.g. generation, vegetation) are the source of design.[4] Hence, to show that the design of the world has an intelligent cause of design, Cleanthes must establish that the design of the world bears a sufficient resemblance to a particular type of machine, so that the world can be classified as a machine of that sort. Only in this way, Philo insists, can the principle 'like effects prove like causes' be employed to prove that God resembles human intelligence. Within the discussion, Philo shows that the features of design present in the world are insufficient to classify the world as a (particular kind of) machine, and, for that matter, as any kind of object whose cause of design is known. Accordingly, Philo argues that all arguments by analogy fail to establish the nature of the cause of the design of the world. And, therefore, when he puts forth any arguments of this sort (Parts 6, 7, 8) it is not done to support a particular hypothesis about the Designer of the world, but to argue against Cleanthes' Design Argument.

In Part 10, the issue of how the design of the world is to be classified does not arise. All three speakers agree that the world contains both good and evil ('mixed phenomena'), and Cleanthes argues that the hypothesis of an infinite benevolent Deity can explain this situation. Philo shows that the *only* world which can be inferred from Cleanthes' hypothesis is one containing only good, and, therefore, no evil. Hence, there is no need for a pyrrhonian approach to Cleanthes' hypothesis in Part 10.

3 See, for example, D. 108-11.
4 This is particularly evident in Parts 2, 6, and 8 of the *Dialogues*.

Philo's argument in Part 11 is divided into three parts: (1) he argues against Cleanthes' hypothesis of a finite benevolent Deity; (2) he attacks the Manichaean account of the causes of good and evil; and (3) he argues for the indifference of the Designer of the world. I will now show that nowhere in his argument in Part 11 is Philo proceeding as a Pyrrhonian.

(1) The discussion between Philo and Cleanthes on the hypothesis of a finite benevolent cause of design of the world focuses on the four causes of evil in the world and whether these causes are necessary and unavoidable. Now, when Philo argued against Cleanthes' 'intelligence' hypothesis, he made it clear that the number of counter-hypotheses he could put forth regarding the origin of the design of the world is indefinitely large: '[I]n such questions as the present, a hundred contradictory views may preserve a kind of imperfect analogy; and invention has here full scope to exert itself' (D. 143). On the other hand, when he begins his attack on Cleanthes' claim that evil is necessary and unavoidable, he urges 'not to admit of any hypothesis, whatever; much less, of any which is supported by no appearance of probability' (D. 163). In other words, Philo maintains that there is no hypothesis which can support the necessity of evil with any degree of success. This difference in Philo's approach will be explained shortly.

Cleanthes' position[5] on the necessity and unavoidability of evil always takes the following form: (a) isolate a particular feature in the world (pain, general laws, powers and faculties, the adjustments present in all parts of the world), and make the (obvious) point that the feature contributes substantially to the survival of sensible creatures; (b) acknowledge that there are occasions when each feature contributes to the destruction, rather than to the survival, of sensible creatures; (c) argue that, to eliminate the evil consequences associated with each feature, the feature itself would have to be eliminated; (d) conclude that if (c) were adopted by the Designer, more evil than exists at present would result, since our survival would encounter even greater challenges than it currently faces. Philo, on the other hand, shows that, for each cause of evil in the world, some alteration, which it is within the Designer's power to bring about, would greatly decrease the quantity of evil, without threatening the quantity of good which obtains. In this way, he shows that evil is neither necessary nor unavoidable.

---

5 D. 163–8 are the pages covering this portion of the discussion of evil. See also the Introduction in this volume, pp. 74–9.

Philo's arguments here are not those of the sceptic. Furthermore, his arguments are, in fact, only indirectly related to God. When arguing against Cleanthes' intelligence hypothesis, Philo maintained that we cannot know anything about God, because the dissimilarities between the design of the world and machines are too great to enable us to reason analogically to the nature of God. When dealing with the question of why there is evil in the world, Philo's argument focuses on the four *natural* causes of evil – on features of the world with which scientists and philosophers are concerned. It is, therefore, our causal knowledge of the world which disproves Cleanthes' hypothesis that this is the best world possible. It is, for example, because we know that people pursue pleasure as eagerly as they avoid pain, that Philo can suggest that avoidance could be accomplished through the prospect of a diminution of pleasure; it is because we know that general laws operate in accordance with the 'secret powers' in objects, that he can propose that particular changes in the secret powers of objects would avoid the evil to be brought about by the operation of certain general laws; and so on. A finitely perfect Deity who is benevolent could bring these alterations about: Philo finds nothing in the concept of such a being which is incompatible with the proposed changes. These proposals, however, are not based on our knowledge of the Deity, but on our (causal) understanding of the world. It is in this sense that Philo's arguments are indirectly related to God. And it is because all suggested improvements to the design of the world are based on our understanding of how the world operates, that Philo does not resort to pyrrhonian arguments. Cleanthes' 'intelligence hypothesis' has 'some appearance of probability', given that we find design originating in intelligence manifests means to ends relations and a coherence of parts. On the other hand, our causal understanding of the world reveals no basis for holding that any of the causes of evil is unavoidable. Accordingly, hypotheses regarding the unavoidability of evil are 'supported by no appearance of probability'. On the topic of evil, there is no hypothesis which requires the counterbalancing achievable through pyrrhonian arguments.

(2) Philo's attack on Manichaeanism[6] proceeds in two stages. In the first, he asks what we should expect to find in the world if Manichaeanism is true. Because Manichaeanism offers a causal account of the presence of good and evil through the hypothesis of a benevolent and a malevolent being, we should find marks of combat between these

---

6 Philo's attack on Manichaeanism appears in one (highly condensed) paragraph, D. 169.

opposing causal forces. Philo argues that the absence of such marks of combat in nature disproves the Manichaean hypothesis. This mode of argumentation is but a further use of the hypothetico-deductive method for testing hypotheses.

Philo concedes that there is an 'opposition' between good and evil in nature; in examining this hypothesis as a defence of Manichaeanism, he puts forth the second stage of his argument against this doctrine. He shows that, logically, good and evil do not differ from other opposites, e.g. hot and cold, moist and dry. That is, just as hot and cold are adequately explained through opposing *immediate* causes, without reference to opposing *original* causes, so good and evil can be explained through opposing immediate causes. Whenever a satisfactory causal account is obtainable without reference to original causes, these latter are not included in our explanation. Given that there are physical causes of good and evil, no reason can be put forth to show that good and evil should be explained through opposing original causes.

Philo makes an additional point on this topic. If a satisfactory causal account for a pair of opposites can be had without reference to any original cause, then there is no basis for arguing that the original source of all things has a preference for one of the immediate causes over the other. Alternatively, only a known unique (causal) relationship between an original cause and one member of a pair of opposites (such as Manichaeanism attempts to establish) can prove that the original cause has a preference for one member of the pair over the other. It is because we lack knowledge of such unique causal relations, that Philo concludes 'The true conclusion is, that the original source of all things is entirely indifferent to all these principles, and has no more regard to good above ill than to heat above cold, or to drought above moisture, or to light above heavy' (D. 169).

Throughout his attack on Manichaeanism, Philo proceeds in a scientific manner – insisting that hypotheses be stated in such a manner that they can be confirmed or refuted by having recourse to observation. His point is that no observation or set of observations supports Manichaeanism, and that all observations are compatible with but one hypothesis regarding the Deity: indifference. The Deity may, in fact, have a preference for good over evil: Philo argues that nothing within our experience reveals that such is the case, for nothing within our experience reveals a unique relationship between the Deity and the production of goodness.

(3) The 'indifference hypothesis', as we have seen, was first developed in the context of his critique on Manichaeanism. Philo argues for this

position, once again, in the third stage of his argument. Considerations of the Deity's power (infinite, finite) have not assisted Cleanthes' efforts to argue for benevolence of the Deity; hence, in this stage of Philo's argument, no reference is made to God's power. Philo now is concerned only with the moral attributes of the Deity, and with whether any attributes or combination of attributes is either compatible with, or can be proved from, the mixed phenomena we find in the world. The most probable conclusion appears to be that the Deity is neither good nor malicious, i.e. that the Deity is indifferent to the good and evil in the world:

> There may *four* hypotheses be framed concerning the first causes of the universe: *that* they are endowed with perfect goodness, *that* they have perfect malice, *that* they are opposite and have both goodness and malice, *that* they have neither goodness nor malice. Mixed phenomena can never prove the two former unmixed principles. And the uniformity and steadiness of general laws seem to oppose the third. The fourth, therefore, seems by far the most probable. (D. 169)

The inquiry into the moral attributes of the Deity, therefore, ends without having recourse to pyrrhonian arguments or objections.

We are now able to understand why there is a fundamental methodological difference between the first eight sections of the *Dialogues,* in which the intelligence hypothesis is discussed, and Parts 10 and 11, in which the moral attributes of the Deity are discussed. In the first eight sections, Philo argues against Cleanthes' hypothesis by advancing his own hypotheses. His effort to advance hypotheses must be assessed in light of the fact that (by his own admission) all such hypotheses are based on insufficient data, and, therefore, none is, strictly speaking, acceptable. Their use is not to establish truths about the nature of God, but to establish the conclusion which we find at the end of Part 8, that 'A total suspense of judgment is here our only reasonable resource.' The design of the world is compatible with, and could have arisen from, an indefinite number of designing principles. On the other hand, we have seen that in dealing with Cleanthes' hypotheses in Parts 10 and 11 we are able to proceed more scientifically, and, in this manner, eliminate all but one of the hypotheses which can be introduced to explain the design of the world.

Scientific investigations never yield certainty. Accordingly, when Philo argues for the indifference of the Deity, he emphasizes that this position 'seems by far the most probable'. What cannot be doubted is that Philo is more satisfied with his arguments in Parts 10 and 11, than he is with those in the first eight sections. This can be shown by noting that in Part 12 he acknowledges a willingness to assess the arguments of the first eight sections, but gives no indication that Parts 10 and 11 will also be reviewed. His former lack of caution (mentioned in the second paragraph of Part 12) does not extend to Parts 10 and 11.

GOING OUT THE WINDOW:
A COMMENT ON TWEYMAN

John W. Davis

> Whether your scepticism be as absolute and sincere as you pretend,
> we shall learn bye and bye, when the company breaks up: We shall
> then see, whether you go out at the door or the window; and
> whether you really doubt; if your body has gravity, or can be
> injured by its fall; according to popular opinion, derived from our
> fallacious senses and more fallacious experience. (D. 99)[1]

My paper is divided into two sections. In the first section I will
summarize and comment on Stanley Tweyman's paper[2] and in the
second section present an alternative reading of Parts 10 and 11 of the
Dialogues.

SECTION I

In his paper Tweyman claims that, although Philo's argument in Parts
1–9 of the *Dialogues* are pyrrhonian, in Parts 10 and 11 a major change of
strategy occurs in which pyrrhonian arguments are replaced by
hypothetico-deductive ones.

Recent scholarship on Hume's *Dialogues* has revolved around two
questions: (1) the identification of the sources and personages of the
Dialogues and (2) Hume's attitude toward religion. Tweyman and I
agree that Philo speaks for Hume. We differ on the character of Philo's
challenge to Cleanthes' experimental theism.

Philo's methodological shift in Parts 10 and 11 is said to consist in his
presentation of scientific hypotheses for appraisal, in contrast to the

---

1 All references to the *Dialogues* are to the version printed above in this volume.
2 Stanley Tweyman, 'Hume's Dialogues on Evil,' in this volume. All references in
the text to this paper will be cited as 'Tweyman' followed by the relevant page
number(s).

alternative hypotheses of the earlier Parts, where sceptical arguments are used to undermine Cleanthes' position. I take it that the scientific hypotheses in question are construed realistically and not instrumentally; they are supposedly true or false and permit deductions to be made from them.

The first evidence of the methodological shift, we are told, occurs in Part 8 in which Philo speaks in the third and not the first person, 'a clear signal to the reader . . . that his pyrrhonism . . . has now been abandoned' (Tweyman, 189). I find this claim unconvincing since in the majority of instances throughout the passage Philo speaks in first-person fashion. Any detectable changes here seem to me to be purely stylistic in character.

Tweyman uses the terms 'scepticism' and 'pyrrhonism' inter-changeably. His account of pyrrhonism involves two theses, the second of which is derived from the first: (1) scepticism involves suspense of judgement between alternative beliefs; and (2) Philo presents his 'position in order to show that the hypotheses advanced by Cleanthes are false' (Tweyman, 189). In his sceptical mode in Parts 1–8 Philo makes no truth claim for the hypothesis he sets out. But, according to Tweyman,

> this does not establish that Philo is a Pyrrhonian throughout the *Dialogues,* and that he *always* supports positions . . . to argue against the hypothesis advanced by Cleanthes. (Tweyman, 189)

Tweyman gives two examples of Philonian scepticism in Parts 1–8. The first is the debate in Part 4 over the Deity's relation to the world. Cleanthes contends that the Deity is external to his creation, and Philo questions the validity of Cleanthes' causal inferences (D. 125). The second is the argument in Parts 6 and 7 in which Philo argues that the available data do not support the hypothesis of an intelligent designer. I find the account at this point unexceptionable.

The first example in which Philo's arguments become 'distinctly unpyrrhonian' (Tweyman, 189) is the passage in which Philo details the 'inconveniences' of anthropomorphism. Philo begins by saying:

> you can still persevere in your anthropomorphism and assert the moral attributes of the Deity, his justice, benevolence, mercy, and rectitude, to be of the same nature with these virtues in human creatures? (D. 156)

But, he continues, 'the course of nature tends not to human or animal felicity (ibid.). Cleanthes has asserted human happiness, a thesis which

197

Philo denies. We are no longer dealing with an alternative hypothesis designed to undermine Cleanthes' account but with 'the hypothetico-deductive method for testing Cleanthes' hypothesis' (Tweyman, 190).

Part 11 divides into the three sections which are each discussed to show that Philo's arguments are not pyrrhonian. Since the argument is similar in all three cases, I will remark only on the discussion of the 'indifference hypothesis', Philo's argument that the Deity is 'indifferent' to the good and evil in the world. The moral attributes of the Deity are under examination and not his existence or power. The probable conclusion that Philo draws is that the Deity is neither good nor malicious but is 'indifferent' to the good and evil in the world. Philo eliminates all hypotheses but one – the indifference of the Deity – and claims that this hypothesis 'seems by far the most probable'.

Although there is much in this reading with which I can agree, I find Tweyman's account misleading in its treatment of Hume's scepticism in the *Dialogues*.

SECTION II

I will begin an alternative account of Parts 10 and 11 with a brief account of Hume's scepticism. Scepticism, as described in Pyrrho's *Outlines of Pyrrhonism*, involves two stages: (1) suspension of judgement, 'a standstill of the intellect as a result of which we neither deny nor affirm anything';[3] (2) the famous ten modes or tropes of scepticism were to bring about the production of oppositions among the appearances of things, where 'appearances' simply refer to the impressions things make upon us. Scepticism is conceived of as *a way of life* for troubled (and untroubled) times. The sceptic contrasts his view with his opponent the dogmatist. A dogmatist has beliefs, but a sceptic neither affirms nor denies. Sceptics are doubters. The word 'dogmatist' in antiquity simply referred to someone with beliefs, not someone who refuses to consider evidence. When Philo calls Cleanthes a 'dogmatist' the term should be taken in its antique sense. To live as a Pyrrhonist required suspension of judgement, a suspense which will lead to tranquillity of spirit or unperturbedness. The suspension of judgement includes not only reactions to sensory experiences but also to logic, physics, and ethics, i.e. the systematic bodies of knowledge recognized by antique science. Hume agreed with the Pyrrhonists that no rational

3 Quoted in Annas and Barnes, *The Modes of Scepticism* (Cambridge, 1985), p. 25.

justification could be given either for the beliefs of common life or for scientific and philosophical beliefs. Here Hume is a 'theoretical sceptic'. Theoretical scepticism is wholly unmitigated except for immediate sensory beliefs[4] and is the proper stance toward scientific hypotheses, including those set out in the *Dialogues*.

But, unlike the Pyrrhonians, Hume feels we are unable to withhold assent from the beliefs of common life. The result is a view he calls variously 'mitigated' or 'moderate scepticism'. This leads to the famous statement in the *Treatise* that 'Nature, by an absolute and uncontroulable necessity has determin'd us to judge as well as to breathe and feel' (T. 183).

The double nature of Humean scepticism, its denial and its assent, is expressed in the following passage from Part I:

> To whatever length any one may push his speculative principles of scepticism, he must act, I own, and live, and converse like other men; and for this conduct he is not obliged to give any other reason than the absolute necessity he lies under of so doing. . . . To philosophise on such subjects [natural or moral subjects] is nothing essentially different from reasoning on common life. . . . All sceptics pretend, that, if reason be considered in an abstract view, it furnishes invincible arguments against itself, and that we could never retain any conviction or assurance, on any subject, were not the sceptical reasonings so refined and subtile, that they are not able to counterpoise the more solid and more natural arguments, derived from the senses and experience. But it is evident, whenever our arguments lose this advantage, and run wide of common life, that the most refined scepticism comes to be upon a footing with them, and is able to oppose and counterbalance them. The one has no more weight than the other. The mind must remain in suspense between them; and it is that very suspense or balance, which is the triumph of scepticism. (D. 101–2)

In effect, two kinds of scepticism are examined in this passage: pyrrhonian and moderate scepticism. Philo argues throughout that Cleanthes is the Pyrrhonist and he is the moderate sceptic. The passage is the key to Philo's scepticism about the Deity's moral attributes in Parts 10 and 11 of the *Dialogues*.

4 I borrow the term from Robert J. Fogelin, *Hume's Scepticism in the Treatise of Human Nature* (London, Routledge & Kegan Paul, 1985), Ch. 1.

To support this contention I will cite two passages from Parts 1–8 and compare them with a later passage to show that Philo's stance toward Cleanthes' arguments is consistent throughout the *Dialogues*. The first passage runs as follows:

> [W]ere I obliged to defend any particular system of this nature (which I never willingly should do), I esteem none more plausible than that which ascribes an eternal, inherent principle of order to the world; though attended with great and continual revolutions and alterations. (D. 136–7)

Philo here exhibits reluctance to give causal hypotheses a high degree of probability, his usual stance. The second passage I have in mind is at the end of Part 6. Philo once again claims that Cleanthes is the real Pyrrhonian:

> All these systems, then, of scepticism, polytheism, and theism, you must allow, on your principles, to be on a like footing, and that no one of them has any advantages over the others. You may thence learn the fallacy of your principles. (D. 137)

But precisely the same picture emerges in Philo's speech at the end of Part 10, the speech in which Philo tells Cleanthes it is now his turn 'to tug the labouring oar' (D. 160):

> I must use the freedom to admonish you, CLEANTHES, that you have put this controversy upon a most dangerous issue, and are unawares introducing a total scepticism into the most essential articles of natural and revealed theology. . . . [B]y your resting the whole system of religion on a point, which, from its very nature, must for ever be uncertain, you tacitly confess, that that system is equally uncertain. (D. 159)

The labouring oar that Cleanthes must now tug is to show that he is not a Pyrrhonian, as Philo claims.

Hume's complex attitude toward religion is consistent throughout his writings. His central purpose in discussing religion was to isolate the subject so that it would have no real effect on social and moral life. Hume's main rational argument, in contrast to whatever emotional or psychological attitudes influenced him, was the ever-intractable problem of evil. This is the problem which gives Hume such a low opinion of religion. Philo says in Part 10:

> I will allow, that pain or misery in man is *compatible* with infinite

power and goodness in the Deity, even in your sense of these attributes: What are you advanced by all these concessions? . . . You must *prove* these pure, unmixed, and uncontrollable attributes from the present mixed and confused phenomena, and from these alone. A hopeful undertaking! (D. 159–60)

However, Cleanthes and Philo share a belief in an empirical theism. In Part 12 Philo says:

that the cause or causes of order in the universe probably bear some remote analogy to human intelligence. (D. 184)

We know that this is Hume's own position from what he tells us in *The Natural History of Religion:*[5]

The whole frame of nature bespeaks an intelligent author; and no rational enquirer can after serious reflection, suspend his belief a moment 'with regard to the primary principles of genuine theism and religion.'

The argument in the *Dialogues* can be divided into four sections. The first section, running from Parts 1 to 2, examines the argument from analogy, with Philo showing the weakness of the analogy as an inductive argument. The second division of the argument occurs in Part 3 in which Cleanthes introduces the 'irregular argument':

Whatever cavils may be urged; an orderly world, as well as a coherent, articulate speech, will still be received as an incontestable proof of design and intention. (D. 119)

In the third division, Parts 10 and 11, the moral attributes of the Deity are examined. The final section, Part 12, summarizes the discussion.

Philo's argument in Parts 10 and 11 is designed primarily to show that we cannot have *knowledge* of the moral attributes of the Deity, his providence, justice, love, and mercy. All we can comprehend are his natural attributes, his intelligence and power. The existence of the Deity is accepted because of entirely non-rational tendencies in human nature, not because of rational proofs. (I will bypass discussion of the moot question of whether belief in the Deity is a so-called 'natural belief' or not.)

The result is that, although both Cleanthes and Philo claim the title 'theist', they mean quite different things by the term. Cleanthes

5 *Natural History of Religion*, reprinted in *Hume on Religion*, ed. Richard Wollheim (New York, Fontana Library, 1963), p. 31.

believes that we can know both the natural and the moral attributes of the Deity by an inductive argument similar to those found in science, a version of the so-called 'parity' argument. Philo denies this because he has a very different conception of the Deity.

Philo speaks of God both as divine Being and a supreme intelligence. In Part 10 the divine attributes are said to be infinitely perfect but incomprehensible. But since these attributes are incomprehensible the most we can have is a natural piety toward the Deity. As Philo says in Part 2:

> Nothing exists without a cause; and the original cause of this universe (whatever it be) we call GOD; and *piously ascribe* to him every species of perfection. . . . But as all perfection is entirely relative, we ought never to imagine, that we comprehend the attributes of this divine Being, or to suppose, that his perfections have any analogy or likeness to the perfections of a human creature. (D. 108, my emphasis)

At this point the famous incomplete syllogism is introduced:

> Our ideas reach no farther than our experience: We have no experience of divine attributes and operations: I need not conclude my syllogism. (D. 108)

One might ask, if God is not the God to whom one can bend the knee, nor is he the metaphysical God of the philosophers, what function does he perform for the Philonian Hume? The answer is given at the end of Part 12: be a Humean philosophical sceptic. When Hume talks of religion we occasionally hear the 'other voice', the rueful voice of natural piety:

> [B]elieve me, CLEANTHES, the most natural sentiment, which a well-disposed mind will feel on this occasion, is a longing desire and expectation, that Heaven would be pleased to dissipate, at least alleviate, this profound ignorance, by affording some more particular revelation to mankind, and making discoveries of the nature, attributes, and operations of the divine object of our faith. (D. 185)

This last point can be emphasized by recalling Philo's contrast between true religion and the 'vulgar superstition' which he despises. The former is described in Philo's last speech in the *Dialogues:*

> To be a philosophical sceptic is, in a man of letters, the first and

most essential step towards being a sound, believing Christian. (D. 185)

The latter, however, is totally pernicious:

> How happens it then . . . if vulgar superstition be so salutary to society, that all history abounds so much with accounts of its pernicious consequences on public affairs? Factions, civil wars, persecutions, subversions of government, oppression, slavery; these are the dismal consequences which always attend its prevalency over the minds of men. (D. 177)

The causal hypotheses under review throughout concern the value of the observational evidence that can be adduced for the Deity's nature. For Philo, the sceptic, the probability of the observational evidence confirming the hypothesis is low; for Cleanthes, the dogmatist, it is high. Philo states his own position in a well-known and controversial passage from Part 12:

> It seems evident, that the dispute between the sceptics [Philo] and dogmatists [Cleanthes] is entirely verbal, or at least regards only the degrees of doubt and assurance, which we ought to indulge with regard to all reasoning: And such disputes are commonly at the bottom, verbal, and admit not of any precise determination. No philosophical dogmatist denies, that there are difficulties both with regard to the senses and to all science: and that these difficulties are in a regular, logical method, absolutely insolveable. No sceptic denies, that we lie under an absolute necessity, notwithstanding these difficulties, of thinking, and believing, and reasoning with regard to all kind of subjects, and even of frequently assenting with confidence and security. The only difference, then, between these sects, if they merit that name, is, that the sceptic, from habit, caprice, or inclination, insists most on the difficulties; the dogmatist, for like reasons, on the necessity. (D. 177)

We know from the researches of Kemp Smith that this passage was probably written in 1776, after the manuscript was completed, and that Hume attached considerable importance to it. The operative phrase in this long passage is that the causal hypotheses at the basis of the dispute *'admit of no determination'*.

The result of my analysis is in no way novel. Although Philo–Hume does not destroy the Design Argument, he delivered it a blow from which it has never recovered. There is a consensus, after Hume, that the Argument from Design is too weak an inductive argument for a successful case to be built upon it. Moreover, in Parts 10 and 11 Philo–Hume showed the weaknesses of inferences about either the Deity's intelligence and power – his natural attributes – or his moral attributes, like providential care.

The substantive differences between Philo and Cleanthes remain immense. The reason is simple: a Philonian causal hypothesis about the creation of the world or the character is worthless as a rational argument. Its probative force arises only from the passional side of our nature. The bed-rock difference between Philo and Cleanthes arises from Philo's theoretical scepticism about all causal hypotheses. Because Cleanthes does not recognize the distinction he is continually forced, albeit from Philo's malice, into the position of an extreme pyrrhonism – a position which Philo (and Hume himself) had weighed and found wanting.

Although no hypotheses can escape Humean scepticism, the causal hypotheses in religion and those in science are fundamentally different for Hume. Scientific causal hypotheses can be judged by general rules and the rules by which we judge of causes and effects. But religious hypotheses cannot be so analysed since they lack precise determination. The result is that, although Tweyman has made an interesting suggestion about the role of scientific hypotheses in Parts 10 and 11, the application by Cleanthes to religion of results drawn from science is minimally effective. Philo shows the greatest respect for scientific results understood in his own sceptical terms, but science does not give anything of value to religion.

COMMENTS ON TWEYMAN
AND DAVIS

George Nathan

Tweyman contends that in Parts 10 and 11 of the *Dialogues* Philo sets
aside his pyrrhonian or sceptical approach to theology, which consists
in falsifying or casting doubt on the hypothesis of Cleanthes, and
instead argues for a thesis of his own, viz. what we might call the
'indifference thesis', that the original source of all things is morally
indifferent.[1] Davis counters with an alternative interpretation of
these two Parts of the *Dialogues,* arguing that Philo's approach to
Cleanthes' arguments is consistent throughout the *Dialogues* and that
Philo's aim is always the same, viz. to show that, if Cleanthes remains
true to his principles and accepts their logical consequences, it is
Cleanthes who is the Pyrrhonian and Philo who is the moderate
sceptic. My position is that neither Tweyman nor Davis has given a
proper analysis of Parts 10 and 11.

I would agree with Davis that Tweyman's position does seem to have
an initial implausibility to it for at least two reasons. First of all, in Part 2
Philo commits himself to the 'mystical incomprehensibility thesis' that
the attributes of God are perfect but incomprehensible; and the mystical
incomprehensibility thesis is incompatible with the indifference thesis. It
cannot be the case both that God has perfect but incomprehensible
attributes and that we also know he is morally indifferent. Moreover, the
mystical incomprehensibility thesis is reiterated in Part 6 and, more
importantly, in Part 10: 'None but we mystics, as you were pleased to
call us, can account for this strange mixture of phenomena, by deriving it
from attributes, infinitely perfect, but incomprehensible' (D. 157).[2]
Since Philo appears to stick to the mystical incomprehensibility thesis,

<hr>

1 Stanley Tweyman, 'Hume's Dialogues on Evil,' in this volume. All references in
  the text to this paper will be cited as 'Tweyman' followed by the relevant page
  number(s).
2 All page references to the *Dialogues* refer to the version printed in this volume.

Tweyman has a problem explaining how Philo can hold one position on the attributes of God in Part 10 (the mystical incomprehensibility thesis) and then supposedly reverse himself in Part 11 to argue for another (the indifference thesis). Second, Tweyman's position seems to contradict the strategic position outlined by Philo in Part 2: 'You seem not to apprehend, replied Philo, that I argue with Cleanthes in his own way; and by showing him the dangerous consequences of his tenets, hope at last to reduce him to our opinion' (D. 111). The strategy is to show Cleanthes that any position but that of the mystics has dangerous, i.e. sceptical or theologically unwelcome consequences, and so should be abandoned. Philo's strategy is not to defend his own position, but rather to reveal the weaknesses in Cleanthes' position.

Thus far I would agree that Davis's interpretation is more consistent with both Philo's strategic position and with his mystical incomprehensibility thesis. Yet Davis does not directly take up the important point about Parts 10 and 11 which Tweyman raises: that Philo changes his way of arguing in Parts 10 and 11 from that which he had been employing previously in the first eight sections, i.e. that he changes from a pyrrhonian to a non-pyrrhonian way of arguing. This is how Tweyman puts it:

> In the first eight sections, Philo argues against Cleanthes' hypothesis by advancing his own hypotheses. His effort to advance hypotheses must be assessed in light of the fact that (by his own admission) all such hypotheses are based on insufficient data, and, therefore, none is, strictly speaking, acceptable. Their use is not to establish truths about the nature of God, but to establish the conclusion which we find at the end of Part 8 that 'a total suspense of judgment is here our only reasonable resource.' The design of the world is compatible with, and could have arisen from, an indefinite number of designing principles. On the other hand, we have seen that in dealing with Cleanthes' hypotheses in Parts 10 and 11 we are able to proceed more scientifically, and, in this manner, eliminate all but one of the hypotheses which can be introduced to explain the design of the world. (Tweyman, 194)

Now Tweyman does seem to have a point here. It is true that Philo takes his arguments in Parts 10 and 11 to have a conclusiveness which he did not attribute to his arguments in Parts 1–8. But at least part of the explanation for Philo's confidence in his arguments about God's moral attributes, as Tweyman himself recognizes, is that there is no dispute about the data from which inferences are to be drawn: all the participants agree that the world contains both good and evil and that the data, therefore, consist of mixed phenomena. Consequently, one source of sceptical argument, viz. how the data are to be classified, has been eliminated, and, therefore, it is not surprising that one of Philo's typical modes of sceptical argumentation cannot be found in Parts 10 and 11. But ambiguities in the data are not the only source of dispute between Philo and Cleanthes. Something that both Tweyman and Davis overlook is that one of the major differences between Philo and Cleanthes is over the question of mysticism versus anthropomorphism, i.e. whether the attributes of God are to be conceived as strongly resembling those of man. This difference is obvious in Part 10 where Philo attempts to dislodge Cleanthes from his anthropomorphism:

> And is it possible, Cleanthes, said Philo, that after all these reflections, and infinitely more, which might be suggested, you can still persevere in your anthropomorphism, and assert the moral attributes of the Deity, his justice, benevolence, mercy, and rectitude, to be of the same nature with these virtues in human creatures? (D. 156)

Cleanthes' first response to this challenge is not to deny his anthropomorphism, but to deny the data, i.e. 'to deny absolutely the misery and wickedness of man' (D. 158). At this juncture Philo introduces the point noted by Davis, viz. that Cleanthes' position is verging on scepticism, because to the extent that the foundations of religion depend on establishing the unestablishable, that the quantity of goodness or pleasure in the world exceeds the quantity of evil or pain, Cleanthes is introducing total scepticism into the foundations of religion. The important point here, not noticed by Davis, is that Philo is forcing Cleanthes into a sceptical position, not because he wants to ironically present Cleanthes as the Pyrrhonian and he as the moderate sceptic, but rather in order to get Cleanthes to abandon his anthropomorphism by showing him its dangerous consequences. In the ensuing Part 11, Cleanthes acknowledges the point and the force of Philo's argument:

> *If we preserve human analogy,* we must for ever find it impossible to reconcile any mixture of evil in the universe with infinite attributes, much less, can we ever prove the latter from the former (D. 161, my emphasis).

His point is that Philo's arguments are taken to be decisive against an anthropomorphism which Cleanthes cannot discard. Since he cannot abandon anthropomorphism, Cleanthes' only remaining out is to abandon the claim that God has infinite attributes. But even this will not save Cleanthes' position. Philo's point in Part 11 is that, on the agreed-upon data, the most probable inference is that God lacks both moral goodness and moral malice, *when those moral attributes are characterized anthropomorphically*. Philo says: 'so long as there is any vice at all in the universe, it will very much puzzle you anthropomorphites, how to account for it' (D. 169). Philo's point, then, is a sceptical, not a metaphysical one: if Cleanthes persists in his anthropomorphism and experimental theism on the topic of the moral attributes of God, the consequences are the undermining of his own position. Cleanthes must choose: abandon religion or anthropomorphism.

Both Davis and Tweyman fail to pay enough attention to the issue of Philo's anti-anthropomorphism. This leads them in opposite directions: Davis sees correctly that Philo continues to argue sceptically in Parts 10 and 11, but mistakenly focuses on the question of scepticism as the lesson of these parts and fails to notice that the issue of anthropomorphism is central. Tweyman, on the other hand, although noting correctly that a certain type of sceptical argument is irrelevant to Parts 10 and 11, is mistakenly led to interpret Philo as abandoning all sceptical arguments and instead embracing scientific proofs of the moral indifference of God. However, that mine is the more plausible interpretation of Philo's moves in Part 11 is confirmed by reference to Part 12 of the *Dialogues,* to which Tweyman himself appeals to shore up his interpretation. But, if Tweyman were correct in his interpretation, we should expect Philo in Part 12 to be endorsing, or at least saying things consistent with, the indifference thesis. What we actually find is Philo continuing to maintain the moral perfection of God: 'For, as the supreme Being is allowed to be absolutely and entirely perfect, whatever differs most from him departs the farthest from the supreme standard of rectitude and perfection' (D. 176-7).

I conclude, then, that Tweyman is correct about Philo's abandoning sceptical argument only to the extent that he is correct that Philo has abandoned one kind of sceptical argument, that based on the ambiguity of the data; but he is not correct that Philo has ceased to argue sceptically at all in those Parts of the *Dialogues,* inasmuch as Philo does continue to present, not his own view, but rather 'inconveniences of anthropomorphism'. What is puzzling, however, and not accounted for by either Tweyman or Davis is the nature of and justification for

Philo's 'mystical incomprehensibility thesis'. Unlocking the mysteries of Philo's mysticism may yet give access to the key to the *Dialogues*.

COMMENTARY ON
PROFESSOR TWEYMAN'S
'HUME ON EVIL'

P. S. Wadia

Philo concludes his long and celebrated debate with Cleanthes on the problem of evil (Parts 10 and 11 of Hume's *Dialogues*) with the assertion that the 'true conclusion' to be drawn from the 'mixed phenomena' in the world is that 'the original source' of whatever order we find in the world is 'indifferent' to matters of good and evil. From what Philo says immediately thereafter it is clear that by the phrase 'The true conclusion is . . .' he does not mean 'The truth is . . .' but rather something like 'The conclusion best supported by the available evidence is . . .' (D. 169)[1].

Now, according to both Nelson Pike and Stanley Tweyman, the claim made by Philo in these passages involves him in a shift or departure from the procedure he adopted in earlier dialogues when he examined the Design Argument set forth by Cleanthes. It is claimed that whereas in the earlier dialogues Philo emphatically professed a sceptical outlook – 'the view requiring that one embrace no metaphysical position of one's own' (to quote Nelson Pike)[2] – in the quoted passage he seems to abandon this scepticism in favour of embracing what amounts to being a metaphysical position in natural theology. Pike thinks that this alleged shift is only an apparent one, that the central import of these passages is sceptical rather than metaphysical, and that, as elsewhere in the earlier dialogues, Philo's sole purpose in offering a more plausible counter-hypothesis is to show that Cleanthes' hypothesis is false. Tweyman, on the other hand, argues that the shift is a very real one and that Hume does indeed 'intend Philo's conclusion in Part XI to be a truth in natural theology. . . . Philo is not

---

1 All references to the *Dialogues* refer to the version printed in this volume.
2 See Nelson Pike's Commentary on the *Dialogues Concerning Natural Religion* (New York: Bobbs-Merrill 1970), p. 201. All page references to Pike in the body of this paper are to this extended commentary which includes a slightly revised version of the relevant passages from his 'Hume on Evil' referred to by Tweyman on p. 188 of this volume.

arguing as a sceptic; rather he is employing the hypothetico-deductive method for testing Cleanthes' hypothesis'.[3]

Let me say at once that I agree with Tweyman, as against Pike, that in these passages Philo does claim to put forward a truth *in* natural theology, and I also agree with just about everything that Tweyman says in his paper concerning the proper interpretation of Philo's views in Parts 10 and 11 leading up to this conclusion. I follow the lead of those scholars who, at least since Kemp Smith, have argued that Philo's whole purpose in demonstrating such 'truths' is to discredit natural theology in the eyes of a true Christian believer by dramatizing the enormous gulf between the very attenuated form of theism ('diaphonous deism', one scholar calls it), which is the most one can hope to get out of Cleanthes' experimental approach to religion, and the claim of Christian theism to which Cleanthes aspires. But I do not accept the view that Philo's claim in these dialogues represents any sort of sudden departure (and certainly not a 'fundamental methodological difference') from his critical stance against the Design Argument in earlier dialogues. What I hope to show below is that not only does this view distort what Philo does in the earlier dialogues, but it also distracts our attention from the true nature of Hume's achievement in Parts 10 and 11 of the *Dialogues*. (Incidentally, I will assume throughout the sequel that Kemp Smith's identification of Hume with Philo is essentially correct.)

It would indeed be extremely paradoxical, in the face of Philo's famous (or notorious) peroration at the end of Part 8 proclaiming the 'complete triumph of the sceptic' in regard to 'all religious systems', to raise any doubts about Philo's acceptance of the sceptical import of his own earlier arguments. But this still leaves unsettled the question as to what sort of scepticism it is whose triumph Philo proclaims at this point and whether it is inconsistent with the conclusion he reaches at the end of his discussion of evil.

One would have hoped that, at this late stage in the scholarship on the *Dialogues,* if there is one issue on which all of us could agree it is that Philo at no time in the *Dialogues* takes the (easy) pyrrhonian line against Cleanthes' 'hypothesis of experimental theism'. I mention this because at several places in his paper Tweyman characterizes Philo's scepticism in the first eight parts of the dialogues as being of the pyrrhonian variety. I will assume that this is simply a lax way of using the term 'pyrrhonian,' as if it were synonymous with 'scepticism,' and let it go at that. If, now, we turn to Pike, whose view Tweyman is criticizing after all, it is clear (see the quote above) that for him the view Philo

3 Stanley Tweyman, 'Hume's Dialogues on Evil,' in this volume, pp. 187–95.

pretends to depart from in the dialogues on evil is *mitigated* scepticism, whose positivistic prescriptions require us to eschew all metaphysical speculations and confine our philosophizing to the 'unavoidable' reasoning of 'common life and experience'.

The puzzling thing about Pike's position is that, in his detailed and very useful discussion of the early dialogues in his longer commentary on them, Philo is shown as agreeing to drop his principled opposition to metaphysical speculations with which he opens his criticism of Cleanthes' proof of God's existence, long before the dialogues on evil. I cannot of course do any justice to Pike's commentary but very, very briefly the situation with regard to the early dialogues he describes may be summed up as follows. Cleanthes' proof is offered as an 'argument from experience' and, as such, it is subjected by Philo to a rigorous examination in accordance with 'the normal canons of adequacy that apply to all inferences of this general sort' (Pike, 134). At the centre of this proof is the claim that the universe as a whole belongs to the class of ordered systems whose other members are human artefacts such as watches and houses. Now, according to Pike, the central thrust of Philo's criticisms in Part 2 of the *Dialogues* is that Cleanthes' 'hypothesis of design' is '*conceptually immature*' because order in the universe is not 'an empirically identifiable datum' (Pike, 156–7 and 164). So far Philo cannot be said to have gone beyond the narrow confines of mitigated scepticism. To continue with Pike's account, he says that after two interludes when Philo returns to his attack on Cleanthes' hypothesis (Parts 5 to 8) he assumes, though only for the sake of argument, that this 'hypothesis is a possible explanation of a genuine fact' (Pike, 175). What Philo now does is to subject Cleanthes' hypothesis to a comparative test with other putative explanations for order in the universe and concludes that none of these explanations, and certainly not Cleanthes', is a clear winner in this competition. He ends with the peroration mentioned above recommending a 'total suspense of judgement' in regard to all such explanations.

I have no quarrel with Pike's description of what takes place in Parts 1 and 2 and from Parts 5 to 7. I would argue, however, that when Philo accepts there must be *some* explanation for order in the universe, he is genuinely conceding this point to Cleanthes, although Pike's contention is that Philo is doing this simply to move the argument forward. My difference with Pike here stems from our radically different readings of Part 2 of the *Dialogues*,[4] an issue I do not need to go into here. What I wish to contend here is simply that, given Pike's interpretation of the

4 See my 'Pike on Part III of Hume's *Dialogues*', *Rel. Stud.* 14, pp. 325–40.

relevant earlier dialogues, the scepticism with which Philo concludes Part 8 is altogether different in kind from the scepticism we encounter in Part 2. Whereas the scepticism of Part 8 results from the application of normal procedures of scientific enquiry, Philo's scepticism in Part 2 does not permit such an enquiry even to get off the ground, because of his contention there that we have no clear notion of what it is we are enquiring about. Or, to put the matter slightly differently, even to allow (as Philo is said to allow beginning with Part 5) the mere possibility of a transcendent explanation for the order in the universe being true, is to 'carry our speculations into the two eternities' and, thus, to abandon the strictures against metaphysics laid down by Philo in the first two parts of the *Dialogues*. But then, if what I have just said is correct, what Philo does in Parts 10 and 11, concluding with the claim with which these comments began, does not constitute a radical break from his method of philosophizing in the immediately preceding parts. In other words, to say that he is engaged in doing metaphysics in one place but not in the other is not a proper way of characterizing how Philo's claims in the earlier and later dialogues differ from each other.

To return now to Tweyman, I find that he locates the difference between Philo's viewpoints in these two sets of dialogues in the proper place but that he misdescribes this difference. Tweyman is essentially correct in characterizing this difference by the thesis that the earlier dialogues deal with the natural attributes of the Deity and the available empirical data are insufficient to warrant the acceptance of any explanatory hypothesis. But in the later dialogues on evil, he argues, sufficient empirical evidence is available to enable us 'to proceed more scientifically, and, in this manner, eliminate all but one of the hypotheses.' But Tweyman is altogether mistaken when he says that this explains 'why there is a fundamental methodological difference' between the manner in which Philo proceeds in these dialogues. As a matter of fact, there is no difference in Philo's method in the two places. In both places Philo is using the self-same method – the 'hypothetico-deductive' method as Tweyman prefers to call it – but with different results simply because the data to which the method is applied in the two places are so very different. One is not necessarily proceeding 'less scientifically' simply because the data one happens to be examining do not warrant drawing a definite conclusion!

Let me point out finally what I believe Hume's achievement in these dialogues to be: one part of the achievement is philosophical in a straightforward way, whereas the other can more properly be described as being of a literary kind.

One of the dominant themes in Christian (and most other varieties of) monotheism is that the creator of the universe is a benevolent and just being who is morally concerned with the ultimate well-being of his creatures. Philo's philosophical achievement in Parts 10 and 11 of Hume's *Dialogues* consists in his demonstrating to a natural theologian like Cleanthes that his preferred method of experimental proof for the existence of a designer for the order in the universe can be turned against him when it comes to proving the moral attributes of such a designer. Grant to Cleanthes that we cannot reject his hypothesis of design, 'without the greatest violence' to common sense (D. 119) – where does that get him? As long as there is even a smidgen of what Philo calls 'avoidable' evil in the world, inference to God's moral attributes remains problematic. Cleanthes cannot appeal to common sense and the argument from experience at one stage and deny the consequences of just this sort of appeal at the next stage in the discussion. That Philo is perfectly aware he has set just this trap for Cleanthes is quite evident from the well-known final paragraph of Part 10, wherein he concedes to Cleanthes that 'Formerly, when we argued concerning the natural attributes of intelligence and design, I needed all my sceptical and metaphysical subtilty to elude your grasp.' But, he goes on, it is Cleanthes' 'turn now to tug the labouring oar, and to support your philosophical subtilties against the dictates of plain reason and experience' (D. 160). Cleanthes' only response to this challenge is to propose a 'new theory' of a 'finitely perfect' but omni-benevolent deity to account for the existence of evil – a move, as we have just been shown, which gets him nowhere.

What I have called the more literary side of Hume's achievement in the dialogues on evil has to do with the confrontation between Philo and Demea that takes place toward the very end of Part 11. As happens not infrequently in these *Dialogues*, Hume is at this point taking advantage of the dialectical interplay which is inherent in the logical structures of the arguments he is dealing with, in order to make what, broadly speaking, we may call a literary point. In the confrontation between Philo and Demea, Hume, I believe, is using this kind of an interplay as a device deliberately to unmask Philo and thus, since I identify Hume with Philo, reveal his own views in this matter. By the time the discussion on evil is brought to a close, it has begun to dawn on the slow-witted Demea that Philo, without putting it in so many words, has confronted him with a dilemma: either go along with Cleanthes' 'experimental theism', in which case the most you can get is a Deity who is indifferent to moral good and evil, or go the whole hog with your 'sceptical fideism', in which case you end with a Deity whose moral, no less than natural, 'attributes [are] infinitely perfect but incomprehensible'. Demea, who has obviously not confronted the lesson of the biblical story of Job and his three worldly-wise friends, has no stomach for this dilemma and leaves the company much distraught and perplexed. Meantime, Hume has exposed the fatal flaws both in Cleanthes' 'anthropomorphism' and Demea's 'mysticism' which leave no middle ground for the ordinary Christian believer to stand upon. Only later will an extraordinary Christian believer like Hamann (followed much later still by Kierkegaard and his modern-day progeny) have the courage of Demea's convictions to revel in the 'adorable mystery' and 'absolute incomprehensibility' of the God of religious faith. But that is a different story. All I wanted to do here was to show that there is a price to be paid for this misreading of the *Dialogues* that denies that Philo consistently uses the same method when dealing with the natural as well as moral attributes of the original source or sources of order in the universe.

BIBLIOGRAPHY

Agassi, J. 'A Note on Smith's Term "Naturalism".' *Hume Studies*, 12, 1986, 92–6.

Aiken, H. D. ed. *Dialogues Concerning Natural Religion by David Hume*, with Introduction. New York: Hafner Publishing Co., 1948.

Anderson, R. F. *Hume's First Principles*. Lincoln: University of Nebraska Press, 1966.

Andic, M. 'Experimental Theism and the Verbal Dispute in Hume's "Dialogues".'*Archiv für Geschichteder Philosophie*, 56, 1974, 239–46.

Austin, W. 'Philo's Reversal.' *Philosophical Topics*, 13, 1985, 103–12.

Ayer, A. J. *Hume*. Oxford: Oxford University Press, 1980.

Badia-Cabrera, M. 'Hume's Natural History of Religion: Positive Science or Metaphysical Vision of Religion.' *Dialogos*, 45, 1985, 71–7.

Barker, S. 'Hume on the Logic of Design.' *Hume Studies*, 9, 1983, 1–18.

Basu, D. K. 'Who is the Real Hume in the Dialogues?' *Indian Phil. Quarterly*, 6, 1978, 21–8.

Battersby, C. 'The *Dialogues* as Original Imitation: Cicero and the Nature of Hume's Skepticism,' in *McGill Hume Studies*, ed. D. F. Norton, N. Capaldi & W. Robison. San Diego: Austin Hill Press, 1979, 239–53.

Beaty, M. D. 'The Problem of Evil: The Unanswered Questions Argument.' *Southwest Philosophical Review*, 4, 1988, 57–64.

Boys Smith, J. S. 'Hume's Dialogues Concerning Natural Religion.' *Journal of Theological Studies*, 37, 1936, 337–49.

Bricke, J. 'On the Interpretation of Hume's Dialogues.' *Religious Studies*, 11, 1975, 1–18.

Bricke, J. 'Hume on Self-Identity, Memory and Causality,' in *David Hume: Bicentenary Papers*, ed. G. P. Morice. Edinburgh: Edinburgh University Press, 1977.

Burch, R. 'Bayesianism and Analogy in Hume's Dialogues.' *Hume Studies*, 6, 1980, 32–44.

Butler, R. 'Natural Belief and the Enigma of Hume.' *Archiv für Geschichteder Philosophie*, 14, 1983, 65–70.

Calvert, B. 'Another Problem About Part IX of Hume's Dialogues.' *International Journal of the Philosophy of Religion*, 14, 1983, 65–70.

Capaldi, N. 'Hume's Philosophy of Religion: God Without Ethics.' *International Journal of the Philosophy of Religion*, 1, 1970, 233–40.

Capaldi, N. *David Hume, The Newtonian Philosopher*, Boston: Twayne, 1975.

Capitan, W. H. 'Part X of Hume's Dialogues.' *American Philosophical Quarterly*, 3, 1966, 82–6.

Carter, W. B. 'The Structure of Hume's Dialogues,' in *Early Modern Philosophy*, ed. G. Moyal & S. Tweyman. Delmar, NY: Caravan Books, 1985, 289–336.

Clarke, B. L. 'The Argument from Design: A Piece of Abductive Reasoning.' *International Journal of the Philosophy of Religion*, 5, 1974, 65–78.

Clarke, B. L. 'The Argument from Design.' *American Journal of Theo. Philosophy*, 1, 1980, 98–108.

Clive, G. 'Hume's Dialogues Reconsidered.' *Journal of Religion*, 39, 1959, 110–19.

Cohen, D. *The Essential Works of David Hume*. Bantam Books, 1965.

Coleman, D. 'An Interpretation of Hume's *Dialogues*.' *Religious Studies*, 25, 1989, 179–90.

Costa, M. J. 'Hume and Justified Belief.' *Canadian Journal of Philosophy*, 11, 1981, 219–28.

Davis, J. W. 'Going Out the Window: A Comment on Tweyman.' *Hume Studies*, 13, 1987, 86–97.

Doore, G. 'The Argument from Design: Some Better Reasons for Agreeing with Hume.' *Religious Studies*, 16, 1980, 145–61.

Duerlinger, J. 'The Verbal Dispute in Hume's Dialogues.' *Archiv für Geschichte der Philosophie*, 53, 1971, 22–34.

Dye, J. 'Superhuman Speech and Biological Books.' *History of Philosophy Quarterly*, 5, 1988.

Dye, J. 'A Word on Behalf of Demea.' *Hume Studies*, 15, 1989, 120–40.

Flew, A. 'Hume's Philosophy of Religion,' in *Philosophers Ancient and Modern*, ed. G. Vesey. New York: Cambridge University Press, 1986, pp. 129–46.

Flew, A. *Hume's Philosophy of Belief*. London: Routledge & Kegan Paul, 1961.

Force, James E. 'Hume in the *Dialogues*, the Dictates of Convention, and the Millennial Future State of Biblical Prophecy.' *Southwest Journal of Philosophy*, 8, 1977, 131–41.

Franklin, J. 'More on Part IX of Hume's Dialogues.' *Philosophical Quarterly*, 30, 1980, 69–71.

Gaskin, J. C. 'God, Hume and Natural Belief.' *Philosophy*, 49, 1974, 281–94.

Gaskin, J. C. 'The Design Argument: Hume's Critique of Poor Reason.' *Religious Studies*, 12, 1976, 331–45.

Gaskin, J. C. 'Hume's Criticism of the Argument from Design.' *Revue Internationale de Philosophie*, 30, 1976, 64–78.

Gaskin, J. C. 'Hume's Critique of Religion.' *Journal of the History of Philosophy*, 14, 1976, 301–11.

Gaskin, J. C. *Hume's Philosophy of Religion*. London: Macmillan, 1978.

Gaskin, J. C. 'Hume's Attenuated Design.' *Archiv für Geschichte der Philosophie*, 65, 1983, 160–73.

Gaskin, J. C. *Hume's Philosophy of Religion*. 2nd edn. New Jersey: Humanities Press International, 1988.

Gawlick, G. 'Hume and the Deists: a Reconsideration,' in *David Hume: Bicentenary Papers*, ed. G. P. Morice, Edinburgh: Edinburgh University Press, 1977.

Ginsberg, M. *Mind and Belief: Psychological Ascription and the Concept of Belief*. New York: Humanities Press, 1972.

Grieg, Y., ed. *The Letters of David Hume*, Oxford: Oxford University Press, two vols, repr. 1969.

Hambourger, R. 'The Argument from Design,' in *Intention and Intentionality*, ed. C. Diamond. Ithaca: Cornell University Press, 1979, pp. 109–31.

Harris, H. S. 'The "Naturalness" of Natural Religion.' *Hume Studies*, 13, 1987, 1–29.

Harward, D. W. 'Hume's Dialogues Revisited.' *International Journal of the Philosophy of Religion*, 6, 1975, 137–53.

Hearn, T. K. 'Norman Kemp Smith on Natural Belief.' *Southern Journal of Philosophy*, 7, 1969, 3–7.

Heath, P. 'The Incredulous Hume.' *American Philosophical Quarterly*, 13, 1976, 159–63.

Hendel, C. W. *Studies in the Philosophy of David Hume*. Indianapolis: Bobbs-Merrill, 1963.

Henze, D. F. 'On Some Alleged Humean Insights and Oversights.' *Religious Studies*, 6, 1970, 369–77.

Hiley, D. R. *Philosophy in Question*. Chicago: University of Chicago Press, 1988.

Hodges, M. & Lachs, J. 'Hume on Belief.' *Review of Metaphysics*, 30, 1976, 3–18.

Hurlbutt, R. H. 'David Hume and Scientific Theism.' *Journal of the History of Ideas*, 47, 1956, 486–97.

Hurlbutt, R. H. *Hume, Newton and the Design Argument*. 2nd edn, Lincoln: University of Nebraska Press, 1985.

Hurlbutt, R. H. 'The Careless Skeptic – the "Pamphilian" Ironies in Hume's Dialogues.' *Hume Studies*, 14, 1988, 207–50.

Immerwahr, J. 'David Hume on Incompatible Religious Beliefs.' *International Stud. Phil.*, 16, 1984, 25–34.

Jacobson, N. P. 'The Uses of Reason in Religion: A Note on David Hume.' *Journal of Religion*, 39, 1959, 103–9.

Jacquette, D. 'Analogical Inference in Hume's Philosophy of Religion.' *Faith and Philosophy*, 2, 1985, 287–94.

James, E. D. 'Scepticism and Religious Belief: Pascal, Bayle, Hume,' in *Classical Influences on Western Thought A. D. 1650–1870*, ed. R. R. Bolgar, Cambridge, 1979.

Jeffners, A. *Butler and Hume on Religion*. Stockholm: Diakonistyrelsens, 1966.

Jeffners, A. 'Butler and Hume on Religion: A Comparative Analysis.' *Philosophical Review*, 77, 1966, 369–72.

Johnson, A. L. 'Hume's Response to the Pressure to Conform in Religious Beliefs.' *Southwest Philosophical Studies*, 2, 1977, 95–101.

Jones, P. 'Hume's Two Concepts of God.' *Philosophy*, 47, 1972, 322–33.

Jones, P. *Hume's Sentiments*. Edinburgh: Edinburgh University Press, 1982.

Jooharigian, R. B. *God and Natural Evil*. Wyndham Hall Press, 1985.

Keen, C. N. 'Reason in Hume's Dialogues.' *Philosophical Papers*, 5, 1976, 121–24.

Kekes, J. 'Belief and Scepticism.' *Philosophy Forum*, 1, 1969, 353–8.

Kemp Smith, N. 'The Naturalism of David Hume.' *Mind*, 14, 1905, 149–73 & 335–47.

Kemp Smith, N. *The Philosophy of David Hume*. London: Macmillan, 1941.

Kemp Smith, N. *Hume's Dialogues Concerning Natural Religion*. Indianapolis: Bobbs Merrill, 1947.

Klibansky, R. & Mossner, E. C. eds. *New Letters of David Hume*. Oxford: Clarendon Press, 1954, repr. 1970.

Klinefelter, D. S. 'Scepticism and Deism in Hume's Philosophy of Religion.'

Journal of American Acad. Religion, 45, 1977, 222.

Laing, B. M. 'Hume's Dialogues Concerning Natural Religion.' *Philosophy,* 12, 1937, 175–90.

Laird, J. *Hume's Philosophy of Human Nature.* London: Methuen, 1932.

Langston, D. 'The Argument from Evil: Reply to Professor Richman.' *Religious Studies,* 16, 1980, 103–13.

Le Mahieu, D. L. *The Mind of William Paley: A Philosopher and His Age.* Lincoln: University of Nebraska Press, 1976.

Levy, S. E. 'Dialogues Concerning Unnatural Uniformity.' *Philosophy Research Archives* 4, 1978.

Livingston, D. W. & King, J. T. *Hume: A Re-evaluation.* New York: Fordham University Press, 1976.

Lucas, F. L. *The Art of Living, Four Eighteenth Century Minds.* London: Cassell, 1959.

Maclagan, W. C. 'Hume's Attitude to Religion.' *Proceedings of Royal Philosophical Society of Glasgow,* 74, 1949, 83.

McPherson, T. 'The Argument from Design.' *Philosophy,* 32, 1957, 218–28.

Matthews, G. 'Theology and Natural Theology.' *Journal of Philosophy,* 61, 1964, 99–108.

Merrill, K. R. & Shahan, R. W., eds. *Hume: Many Sided Genius.* Norman: University of Oklahoma Press, 1976.

Michael, S. J. *An Examination of the Role of Natural Belief in David Hume's Philosophy of Religion* (diss.). Harvard University, 1969.

Michaud, Y. 'How to Become a Moderate Skeptic.' *Hume Studies,* 11, 1985, 33–46.

Miller, H. 'The Naturalism of Hume.' *Philosophical Review,* 38, 1929, 469–82.

Moore, A. 'Mysticism and Philosophy.' *Monist,* 59, 1976, 493–506.

Morice, G. P., ed. *David Hume: Bicentenary Papers.* Edinburgh: Edinburgh University Press, 1977.

Morrisroe, M. 'Hume's Rhetorical Strategy.' *Texas Studies in Literature and Language,* 11, 1969, 963–7.

Morrisroe, M. 'Characterization as Rhetorical Device in Hume's Dialogues.' *Enlightenment Essays,* 1, 1970, 95–107.

Mossner, E. C. 'The Enigma of Hume.' *Mind,* 45, 1936, 334–49.

Mossner, E. C. 'Hume's Dialogues Concerning Natural Religion.' *Philosophy,* 13, 1938, 84–6.

Mossner, E. C. 'Hume and the Legacy of the *Dialogues*', in *David Hume: Bicentenary Papers,* ed. G. P. Morice. Edinburgh: Edinburgh University Press, 1977, 1–22.

Mossner, E. C. 'The Religion of David Hume.' *Journal of the History of Ideas,* 39, 1978, 653–63.

Nathan, G. 'Hume's Immanent God,' in *Hume: A Collection of Critical Essays,* ed. V. C. Chappell. New York: Doubleday, 1966, 396–423.

Nathan, G. *Hume's Genuine Theism and Religion* (diss.). University of Toronto, 1972.

Nathan, G. 'The Existence and Nature of God in Hume's Theism,' in *Hume: A Re-evaluation,* ed. D. W. Livingston & J. T. King. New York: Fordham University Press, 1976, 126–49.

Nathan, G. 'A Humean Pattern of Justification.' *Hume Studies,* 9, 1983, 150–70.

Nathan, G. 'Comments on Tweyman and Davis.' *Hume Studies,* 13, 1987, 98–103.

Nelson, J. O. 'The Role of Part XII in Hume's "Dialogues Concerning Natural Religion".' *Hume Studies,* 14, 1988, 347–71.

Norton, D. F. *David Hume: Common-Sense Moralist, Sceptical Metaphysician.* Princeton, NJ: Princeton University Press, 1982.

Norton, D. F., Capaldi, N. & Robison, W. L., eds. *McGill Hume Studies.* San Diego: Austin Hill Press, 1979.

Noxon, J. 'Hume's Agnosticism.' *Philosophical Review,* 73, 1964, 248–61.

Noxon, J. 'In Defence of Hume's Agnosticism,' in *Hume: A Collection of Critical Essays,* ed. V. C. Chappell. University of Notre Dame Press, 1968, 361–83.

Noxon, J. *Hume's Philosophical Development: A Study of his Methods.* Oxford: Clarendon Press, 1973.

Noxon, J. 'Hume's Concern with Religion,' in *David Hume: Many Sided Genius,* ed. K. R. Merrill & R. W. Shahan. Norman: University of Oklahoma Press, 1976, 59–82.

Pakaluk, M. 'Philosophical Types in Hume's Dialogues,' in *Philosophers of the Scottish Enlightenment,* ed. V. Hope. Edinburgh: Edinburgh University Press, 1984.

Pakaluk, M. 'Cleanthes' Case for Theism.' *Sophia* (Australia), 27, 1988, 11–19.

Parent, W. A. 'An Interpretation of Hume's Dialogues.' *Review of Metaphysics,* 30, 1976, 96–114.

Parent, W. A. 'Philo's Confession.' *Philosophical Quarterly,* 26, 1976, 63–8.

Parsons, J. E. 'Hume's Dialogues Concerning Natural Religion: I.' *Independent Journal of Philosophy,* 2, 1978, 113–17.

Parsons, J. E. 'Hume's Dialogues Concerning Natural Religion: II.' *Independent Journal of Philosophy,* 3, 1979, 119–26.

Passmore, J. *Hume's Intentions.* 3rd edn. London: Duckworth, 1980.

Pearl, L. 'Hume's Criticism of the Design Argument.' *Monist,* 54, 1970, 270–84.

Pears, D. ed. *David Hume: A Symposium.* London: Macmillan, 1963.

Penelhum, T. *Hume.* London: Macmillan, 1975.

Penelhum, T. 'Skepticism and the Dialogues,' in *McGill Hume Studies,* ed. D. F. Norton, N. Capaldi & W. L. Robison. San Diego: Austin Hill Press, 1979, 253–78.

Penelhum, T. 'Natural Belief and Religious Belief in Hume's Philosophy.' *Philosophical Quarterly,* 33, 1983, 166–81.

Penelhum, T. 'Butler and Hume.' *Hume Studies,* 14, 1988, 251–76.

Peters, R. S. 'Hume's Argument from Design', in *Hume and the Enlightenment: Essays Presented to Ernest Campbell Mossner,* ed. W. B. Todd. Edinburgh: Edinburgh University Press, 1974.

Pike, N. 'Hume on Evil.' *Philosophical Review,* 72, 1963, 180–97.

Pike, N. *David Hume, Dialogues Concerning Natural Religion.* New York: Macmillan, 1985.

Plantinga, A. *God and Other Minds.* Ithaca: Cornell University Press, 1974.

Popkin, H. *The High Road to Pyrrhonism.* San Diego: Austin Hill Press, 1980.

Popkin, R. 'David Hume and Pyrrhonian Controversy.' *Review of Metaphysics,* 6, 1952, 65–81.

Popkin, R. M. *David Hume, Dialogues Concerning Natural Religion and the Posthumous Essays.* Indianapolis: Hackett, 1980.

Prado, C. G. 'Hume and the God-Hypothesis.' *Hume Studies,* 7, 1981, 154–63.

Price, H. H. *Hume's Theory of the External World.* Oxford: Clarendon Press, 1940.

Price, J. V. 'Sceptics in Cicero and Hume.' *Journal of the History of Ideas*, 25, 1964, 97–106.

Price, J. V. *David Hume*. New York: Twayne Publishers, 1968.

Price, J. V. 'The First Publication of David Hume's Dialogues.' *Papers of the Bibliographical Society of America*, 68, 1974, 119–27.

Price, J. V. *David Hume, Dialogues Concerning Natural Religion*. Oxford: Clarendon Press, 1976.

Priest, G. 'Hume's Final Argument.' *History of Philosophy Quarterly*, 2, 1985, 349–51.

Robison, W. 'Hume's Ontological Commitments.' *Philosophical Quarterly*, 26, 1976, 39–47.

Rohatyn, D. 'Hume's Dialogical Conceits: The Case of Dialogues XIII.' *Philosophy and Phenomenological Research*, 43, 1983, 519–32.

Root, H. E. *David Hume and the Natural History of Religion*. Stanford: Stanford University Press, 1956.

Salmon, W. E. 'Religion and Science: A New Look at Hume's "Dialogues".' *Philosophical Studies*, 33, 1978, 143–76.

Salmon, W. E. 'Experimental Atheism.' *Philosophical Studies*, 35, 1979, 101–4.

Siddiqui, Z. A. 'Causal Argument in Hume's Dialogues.' *Philosophical Quarterly India*, 29, 97–100.

Soles, D. H. 'Hume, Language and God.' *Philosophical Topics*, 12, 1981, 109–20.

Solon, T. P. & Wertz, S. K. 'Hume's Argument from Evil.' *Personalist*, 50, 1969, 383–92.

Sprague, E. 'Hume, Henry More and the Design Argument.' *Hume Studies*, 14, 1988, 305–27.

Stahl, D. E. 'Hume's Dialogues IX Defended.' *Philosophical Quarterly*, 34, 1984, 505–7.

Stanley, P. 'The Skepticisms of David Hume.' *Journal of Philosophy*, 32, 1935, 421–31.

Steinberg, E. 'Hume on Liberty, Necessity and Verbal Disputes.' *Hume Studies*, 13, 1987, 113–37.

Stove, D. C. 'Part IX of Hume's Dialogues.' *Philosophical Quarterly*, 28, 1978, 300–9.

Sutherland, S. R. 'Penelhum on Hume.' *Philosophical Quarterly*, 33, 1983, 131–6.

Swinburne, R. E. 'The Argument from Design.' *Philosophy*, 43, July 1968, 199–212.

Taylor, A. E., Laird, J. & Jessop, T. E., 'The Present-day Relevance of Hume's Dialogues Concerning Natural Religion.' *Proceedings of the Aristotelean Society*, 18, 1939, 179–228.

Tweyman, S. *Reason and Conduct in Hume and his Predecessors*. The Hague: Martinus Nijhoff, 1974.

Tweyman, S. 'L'Incidence des organismes sur la croyance dans une intelligence creatrice.' *Revue de l'Université de Moncton*, 2 (3), 1978, 113–20.

Tweyman, S. 'The Vegetable Library and God.' *Dialogue* (Canada), 18, 1979, 517–27.

Tweyman, S. 'Remarks on Wadia's Philo Confounded.' *Hume Studies*, 6, 1980, 155–61.

Tweyman, S. 'La Sceptique comme pedagogue – I,' *Revue de l'Université de Moncton*, 13 (1), 1980, 115–25.

Tweyman, S. 'The Sceptic as Teacher,' *Spindrift,* 1 (1), 1981, 16–28.

Tweyman, S. 'La Sceptique comme pedagogue – II.' *Revue de l'Université de Moncton,* 14 (1), 1981, 85–95.

Tweyman, S. 'The Articulate Voice and God.' *Southern Journal of Philosophy,* 20, 1982, 263–75.

Tweyman, S. 'An Inconvenience of Anthropomorphism.' *Hume Studies,* 8, 1982, 19–42.

Tweyman, S. 'The 'Reductio' in Part V of Hume's "Dialogues".' *Southern Journal of Philosophy,* 21, 1983, 453–60.

Tweyman, S. 'A propos d'une difficulté logique dans l'argument de Cleanthe.' *Hume Studies,* 10, 1984, 69–80.

Tweyman, S. 'An Enquiry Concerning Hume's Dialogues,' in *Early Modern Philosophy,* ed. G. Moyal & S. Tweyman, Caravan Books, 1985, 155–75.

Tweyman, S. *Scepticism and Belief in Hume's Dialogues Concerning Natural Religion.* The Hague: Martinus Nijhoff, 1986.

Tweyman, S. 'Hume's Dialogues on Evil.' *Hume Studies,* 13, 1987, 74–85.

Tweyman, S. 'David Hume on Science, Theology and Society,' in *Studies on Voltaire and the Eighteenth Century.* Oxford, The Voltaire Foundation, at the Taylor Institute, 1989, 486–8.

Tweyman, S. *Descartes and Hume: Selected Topics.* Delmar, NY: Caravan Press, 1989.

Vink, A. G. 'The Literary and Dramatic Character of Hume's Dialogues Concerning Natural Religion.' *Religious Studies,* 22, 1986, 387–96.

Wadia, P. S. 'Professor Pike on Part III of Hume's Dialogues.' *Religious Studies,* 14, 1978, 325–42.

Wadia, P. S. 'Philo Confounded,' in *McGill Hume Studies,* ed. D. F. Norton, N. Capaldi & W. L. Robison. San Diego: Austin Hill Press, 1979, 279–90.

Wadia, P. S. 'Commentary on Professor Tweyman's "Hume on Evil".' *Hume Studies,* 13, 1987, 104–12.

Wilson, F. 'Is Hume a Sceptic with Regard to Reason?' *Philosophical Research Archives,* 10, 1984, 275–320.

Winters, B. A. 'Hume's Argument for the Superiority of Natural Instinct.' *Dialogue,* 20, 1981, 635–43.

Wollheim, R. *Hume on Religion.* London: World Publishing Co., 1963.

Wood, F. E. 'David Hume's Philosophy of Religion as Reflected in the Dialogues.' *Southwest Journal of Philosophy,* 2, 1971, 186–93.

Wright, J. P. 'Hume's Academic Skepticism.' *Canadian Journal of Philosophy,* 16, 1986, 407–35.

Wright, J. P. *The Sceptical Realism of David Hume.* Minneapolis: University of Minnesota Press, 1983.

Yandell, K. E. 'Hume on Religious Belief,' in *Hume: A Re-evaluation,* ed. D. W. Livingston & J. T. King. New York: Fordham University Press, 1976.

Yandell, K. E. 'Hume's Explanation of Religious Belief.' *Hume Studies,* 5, 1979, 94–109.

Yandell, K. E. *The Inexplicable Mystery.* Philadelphia: Temple University Press, 1990.

INDEX

Page references in italic refer to the text of Hume's *Dialogues Concerning Natural Religion*